SHAKESPEARE'S IDEAS

W9-BNM-926

Blackwell Great Minds
Edited by Steven Nadler

The Blackwell Great Minds series gives readers a strong sense of the fundamental views of the great western thinkers and captures the relevance of these figures to the way we think and live today.

1 *Kant* by Allen W. Wood
2 *Augustine* by Gareth B. Matthews
3 *Descartes* by André Gombay
4 *Sartre* by Katherine J. Morris
5 *Charles Darwin* by Michael Ruse
6 *Schopenhauer* by Robert Wicks
7 *Shakespeare's Ideas* by David Bevington

Forthcoming
Camus by David Sherman
Kierkegaard by M. Jamie Ferreira
Mill by Wendy Donner and Richard Fumerton

SHAKESPEARE'S IDEAS

More Things in Heaven and Earth

David Bevington

⟨W⟩WILEY-BLACKWELL

A John Wiley & Sons, Ltd., Publication

822.33
BEV

This edition first published 2008
© 2008 David Bevington

Blackwell Publishing was acquired by John Wiley & Sons in February 2007. Blackwell's publishing program has been merged with Wiley's global Scientific, Technical, and Medical business to form Wiley-Blackwell.

Registered Office
John Wiley & Sons Ltd, The Atrium, Southern Gate, Chichester, West Sussex, PO19 8SQ, United Kingdom

Editorial Offices
350 Main Street, Malden, MA 02148-5020, USA
9600 Garsington Road, Oxford, OX4 2DQ, UK
The Atrium, Southern Gate, Chichester, West Sussex, PO19 8SQ, UK

For details of our global editorial offices, for customer services, and for information about how to apply for permission to reuse the copyright material in this book please see our website at www.wiley.com/wiley-blackwell.

The right of David Bevington to be identified as the author of this work has been asserted in accordance with the UK Copyright, Designs, and Patents Act 1988.

Wiley also publishers its books in a variety of electronic formats. Some content that appears in print may not be available in electronic books.

Designations used by companies to distinguish their products are often claimed as trademarks. All brand names and product names used in this book are trade names, service marks, trademarks, or registered trademarks of their respective owners. The publisher is not associated with any product or vendor mentioned in this book. This publication is designed to provide accurate and authoritative information in regard to the subject matter covered. It is sold on the understanding that the publisher is not engaged in rendering professional services. If professional advice or other expert assistance is required, the services of a competent professional should be sought.

Library of Congress Cataloging-in-Publication Data

Bevington, David M.
  Shakespeare's ideas : more things in heaven and earth / David Bevington.
    p. cm. – (Blackwell great minds)
  Includes bibliographical references and index.
  ISBN 978-1-4051-6795-6 (hardcover : alk. paper) – ISBN 978-1-4051-6796-3 (pbk. : alk. paper)
  1. Shakespeare, William, 1564-1616–Philosophy. I. Title.
  PR3001.B48 2008
  822.3'3–dc22

                                                            2008006980

A catalogue record for this title is available from the British Library.

Set in 10.5/13pt Galliard
by Graphicraft Limited, Hong Kong
Printed and bound in Singapore
by Fabulous Printers Pte Ltd

1   2008

To Stanley Wells

Contents

Acknowledgements

My chief debt is to those scholars and critics whom I list in the 'Further Reading' section of this book. What I have written in this book reflects a lifetime of reading and teaching and intellectual conversation, without which I fear I would have learned little. Among those to whom I am most indebted, I should mention Alfred Harbage (my mentor of graduate school days), Sam Schoenbaum, Maynard Mack, Northrop Frye, C. L. Barber, Coppélia Kahn, David Kastan, Fredson Bowers, Arthur Kirsch, Frank Kermode, Barbara Mowat, Janet Adelman, Richard Wheeler, and Stanley Wells, to the last of whom this book is affectionately dedicated. The list here is manifestly inadequate; my obligation is much wider than that. I am most of all indebted to the spirit of collegiality that thrives in the world of Shakespeare studies and at the great universities (Harvard University, the University of Virginia, the University of Chicago, Northwestern University, the University of Hawaii, Dominican University, the University of Victoria) where I have been privileged to teach.

1

A Natural Philosopher

TOUCHSTONE   Hast any philosophy in thee, shepherd?
CORIN   No more but that I know the more one sickens the worse at
ease he is; and that he that wants money, means, and content is
without three good friends; that the property of rain is to wet and
fire to burn; that good pasture makes fat sheep and that a great cause
of the night is lack of the sun; that he that hath learned no wit by
nature nor art may complain of good breeding or comes of a very
dull kindred.
TOUCHSTONE   Such a one is a natural philosopher.

(*As You Like It*, 3.2.21–30)

Even if Shakespeare was not a philosopher in the sense of writing essays
or treatises arguing philosophical positions and proposing an embracing philosophical scheme, we need to take the ideas in his plays and
poems seriously. This book is dedicated to the proposition that the
writings of Shakespeare reveal the workings of a great mind. True, we
have no literary criticism or other theorizing as such from his pen.
Unlike his near-contemporary Ben Jonson, whose theories of dramatic
art are loudly proclaimed in prologues, manifestos, satirical diatribes,
and recorded conversations, Shakespeare never speaks in his own
voice about his ideas on writing or on what we would broadly call his
'philosophy'. That is because he is a dramatist with a special genius
for allowing his characters to speak on their own behalfs without his
editorial intervention.

Shakespeare does not discuss philosophers very often, and may
not have read widely in them. He cites Aristotle twice in throwaway
comments (see Chapter 4). He never mentions Plato or his Academy.
Socrates appears once by name as the hapless henpecked husband of

Xantippe (*The Taming of the Shrew*, 1.2.69–70). Shakespeare's four references to Pythagoras seem to regard his ideas as a bizarre joke. Seneca is named once as the quintessential 'heavy' dramatist, not as a philosopher (*Hamlet*, 2.2.400). Although the concept of stoicism is important to Shakespeare, as we shall see in Chapter 6, he uses the word 'stoics' only in a single comic remark to characterize students who prefer diligent study to fun and games (*Taming*, 1.1.31), and he says nothing about Zeno or his followers. 'Sceptic', 'sceptical', and 'scepticism' form no part of Shakespeare's vocabulary, however much he may have pondered what we would call sceptical ideas, nor does he name Pyrrhon or Pyrrhonism or Sextus Empiricus. Shakespeare tends to use 'epicurean' in its slang sense of 'hedonistic'. Medieval theologians like Abelard, Eusebius, Tertullian, Augustine, Thomas Aquinas, William of Ockam, and Duns Scotus are nowhere to be found. So too with Renaissance neoplatonists like Pico della Mirandola, Marsilio Ficino, and Baldassare Castiglione, or radical thinkers like Giordano Bruno. 'Lutheran' surfaces once (*Henry VIII*, 3.2.100) as a defamatory Catholic-inspired label for Anne Bullen. John Calvin's name is absent, even though his widely-circulated ideas are discernible. 'Machiavel' turns up thrice as a synonym for 'villain' or 'political intriguer'. We hear nothing of Agrippa, or Paracelsus, or Ramus. Shakespeare never names Montaigne, although his debt to one essay at least is evident in *The Tempest*.

Is Shakespeare gently laughing at himself when he has Touchstone describe Corin as a 'natural philosopher'? A 'natural philosopher' need not be a guileless innocent; the phrase can suggest one who is innately gifted and wisely self-taught, even if not schooled in a narrowly pedantic sense. It can also suggest one who studies 'natural philosophy', i.e., knowledge of the natural world.

Learned or not, the plays and poems are full of ideas. Writers on Shakespeare from Dr Samuel Johnson and John Keats to Ralph Waldo Emerson, Virginia Woolf, Northrop Frye, Harold Bloom, Stanley Cavell, and Stephen Greenblatt have lauded Shakespeare as a great moral philosopher. The titles of numerous critical studies underscore the importance of the topic. Kenneth J. Spalding's *The Philosophy of Shakespeare* (Oxford, 1953) discusses the subject under subheadings of 'The Mind of Shakespeare', 'Shakespeare and Man', 'Social Man', 'The Statesman', 'Individual Man', 'Man's Salvation', and 'The Last Question'. Franz Lütgenau's similarly-titled *Shakespeare als Philosoph*

(Leipzig, 1909) asks what Shakespeare's writings have to say about free will versus determinism, relativity vs. certainty, scepticism, Pythagorean doctrine, dualism, Pantheism, astrology, and still more. Ben Kimpel's *Moral Philosophies in Shakespeare's Plays* (Lewiston, ME, 1987) focuses on the duality of good and evil, arguing that Shakespeare ultimately endorses a providential reading of divine justice. John J. Joughin's collection of essays entitled *Philosophical Shakespeares* (London and New York, 2000), devoted to the postmodern proposition that we must acknowledge multiple philosophies in Shakespeare, begins with a foreword by Stanley Cavell addressing the critical problem of how to distinguish the ideas from the literary texts into which they are inseparably woven. Tzachi Zamir's *Double Vision*, subtitled *Moral Philosophy and Shakespearean Drama* (Princeton, 2007), analyzes the epistemological and moral bases of philosophical criticism as necessary groundwork for practical criticism. More studies of this kind are listed in the section on 'Further Reading' at the end of this book.

Important as the ideas are in Shakespeare's plays, we are on far less certain ground in attempting to determine which of them are specifically his own. Do Shakespeare's characters sometimes serve as mouthpieces for his own personal beliefs? The notion is attractive because the things that are said by Hamlet, or Lear, or Macbeth, or just about any other thoughtful character are so wise and stimulating and eloquently expressed that we like to imagine that we can hear the author himself. Yet we must be vigilantly aware that each speaker is a narrative voice, even in the Sonnets and other nondramatic poems. If that is true in nondramatic verse, it is insistently more true in drama. Knowing as little as we do about Shakespeare's personal views outside of his writings, we must exercise great care in assuming that we can hear him asking 'To be, or not to be' with Hamlet, or agreeing glumly with the Earl of Gloucester in *King Lear* that 'As flies to wanton boys are we to the gods; / They kill us for their sport', or endorsing Macbeth's nihilistic conclusion that 'Life's but a walking shadow'. One can as easily and fruitlessly generalize on the basis of Puck's 'Lord, what fools these mortals be!' in *A Midsummer Night's Dream*, or Feste's song, 'Then come and kiss me, sweet and twenty; / Youth's a stuff will not endure' in *Twelfth Night*. Shakespeare's utterances often achieve the status of proverbial speech because they are so persuasively and exquisitely worded.

This, then, is the challenge of this present book, as of other earlier studies that have asked about Shakespeare's ideas. He is a remarkable subject because he has revealed so little directly about himself while at the same time uttering such extraordinary wisdom that we want to understand him as a thinker. Biographical information about him has accumulated in considerable detail, but not in the form of letters written by him, or recorded conversations. Our materials for a study of Shakespeare's ideas must be the plays and poems that he wrote.

Shakespeare was a dramatist in ways that tend to conceal the author behind the work. He generally took his plots from known and published sources. The history plays and to an extent *Macbeth* take their basic narratives from Raphael Holinshed's *The Chronicles of England, Scotland, and Ireland*, newly published in a second edition in 1587. The Roman plays, especially *Julius Caesar, Antony and Cleopatra*, and *Coriolanus*, take their narrative material from Plutarch's *Lives of the Noble Grecians and Romans*, translated into English by Thomas North in 1579. Many other plays, including *The Merchant of Venice, Much Ado About Nothing, Twelfth Night, All's Well That Ends Well, Othello*, and *Cymbeline*, are derived plotwise from Italian or other continental short stories, plentifully available in England in Shakespeare's lifetime and generally in translation. *Romeo and Juliet* takes as its point of departure a long narrative poem in English by Arthur Brooke called *The Tragical History of Romeus and Juliet, written first in Italian by Bandell and now in English by Ar. Br.*, 1562, with a long history of earlier versions prior to that of the Italian short-story writer Matteo Bandello. *Hamlet* owes its plot ultimately to Saxo Grammaticus's *Historia Danica* (1180–1208). *Troilus and Cressida* goes back to Homer, Chaucer, John Lydgate, and William Caxton, among others, for its information about the Trojan War and the doomed love affair of the play's title characters. *Titus Andronicus* is seemingly based on a now-lost prose original of which analogs are still available. *Timon of Athens* seems to have been inspired by a dialogue called *Timon, or The Misanthrope*, by Lucian of Samosata (c. AD 125–80). *The Two Noble Kinsmen*, by Shakespeare and John Fletcher, goes back to Chaucer's 'Knight's Tale'. Sometimes Shakespeare extensively revised an already existing play, as in the case of *Measure for Measure, King John, Henry IV Parts I and II, Henry V, King Lear*, and perhaps *Hamlet*. He adroitly made use of classical and neoclassical comedies by Plautus, Ariosto, and others in such plays as *The Comedy of Errors* and *The Taming of the Shrew*. He showed that he knew how to capitalize on the narrative traditions of pastoral and romance in *The Two Gentlemen of Verona*, *As You Like It*, *Pericles*, and *The Winter's Tale*. Only *Love's Labour's Lost*, *A Midsummer Night's Dream*, *The Merry Wives of Windsor*, and *The Tempest* stand as plays for which no single organizing plot can be found as Shakespeare's source, and even here his borrowing from other writers is extensive.

This wide use of sources was characteristic of other Renaissance dramatists as well. As such it points to an important feature of early modern dramatic writing: the author-dramatist was essentially anonymous, or nearly so. Many plays were published without the author's name on the title page or anywhere in the edition. Shakespeare's name did not make an appearance on a printed play-text by him until 1598, when *Love's Labour's Lost* was published in quarto (a small and relatively inexpensive form of book publishing) as 'Newly corrected and augmented by *W. Shakespere*'. By that time Shakespeare may have been in London for a decade or so, gaining steadily in reputation as a dramatist: as early as 1592 his *1* and *3 Henry VI* caught the attention of his fellow-dramatists Robert Greene and Thomas Nashe, and by 1598 he was lauded by Francis Meres as the Plautus and Seneca of his generation. Yet official recognition in print came slowly. The reason we have no manuscripts of his today, or correspondence, or any biography of him written during his lifetime, is that dramatists like Shakespeare were regarded as popular entertainers. Sophisticated readers did not ordinarily 'collect' Shakespeare. When Thomas Bodley gave to Oxford University the library that today bears his name, instructing that institution to assemble in its collection every book published in England, he specified that they need not bother to include plays. Plays were ephemeral. The situation was perhaps like that of today in our cultural estimation of films: we are likely to know who has directed an important film, and who are its lead actors, but seldom are we able to come up with the name of the script writer or writers, unless they happen to be someone like Tom Stoppard with credentials from the more visibly cultured world of stage drama, fiction, poetry, music, etc.

Popular dramatists were generally known in Shakespeare's day as makers and compilers rather than as artists. They were artisans, often drawn (as in Shakespeare's case) from the ranks of performers, who in turn tended to come from the artisan class. James Burbage, builder of the Theatre in 1576 and father of Shakespeare's longtime leading man, Richard Burbage, had been a joiner or expert carpenter. Some of Shakespeare's colleagues in the company known as the Chamberlain's Men and then the King's Men were members of London's powerful trade guilds, such as the Grocers and the Goldsmiths. Shakespeare's own father had been a manufacturer and seller of leather goods and other commodities in Stratford-upon-Avon. Even Ben Jonson had as his stepfather a mason, and was himself apprenticed for a time, albeit unwillingly, to that craft. Playwriting was a trade, like acting. The dramatist was a journeyman, a craftsman. Our modern conception of creative writing as usually autobiographical in its method and subject would have seemed strange to Shakespeare and his contemporaries. Their job was to fashion theatrical entertainments around popular and familiar stories. Such an idea of authorship tends to distance a play from its writer in terms of personal expression. Can an author who chronicles the story of a Richard II or Hamlet be assumed to be searching out ways to express his own views on politics or human destiny?

Patronage of the drama, and in other arts as well, tended to encourage this same sort of craftsmanship in which the maker subsumed his identity into the work at hand. Many of the great paintings of the Renaissance were executed at the behest of church authorities and wealthy patrons. Artists might be commissioned to provide representations of religious subjects for a particular location in a particular church. The subject might well be dictated, such as the Annunciation, or the Descent from the Cross, in which case the details of composition might also be specified, including the size of the painting and the arrangement of the figures. Where, in such an instance, was there room for what we would call creativity? The results in the best-known instances could be astonishingly beautiful and revelatory of the artist's genius, and yet even here the degree of personal expression can be hard to determine.

The same is true in the drama of the early modern period. Shakespeare wrote for his patrons, who were in his case the playgoing public of London. What kinds of pressures would he have felt? Don Marquis, creator of a delightful newspaper column (1913–37) in the New York *Sun* called 'The Sun Dial' and featuring, among others, Archy the *vers libre* cockroach and Mehitabel the cat, devoted one piece to imagining what it would have been like for Shakespeare to write the kinds of plays demanded of him by his popular audiences. Archy the cockroach narrates the account, using no capitals or punctuation because he is hopping from key to key on Don Marquis's typewriter. He imagines Shakespeare in a tavern, complaining to his drinking companions about the harsh demands placed on him by his unlearned spectators.

> what they want
> is kings talking like kings
> never had sense enough to talk
> and stabbings and stranglings
> and fat men making love
> and clowns basting each
> other with clubs and cheap puns
> and off colour allusions to all
> the smut of the day,

Shakespeare laments. 'give them a good ghost / or two', and 'kill a little kid or two a prince', 'a little pathos along with / the dirt'.

> what I want to do
> is write sonnets and
> songs and spenserian stanzas
> and i might have done it too
> if i hadn t got
> into this frightful show game.

Marquis is of course exaggerating for comic effect, but his main point is still worth considering: a public artist in Shakespeare's situation needed to cater substantially to the tastes of his public. In the title of his 1947 study of Shakespeare, *As They Liked It*, Alfred Harbage adroitly captures the idea that the greatest of English writers achieved his success in good part by telling his audiences what they wanted to hear. To the extent that this is true, what room is left then for saying that the ideas expressed in his popular plays are Shakespeare's own?

The problem of identifying any ideas in the plays or poems as Shakespeare's own is compounded still further by Shakespeare's extraordinary ability to submerge his own personality as writer into the mindset of the characters he creates. He allows Falstaff, or Hotspur, or Cleopatra, or Lady Macbeth to speak his or her innermost thoughts as though without the intervening or controlling perspective of the author. Shakespeare's gift for creating unforgettable characters this way is legendary. It is sometimes called his 'negative capability', meaning his skill as a dramatist in setting aside his own point of view in order to focus entirely on what the character he has created must be thinking at any given moment. The phrase is John Keats's in praise of Shakespeare, in a letter to Keats's brother Thomas written on 17 December 1817. The letter itself actually points in a slightly different direction: Keats writes that negative capability 'is when a man is capable of being in uncertainties, mysteries, doubts, without any irritable reaching after fact and reason', laying stress on the idea of genius as liberated by creative uncertainties. But the difference doesn't really matter; the definitions are alike in praising qualities for which Shakespeare is justly famous, and 'negative capability' has stuck as a way of describing Shakespeare's remarkable talent for showing us what his characters are thinking, not what the dramatist is trying to prove.

Plays vary greatly as to the extent to which they try to make an identifiable point. A central idea in back of Ben Jonson's *Volpone* (1605–6) is that a nearly universal human greed for wealth ultimately consumes itself and is justly punished by its own excesses. We do not seriously distort the evident purpose of Arthur Miller's *The Crucible* (1952) when we say that its aim is to criticize the kind of cultural and political hysteria that led to the Salem witchcraft trials of the late seventeenth century and then much later to the McCarthy witch-hunts of the 1950s. Sophocles's *Oedipus the King* (32 BC) darkly affirms the great commonplace that the will of the gods must be fulfilled, even if in the process Oedipus must suffer a devastating tragic fall. These are all extraordinary plays; to say that they are didactic, in that we can identify an authorial intent, is to make an analytical observation, not to put these plays down as in any way deficient. At the same time, the genre of drama offers a very different alternative. It can encourage the clash of ideas in antithetical debate. Shakespeare is brilliant at this. Is Falstaff right, in *Henry IV Part I*, to celebrate joie de vivre and to revel in the ironies that surround the concept of honour in a time of war, or is Prince Hal right to conclude ultimately that Falstaff is a threat to public order? In *Antony and Cleopatra*, are we to admire Antony for embracing the unrepressed hedonism of Egypt, or should we shake our heads in dismay at his collapse into sensuality? The debate can be internal: is Hamlet right to delay his revenge until he is sure of what he is doing, or is he a coward to put off a duty that he is prompted to 'by heaven and hell' (*Hamlet*, 2.2.585)? He himself is far from sure of the answer. Generally, if we try to determine what is the 'message' of a Shakespeare play, we are on the wrong track. How then can we talk about Shakespeare's ideas?

One approach is to eschew any search for the 'meaning' of a Shakespeare play in favour of asking, instead, what issues are at stake. What is being debated, and what are the arguments advanced on the various sides? Why do these issues matter, and to whom? How are our sympathies directed by the dialogue and the dramatic situation? To say that Shakespeare avoids propounding a 'message' is not to say that his plays avoid ethical and moral alignments. Quite the contrary. Part of Shakespeare's lasting appeal is that he comes across as so deeply humane. His plays surely invite us to deplore murder and senseless bloodshed, to applaud charitable generosity, to dislike characters such as Iago or Edmund who are cunningly vicious and self-serving, to appreciate romantic heroines like Rosalind and Viola who are so patient and good-humoured and resourceful, and to deny our sympathy to tyrannical bullies like Duke Frederick in *As You Like It* or the Duke of Cornwall in *King Lear* while wishing the best for those like Edgar and Cordelia and Kent in *King Lear* who are outcast and persecuted for their courageous if imprudent rightmindedness. This is not to assert that Shakespeare himself can be said to have endorsed those various views; no doubt we are inclined to suppose that he emphatically did, and that he wrote to foster such idealisms, but we simply have no direct evidence about the man himself. In the last analysis, the question is both unanswerable and unimportant.

To be sure, we do have the testimony of Henry Chettle in 1592 that a certain playwright, unidentified by name but almost certainly Shakespeare, was widely regarded as a man of pleasant bearing and honest reputation. 'Myself have seen his demeanor no less civil than he excellent in the quality he professes', wrote Chettle by way of apology for an attack on Shakespeare by Robert Greene in that same year. 'Besides, divers of worship have reported his uprightness of dealing, which argues his honesty and his facetious grace in writing that approves his art' (*Kind-Heart's Dream*, 1592). Other testimonials tend to confirm that Shakespeare was well liked, though we need to remember that Greene seems to have despised Shakespeare as an unprincipled plagiarist. Another tribute lauds Shakespeare as one of the most 'pregnant wits' of his time (William Camden, *Remains of a Greater Work Concerning Britain*, 1605), concentrating on his greatness as a writer without saying anything about him as a person. All in all, these testimonials give us almost nothing to go on in determining whether Shakespeare as a man can be said to stand behind the rich and multitudinous ideas embedded in his writings. We do have the plays and poems, however, and they collectively give evidence of a deep moral commitment that we can locate in what we call 'Shakespeare', meaning not only the plays and poems but the multitudinous responses they have elicited over the four centuries or so since Shakespeare wrote.

The plan of this book will be to proceed topically, asking what the plays and poems suggest in continual debate about an array of topics: sex and gender, politics and political theory, writing and acting, religious controversy and issues of faith, scepticism and misanthropy, and Last Things, including the approach of retirement and death. I take up these topics, broadly speaking, in the order in which they seem to have fascinated Shakespeare. Sex and gender are especially relevant in his early years while he is writing romantic comedies. Politics become the central topic of the history plays that culminate in the great series about Henry V written in the late 1590s. Critical ideas about writing and acting are explored with special cogency in the Sonnets and in the plays of Shakespeare's middle years. Religious controversy and sceptical challenges to orthodoxy come increasingly into focus as Shakespeare turns to the painful dilemmas of the great tragedies in the early years of the seventeenth century. Finally, ideas of closure in both artistic and personal terms seem to be of deep concern to Shakespeare as he contemplates his approaching retirement from the theatre. At the same time, because these topics defy any neat chronological arrangement, and because the topics themselves constantly overlap (as when issues of religion take on political dimensions), the examples and attitudes will range freely over the entire canon.

Implicit in the arrangement of this book is an argument that the ideas presented in Shakespeare's plays and poems develop over time, and do so in ways that would seem to reflect the author's changing intellectual preoccupations if not indeed something approaching his own philosophical outlook on important problems of human existence. In his early plays, he dwells in his romantic comedies on the nature of loving relationships, both opposite-sex and same-sex. What can humans discover about who they really are from the ways they behave when they fall in love? How do young men and women differ from one another as they approach the hazards and rewards of amorous courtship? What indeed is the very nature of gender? Is it inherent in the human constitution, or is it, in part at least, socially constructed? Why are the young women in Shakespeare's comedies often so much smarter and more knowledgeable about themselves than are the young men? To what extent should young people regulate their conduct according to social codes that, in Shakespeare's day especially, mandated marriage as a pre-condition for sexual fulfillment? What role should loving friendship play in the formation of lasting relationships? When two men or two women experience feelings of deep love for one another, should erotic pleasure be embraced also? These are questions that were bound to fascinate a youngish writer still in his late twenties and early thirties when he wrote the plays and poems of the 1590s.

The English history plays are from the same period of Shakespeare's career, in the 1590s. Can we discern in them a developing political philosophy that might seem appropriate to a young author intent on understanding the history of his country and its political institutions, while pondering at the same time what England is like as a place for a young man of ambition to come to terms with the demands of male adulthood? The history plays give Shakespeare immense scope for studying political impasse and the clash of contending ideologies. Is his response that of a political conservative or liberal? These terms change meaning over time, of course; in Shakespeare's case, are we to see him as a defender of the Tudor monarchy? Is he a social conservative in his presentation of class differences, or something more iconoclastic? Is he a defender or critic of war? Is he suspicious of political activism by the common people, or is he sympathetic toward ideas of popular resistance to tyranny, or something of both? Do his ideas about such matters change over time? Perhaps what we should focus on is the development of political ideas in his history plays, as those ideas shift from a broadly providential interpretation of England's civil wars of the fifteenth century to a more pragmatic and even existential view of historical process in the story of Henry IV's usurpation of power from Richard II and its aftermath in the reign of Henry V. To the extent that we can see Shakespeare exploring a more Machiavellian view of historical change, even if as dramatist he withholds his own personal judgement of the matter, we can perhaps see some preparation for the depictions of religious and philosophical scepticism that are to come in the plays of the following decade.

Shakespeare's ideas on his craft as a dramatist and actor, implicit in all he wrote, are explored with special intensity in the Sonnets, in *As You Like It*, and in *Hamlet*, written more or less at the turn of the century when Shakespeare was in the process of shifting genres from romantic comedies and English history plays to problem plays and tragedies. His ideas on art seem well calculated to arm him for the encounter with the large philosophical problems shortly to come in his way. Poetry and drama are, to Hamlet and other eloquent speakers on the subject, ennobling enterprises, deeply moral in the best sense of promoting virtuous behaviour through positive and negative examples. Because great art is immortal, it is able to transcend human mortality and time. To be great art it must address itself to a high-minded audience of those who truly understand; it must not cater to buffoonish tastes or mere popularity. It must approach any classical 'rules' of dramatic structure with great caution, and be ready to construct dramatic genres in a pragmatic and experimental way. Aristotle's notion of *hamartia* (mistake or flaw) can sometimes prove useful in writing tragedy, sometimes not. The important thing, seemingly, is to be flexible and avoid dogmatism. Whether Shakespeare knew Aristotle's *Poetics* is very much open to question, but he must have been acquainted with neo-Aristotelean practice. He makes use of it when it suits his purposes, and often not. He avoids intemperate theorizing.

Questions of religious faith also come into special focus in 1599 and afterwards, as Shakespeare turned increasingly to the writing of problem plays and tragedies. In an age of heated religious controversy, Shakespeare seems to have found himself drawn more and more to the depiction of religious and ideological conflict. He displays a deep knowledge of doctrinal differences, which he generally portrays even-handedly. He makes use of anticlerical humour as did other dramatists and writers, but generally in a more temperate vein. Occasional disparaging remarks about Jews are offset by a characteristic Shakespearean sympathy for those who are the subject of ethnic or racial hatred. Toward Puritans he is less charitable, perhaps because of the virulent opposition of some religious reformers to the stage. His presentation of ghosts, fairies, and other spirits is wittily theatrical, freely admitting them into his plays but in such a way as to leave open the hotly debated issue as to whether such spirits are 'real'. Toward questions of determinism versus free will and the existence of heaven and hell he is equally tactful and indirect. The spiritual and religious values that he seems especially to prize are those to be sought through charitable generosity, penance, and forgiveness rather than through religiously institutional means.

In the period of his great tragedies, Shakespeare explores pessimism, misanthropy, misogyny, and scepticism with devastating candour and ever-increasing intensity. *Troilus and Cressida* offers a totally disillusioning view of the most famous war in history and its demoralizing effects on both sides. Human relationships fall apart. Supposed heroes betray their best selves in vain assertions of manhood. The hero of *Hamlet* is obsessed with the perception that the world in which he lives is nothing but a 'pestilent congregation of vapors'. His mother's desertion of her dead husband's memory prompts him to accuse womankind generally of frailty and sensual self-indulgence. Misogyny assumes a new urgency in these two plays, as also in the 'Dark Lady' Sonnets: whereas before, in the romantic comedies, male fears of womanly infidelity were unfounded and chimerical, those fears now take on the disturbing urgency of fact. The dispiriting ending of *Julius Caesar* seems to illustrate the sad truth that human beings are sometimes their own worst enemies; in the unpredictable swings of history, nobly intended purposes too often result in the destruction of those very ideals for which the tragic heroes have striven. *Othello* and *King Lear* turn to even darker scenarios by introducing us to villains who see no reason to obey the dictates of conventional morality. The unnerving success of Edmund especially, down nearly to the last moment of *King Lear*, seems to demonstrate with frightening clarity that the gods worshipped by traditionalists like Lear and Gloucester will do nothing to aid old men in distress; indeed, the gods may not exist. The deep pessimism and misanthropy of *Timon of Athens* and *Coriolanus* do nothing to relieve the existential angst.

Shakespeare's late plays offer a kind of reply or final countermovement in his career as he moves from thesis (the early work) through antithesis (in the tragedies) to synthesis. In *Antony and Cleopatra*, the pessimism and misogyny of Shakespeare's earlier tragedies are transformed by stage magic into an unstable vision in which a man and a woman reach for mythic greatness by daring to cross the hazardous boundaries of gender difference. The genre of tragicomedy offers Shakespeare a dramatic form in which to fashion a series of happy endings out of the afflictions of his long-suffering characters. The assurances are indeed positive, but should not be read as a simple refutation of the dispiriting circumstances over which they finally prevail. The gods do oversee human actions in these plays, but they are the gods of the artist's creation. Bearing pagan names like Jupiter, Juno, Ceres, Iris, and Diana, they are the stage contrivances of tragicomedy. The self-aware artifice of these plays turns our attention to the dramatic artist and his craft as he prepares for retirement and death. In this sense, even the late plays offer a profoundly sceptical view of the dramatist's world.

2

Lust in Action
Shakespeare's Ideas on Sex and Gender

The question of Shakespeare's ideas on sex and gender is our place to begin, not only because he addresses these matters intently in the ten romantic comedies he wrote in the 1590s as a young man, from *The Comedy of Errors* (early in the decade) down through *Twelfth Night* (around the turn of the century), but also because the business of locating what we might want to call a Shakespearean idea is especially problematic here. First, as we have said, 'Shakespeare' must be understood to mean not the man from Stratford-upon-Avon who became a famous writer but the plays and poems themselves collectively considered. The man who wrote them is largely inaccessible to us; the plays and poems must stand on their own. Then, too, attitudes toward sex and gender are notoriously located in cultural norms or in deviations from those norms. To the extent that Shakespeare was inescapably a man of his time, writing for popular audiences, he was bound to take popular attitudes on sex and gender into account.

Shakespeare may well have sensed a particular constituency in his audience to whom he wished especially to address the concerns embedded in his plays. London was of course not of one mind about matters of sexuality. Many ordinary citizens, including those engaged in the city's bustling commercial life, tended to endorse the church's insistence on sexual restraint before marriage and fidelity within the marriage contract. Citizens of this temperament tended to disapprove of profanity and anything they regarded as obscene or indecorous. They believed in upright dealings, both in their commercial life and in their domestic arrangements. They liked to think of themselves as decent Christians, piously obedient to the Ten Commandments and to the Beatitudes. As Protestants, they generally supported the campaign of the established Anglican church to promote an idea of companionate marriage in which the father was very much the head of household and yet was charged with maintaining a proper mutuality between husband and wife. Sex was no longer generally viewed as an inherently sinful passion, tolerated by the medieval Catholic church only in marriage and even then only under severe restrictions as to time and place. To English Protestants, sex was generally acceptable and even precious as a necessary physical fulfillment of a bond between man and woman that found its highest expression in a spiritual union of souls united for eternity and committed to the raising of a family. Edmund Spenser's 'Epithalamion' and John Donne's 'The Ecstasy' are among the many poetic expressions of this idea.

To be sure, there were differences within the community thus defined, and these difference too could have mattered to Shakespeare and his acting company. Zealous reformers denounced playgoing entirely. Stephen Gosson spoke of plays as 'the invention of the devil, the offerings of idolatry, the pomp of worldlings, the blossoms of vanity, the root of apostasy, food of iniquity, riot and adultery'. 'Detest them', he warned. 'Players are masters of vice, teachers of wantonness, spurs to iniquity, the sons of idleness' (*The School of Abuse, Containing a Pleasant Invective Against Poets, Players, Jesters, and Suchlike Caterpillars of a Commonwealth*, 1579). Philip Stubbes (*The Anatomy of Abuses*, 1583) and later William Prynne (*Histrio-Mastix: The Players' Scourge or Actors' Tragedy*, 1633) kept up the litany of invective. Yet the drama had been used by Protestant officials to further the causes of the Reformation, and plays were undeniably popular in London, so that the adult acting companies could adopt various strategies to placate the more extreme reformers or at least appeal to moderates. Two adult acting companies especially vied for the attention of London's playgoing public. The Admiral's Men, with Edward Alleyn as its chief actor, tended to court a citizenry that leaned toward Puritan values without the extremism of Gosson or Stubbes. Shakespeare's company, the Lord Chamberlain's Men (organized in 1594), with Shakespeare as its chief playwright, occupied a position that, while still broadly popular in its cultural politics, was somewhat more urbane. The plays for this company tended to support what we might call family values, but without pietistic fervour and often with a sense of humour and even a touch of playful daring.

Markedly differentiated from these two adult troupes were the boys' companies, playing indoors in the Blackfriars Theatre and similar venues to comparatively affluent and sophisticated audiences made up in good measure of lawyers, law students, courtiers, and men about town. Partly because the price of admission for nighttime performances was as much as six times the entrance fees at the public adult theatres, the audiences at Blackfriars and similar 'private' playhouses tended to be more select and more attuned to moral and political satire. These theatres catered to what we might today call the avant garde. Their plays were judged so transgressive by the authorities, in fact, that they were closed down during most of the 1590s, especially for political satire but also for trendy views on sexual mores. When allowed to reopen in 1599, the boys' companies went right back to their irreverent ways, with the result that the issue of morality in the theatre was a burning topic in London right around the time that Shakespeare wrote *Hamlet*. In the Folio text of that play, Hamlet is fascinated to learn from Rosencrantz and Guildenstern about a battle involving 'an aerie of children, little eyases' (i.e., the boy actors), who are 'now the fashion' and are 'most tyrannically clapped' for their berattling of 'the common stages' (i.e., the adult companies), with the result that the adult companies find themselves very much on the defensive (2.2.337–62). The passage is unusual in Shakespeare for its topicality, and as such it highlights the sense of alarm that his acting company seems to have felt in its competition with the boy actors in matters of satire and public morality.

What then are the ideas about sex and gender as set down in plays written by Shakespeare for the Chamberlain's Men (subsequently the King's Men, in 1603) in the context of this debate in London about the proper limits of sexual expression in plays offered for public performance? One insight can perhaps be gained from Shakespeare's treatment of his sources. He regularly tones down the sexual explicitness or experimental nature of his sources in a way that seems consistent with the mandate of his acting company and the Londoners to whom they apparently wished to appeal.

An instance of this gentle expurgating is to be found in the Lucentio–Bianca plot of *The Taming of the Shrew* (c.1590–3). This delightful comedy (perhaps acted originally by Pembroke's Men and then passed along to the Chamberlain's Men) features two plots. One is the better-known story of Petruchio's taming of the shrewish Kate. The other centres on Kate's younger sister, Bianca, who, as the attractive and seemingly mild-mannered daughter of the wealthy Baptista Minola, is sought after by several wooers: by the wealthy old pantaloon, Gremio, by the younger Hortensio, and by Tranio. This last wooer, the servant of a gentleman named Lucentio, disguises himself as Lucentio and presents himself as one of the competitors for the hand of Bianca in order that the real Lucentio may take on the disguise of Tranio and thus gain access to the household of Baptista Minola, where he hopes secretly to gain the affection of Bianca. This plot is one that Shakespeare borrowed from an Italian neoclassical play called *I Suppositi* (1509), by Ludovico Ariosto. It had been translated into vigorous and colloquial English by George Gascoigne as *Supposes* (1566).

In the original and its English translation, several aspects are more boldly put forward than in Shakespeare's redaction. The prosperous old wooer, named Gremio in Shakespeare and presented to us as an amiable old codger intent on buying Bianca with his wealth, is in Ariosto an aged and miserly lawyer named Dr Cleander. The script misses no opportunity to laugh at him mercilessly not only for his grasping ways but also for his slovenly personal hygiene, his smelly armpits and crotch, and the like, with the suggestion too that he has a preference for young boys. Even more to the point, the young heroine in Ariosto's play, named Polynesta, is a pretty fast young woman when measured against her demure counterpart, Bianca, in Shakespeare's play. Whereas the disguised Lucentio and Bianca in *Taming* flirt with each other and manage to fall in love, the play offers no suggestion that they consummate their relationship until their marriage night at the close of the play. Polynesta, by contrast, does take her secret wooer Erostrato into her bed, and in fact becomes pregnant, thus confronting her father Damon with a seeming dilemma far more distressing to him than the worries of Baptista in Shakespeare's play. Polynesta is assisted in her affair by Balia, a nurse whose real function, as in many a fabliau, is to serve as a go-between or bawd. No such type appears in *Taming*.

When Shakespeare does present us with a Nurse-duenna, as in *Romeo and Juliet*, he once again expunges the stereotypical function of her acting as a bawd. Juliet's Nurse is a go-between to Romeo, of course, but the situation is emphatically guarded by the premise that Romeo and Juliet are to be quickly married, as indeed they are before they spend their one night together with the Nurse's assistance. The play is still rich in bawdry, as when Mercutio conjures up for Romeo's delectation Rosaline's 'fine foot, straight leg, and quivering thigh, /

And the demesnes that there adjacent lie' (2.1.20–1), or when the Nurse repeatedly recalls how once upon a time the infant Juliet fell and bruised her face, whereupon the Nurse's husband bade her to 'fall backward when thou hast more wit' (1.3.43), but the humour tends to be verbal and punning rather than presenting us with characters in compromising sexual situations.

Shakespeare alters his source material in *Twelfth Night* (1600–2) to similar effect. In his chief source, Barnabe Riche's *Riche His Farewell to Military Profession* (1581), the plot goes much as in Shakespeare's play: a plucky young heroine, Silla, is washed ashore near Constantinople, disguises herself as 'Silvio', and takes service with Duke Apollonius, in which role her most important duty is to convey love messages on behalf of Apollonius to the wealthy lady Julina. This lady falls in love with 'Silvio', as does the Countess Olivia in Shakespeare's play with 'Cesario', Viola's disguise identity. When in Riche's story the twin brother of Silla shows up and is mistaken by Julina for 'Silvio', Julina gladly accepts the twin brother as her wooer. The fact that he is actually named Silvio makes the confusion of identity all the more plausible. The difference is that in Riche's account, Julina and the real Silvio become lovers, and she soon realizes that she is pregnant. Confronting 'Silvio' (i.e., Silla) with this complication (the real Silvio meanwhile having departed in search of his sister), Julina is distraught to hear her supposed lover deny any role in the conception of the expected infant. Imagine Julina's unhappiness when 'Silvio' or Silla, driven to the last extremity to prove herself incapable of fathering a child, exposes her maiden breasts to Julina! Apollonius for his part is so furious at learning of 'Silvio's' apparent success with Julina that he throws his page into prison. Only the eventual return of the actual Silvio to marry Julina resolves these difficulties. The story is much the same in the source and in the play, but in the process of retelling it Shakespeare has eliminated the premarital pregnancy, the desertion, the imprisonment, and much of Riche's pious moralizing about the wages of fleshly sin. Shakespeare passes up a hilarious mixup about alleged fatherhood, seemingly in the interests of decorum. Perhaps he reflected too that the exposing of female breasts would not go well on the Elizabethan stage with a boy actor in the part of Viola.

Much Ado About Nothing (1598–9), like *The Taming of the Shrew*, juxtaposes two plots, one a delightful comedy of sparring between well-matched contestants (Beatrice and Benedick) in the war of love, the other an Italianate tragicomic plot of sexual misunderstanding and deception. An important source for Shakespeare, though not his main source, was Ariosto's *Orlando Furioso* (1516), translated into English by Sir John Harington in 1591. In Shakespeare's play, the innocent Hero is falsely accused of fornication on the eve of her wedding to Claudio by the ill-wishing Don John, who, in order to convince Claudio and his commanding officer Don Pedro of her guilt, arranges for the two of them to witness from afar a man entering Hero's chamber window on the night before her wedding day. What they see is in fact an accomplice of Don John's named Borachio, who prevails on Hero's lady-in-waiting, Margaret, to dress herself in Hero's garments and appear at the window in such a way as to create the impression that she is welcoming the sexual advances of a man – Borachio himself. What Margaret's motives are for consenting to such a charade are not made clear, but evidently she is infatuated with Borachio and accedes to the plan to please his fantasy, figuring that no great harm can come from her doing so. Ariosto's account is more dark and sexually brutal. The villainous deceiver, Polynesso, Duke of Albany, has often made love to Dalinda (the equivalent of Margaret) in the chambers of Dalinda's mistress, Genevra, so that Polynesso has no difficulty persuading Dalinda to receive him when he ascends to her window by a rope ladder in full view of Genevra's noble suitor (Ariodante) and her brother (Lurcanio). Dalinda's motive for doing so is clearer than in the equivalent situation in Shakespeare's play: Dalinda has been duped by Polynesso into believing that he merely wishes to satisfy his craving for Genevra by making love in Genevra's chambers to a woman dressed like Genevra herself. Since no maid or window scene occurs in Shakespeare's main source (an Italian short story by Matteo Bandello, 1554), Shakespeare must have known the Ariosto account. He minimizes its sordid kinkiness. Even the villain in *Much Ado* is made less repellent, while Margaret is more easily forgiven.

Although *The Tempest* (c.1611) is based on no single source, we need no source to see in this play an intense commitment to the idea that marriage must precede sexual fulfillment. Prospero insists on a proper restraint from the very first moment that Ferdinand and Miranda meet. He has arranged the meeting through his magic powers by having Ferdinand come ashore where he will encounter Miranda, and Prospero clearly wishes to promote this match, but at the same time he will make sure that it does not proceed too swiftly. He expresses delight when he perceives that the two young people 'are both in either's powers' at first meeting, but immediately adds, 'this swift business / I must uneasy make, lest too light winning / Make the prize light' (1.2.454–6). His plan of attack and motivation seem abundantly clear throughout: he will invent obstacles, casting himself in the blocking role of the angry father in order to ensure that things do not move too quickly. He accuses Ferdinand of spying, brands him a 'traitor', and threatens to 'mangle' his 'neck and feet together', with seawater only to drink, and mussels, withered roots, and acorn husks as the only source of sustenance (464–8). When Ferdinand resists, attempting to draw his sword, Prospero charms the young man from moving. Miranda has never seen her father so seemingly angry. Later, he brusquely requires Ferdinand to carry logs in obedient servitude for Miranda's sake, even though he again confides to us his delight in their courtship ('Heavens rain grace / On that which breeds between 'em!', 3.1.75–6) and declares in soliloquy, once they have left the stage, 'So glad of this as they I cannot be, / Who are surprised with all; but my rejoicing / At nothing can be more' (93–5). Similarly, when he gives his formal consent to their engagement, just before the wedding masque, saying to Ferdinand, 'Then, as my gift and thine own acquisition / Worthily purchased, take my daughter', he immediately couples this statement with a caveat:

> But
> If thou dost break her virgin-knot before
> All sanctimonious ceremonies may
> With full and holy rite be ministered,
> No sweet aspersion shall the heavens let fall
> To make this contract grow; but barren hate,
> Sour-eyed disdain, and discord shall bestrew
> The union of your bed with weeds so loathly
> That you shall hate it both. Therefore take heed,
> As Hymen's lamps shall light you.   (4.1.14–23)

And, lest we wonder if this insistence on constraint is the neurotic worry of a father about to lose his only daughter to a rival younger male, the play insists on a more broadly-based morality by having the young man embrace the doctrine as avidly as does his prospective father-in-law. Ferdinand is ready with his answer to Prospero's challenge:

> As I hope
> For quiet days, fair issue, and long life,
> With such love as 'tis now, the murkiest den,
> The most opportune place, the strong'st suggestion
> Our worser genius can, shall never melt
> Mine honor into lust, to take away
> The edge of that day's celebration
> When I shall think or Phoebus' steeds are foundered
> Or Night kept chained below.   (4.1.23–31)

The young man willingly acknowledges the eternal spiritual rewards of sexual restraint, even while he freely confesses that his own frenzy of desire for sexual completion on the night of the marriage day will make that day seem the longest of his life. Miranda says nothing, but her own chaste conduct confirms that she too has internalized the moral strictures taught her by her father.

To be sure, other ideas of sexual behaviour are in evidence on the island of *The Tempest*. Caliban, native to the place, has attempted to take Miranda as his sexual partner. Caliban and Ferdinand are thus paired and contrasted as potential mates for the play's young heroine. Both are enslaved by Prospero; both must carry wood. Miranda's choice is clear, but for Caliban the choice seems clear also. He remains impenitent about his attempt: 'Oho, oho! Would't had been done! / Thou didst prevent me; I had peopled else / This isle with Calibans' (1.2.352–4). In his eyes, sexual desire is a natural procreative instinct, one designed to perpetuate the species. It is as natural as eating. Shakespeare characteristically gives ample play to this defence of sex as natural; Caliban is in many ways an attractive character, because he is a child of nature. At the same time, what he tried to do was, in the eyes of Prospero, 'to violate / The honor of my child' (350–1). To Prospero and Miranda, the attempt if successful would have been a rape, since Miranda vehemently objected. She is still quite ready to agree with her father that Caliban is an 'Abhorrèd slave, / Which any print of goodness wilt not take' (354–5).

Two views of sexuality are thus juxtaposed, one belonging to the 'natural' world of the island, the other the conventional view of Western civilization and the Christian church. The contrast invites us to consider how there are two sides to most questions and certainly to this one. Yet the shape of the play itself encourages us to agree that at its very best, as embodied in Miranda and Ferdinand, the 'civilized' view of sexuality has a special merit. Ferdinand does win Miranda, as Caliban does not, and the children of Ferdinand and Miranda will unite the warring kingdoms of Naples and Milan in a way that has seemed heretofore impossible. Civilization has its discontents, of course, and sexual restraint imposes a neurotic limit on desire, but it does so in the interests of preserving marriage as a stabilizing force. The idea is given a kind of divine sanction in *The Tempest* by the presence of the gods at the celebration of Ferdinand's and Miranda's betrothal. Granted that the gods are really the invention of Prospero's art, as performed in a studiously artificial masque by Ariel and his fellow spirits, the dramatic effect is nonetheless one of suggesting a large spiritual dimension to the marriage of the two young people. Whether or not we agree today about denying sex before marriage, we can see in this late play of Shakespeare a debate in which the winning cards appear to be on the side of sexual restraint as a prelude to fulfillment.

Thus far we have been pursuing the evidence of a kind of bedrock orthodoxy in Shakespeare's thought about sexuality and marriage, evidencing itself from first to last, in his early romantic comedies and in the play (*The Tempest*) that seems to have been his more or less official farewell to the stage. Countering these conventional assurances, on the other hand, are many complexities that make for interesting drama. Relationships between men and women in the game of courtship are often embattled. Part of this antagonism is no doubt the result of a need for complications in the plots that will eventually be resolved in the plays' denouements, but some features of male–female conflict begin to sound more particular than that. Let us consider some of the ways in which young men and women in Shakespeare differ from each other.

Generally, in the romantic comedies of the 1590s, the young women are much better at knowing themselves than are the young men. The women are plucky, patient, and good-humoured. They seem to enjoy teasing their young men, but do so knowing that they will submit themselves finally to their wooers. Marriage will put women in a subordinate position. They are aware of this, and accept the conditions of a patriarchal culture. They are intent on marriage, and generally know right away whom it is that they will marry. Although the men nominally take the lead in proposing marriage, the women are better aware of what is at stake. The women seem smarter and more self-possessed. They are wittier and blessed with an ironic sense of humour that serves them well in dealing with masculine frailty. They are ultimately forgiving.

The men, conversely, seem woefully lacking in a sensible perspective on their own desires. They flee ineffectually from romantic attachments, or mistrust the women to whom they are attracted despite themselves, or are fickle in their choices. They seem far more sensitive to the judgement of their male friends then are the women to the judgement of their female peers. Their male egos are painfully insecure. A cutting remark from a woman, or a jeering laugh from a male friend, can unnerve the men utterly. Because they understand themselves so little, Shakespeare's young men can often seem absurd, even while we are invited to be sympathetic. They are their own worst enemies.

In *Love's Labour's Lost* (c.1588–97), for example, the young King of Navarre, together with Berowne and two other companions, sequester themselves in a three-year programme of study from which women are to be rigorously excluded. Romantic desire is too much of a distraction for men, they fear. Yet from the start we perceive that their resolves are hopelessly unrealistic. When the Princess of France and her entourage of three ladies appear at the entrance to Navarre on a diplomatic mission, the men have no idea what to do. Each of the four women knows instantly which of the four men is for her; never do they experience a moment's inner struggle. The men, on the other hand, go through painful contortions to hide from each other the desire they secretly are experiencing. When they are shamed into confessing to each other their weaknesses, they hit on a zany plan of disguising themselves as visiting Russians in order to pay court to the ladies, only to be mocked by the ladies for their pains and their perjuries. At the end, news of the death of the Princess gives the ladies an opportunity to postpone all romantic engagements for a year, in which time the ladies insist that the gentlemen get a better grip on themselves. The most self-aware of the young men, Berowne, freely confesses at last that he and his fellows have 'neglected time' and 'Played foul play with our oaths'. 'Your beauty, ladies, / Hath much deformed us, fashioning our humors / Even to the opposèd end of our intents', so that the gentlemen's behaviour 'hath seemed ridiculous' (5.2.751–5). The men have a lot to learn.

The four young lovers in *A Midsummer Night's Dream* (c.1595) are paired symmetrically two and two, like the four couples of *Love's Labour's Lost*, and with a similarly instructive contrast of male vs. female behaviour. The two women, Hermia and Helena, turn against each other briefly under intense pressure of sexual rivalry, but they never waver in their romantic attachments, Hermia for Lysander and Helena for Demetrius. Helena's loyalty is all the more astonishing in view of the contempt that Demetrius heaps on her for most of the play, along with a warning that he may just rape her if she doesn't stop tagging along after him in the forest. 'Use me but as your spaniel', she pleads, 'spurn me, strike me, / Neglect me, lose me; only give me leave, / Unworthy as I am, to follow you' (2.1.205–7). Hermia is similarly hurt by Lysander's desertion of her; they have eloped into the forest at great personal risk to be with each other, and now he has given her up in order that he may pursue Helena. The temporary break in friendship between Hermia and Helena is all the more painful in that they have been inseparable as childhood friends, growing together 'Like to a double cherry, seeming parted, / But yet an union in partition, / Two lovely berries molded on one stem' (3.2.209–11). The men, conversely, are constant to nothing other than to their aggressive rivalry. Demetrius, once a wooer of Helena, chases fruitlessly after Hermia, though knowing her to be in love with Lysander, until at length he is restored to his first affection. Lysander similarly shifts from his engagement with Hermia to a mad pursuit of Helena and eventually to a renewal of his first love. These changes of affection in the men are occasioned, to be sure, by the love-juice that Puck squeezes on their eyes, but we are surely invited to consider the love-juice as essentially a symbolic anointment betokening the proneness of the male psyche to inconstancy of affection. Lysander leaves Hermia for Helena when Hermia has demurely refused to sleep right next to Lysander on the forest floor (2.2.41–66). Demetrius remains presumably under the spell of Puck's love-juice at the end of the play, suggesting that love-juice acts on the male pretty much the way testosterone does. The love-juice is used only on the young men, and signals their repeated shifts in choosing the female objects of their desire.

The plot complications of *Midsummer* recall those of *The Two Gentlemen of Verona* (c.1590–4), in which the two 'gentlemen' of the title become rivals for a single lady because Proteus, incapable of remaining satisfied with the love of his loyal and patient Julia, strives to take away Silvia from her beloved Valentine. Eventually, Valentine's extraordinary generosity in offering to give up his claim to Silvia persuades Proteus that he is in the wrong. Proteus's namesake in Homer's *Odyssey* (6.351ff.), the 'ancient one of the sea', is infamous for his ability to change shapes at will.

Portia, in *The Merchant of Venice* (c.1596–7), is a self-possessed young woman who submits her fortunes to her father's will as specified in the competition of the three caskets, and then, having been won by Bassanio, the man she would have chosen, gracefully turns over the control of everything she has owned to her new lord and master. 'But now I was the lord / Of this fair mansion, master of my servants, / Queen o'er myself', she tells Bassanio; 'and even now, but now, / This house, these servants, and this same myself / Are yours, my lord's' (3.2.167–71). Bassanio, for his part, is a fine young man, and loyal to Portia, yet even here we encounter the comic subjection of the male. Bassanio is entirely outmanoeuvred by Portia, in her disguise as the legal expert Balthasar, into giving his wedding ring to 'Balthasar' for having saved the life of Antonio from Shylock's threat of exacting the pound of flesh. Bassanio is teased and tortured into acting out a fantasy of marital inconstancy from which Portia can release him by revealing that she herself was the learned doctor who played such a trick on him. At Belmont, in the play's comic finale, Bassanio and his male companion Gratiano are made to beg pardon of their new wives and to acknowledge that their first obligation must be to guard the sacred chastity of their marriages. Portia and Nerissa accede to the patriarchal arrangement demanded by their culture in marriage, but not without making clear their own witty superiority as a form of control. The obligations of chastely sexual union become the mirthful subject of sexual double entendre in the play's closing lines, as Gratiano vows that he will 'fear no other thing / So sore as keeping safe Nerissa's ring'; the ring is at once a symbol of chaste marriage and of the woman's sexual anatomy. No doubt 'sore' has a comically sexual resonance also. As in *Romeo and Juliet*, bawdry can be playfully entertaining in Shakespeare's romantic comedies so long as it is safely circumscribed by a happy ending in a mutually companionate marriage.

Rosalind, in *As You Like It* (1598–1600), shares many views with Portia on sex and marriage. In the play's final ceremony of multiple betrothals, Rosalind acknowledges the lordship of the two most important men in her life: her father, and Orlando, to whom she is now to be married. 'To you I give myself, for I am yours', she tells her father, and then, in the same phrasing, she says to Orlando: 'To you I give myself, for I am yours' (5.4.115–16). Her addressing them both in this fashion dramatizes the customary understanding of marriage in the Anglican Book of Common Prayer: the father gives his daughter to the younger man, transferring ownership and authority. As Prospero says in *The Tempest*, addressing Ferdinand as his prospective son-in-law: 'Then, as my gift and thine own acquisition / Worthily purchased, take my daughter' (4.1.13–14). Rosalind accepts all this, and yet she is indisputably the winner in a contest of wit between herself and Orlando. Especially at the start of the play, she is adept at badinage and wordplay whereas Orlando is ashamed at his lack of refinement and education. 'Cannot I say "I thank you"?' he wonders, when Rosalind has graciously and even invitingly given him a chain from around her own neck. 'My better parts / Are all thrown down, and that which here stands up / Is but a quintain, a mere lifeless block' (1.2.239–41). (A hint of detumescence hovers about this image.) Rosalind must become his teacher. Her disguise in the forest as 'Ganymede' enables her to initiate a discussion on the art of wooing, in which she hopes to instruct Orlando in how to avoid stereotyping and idealizing of women. He must learn that women can be 'more clamorous than a parrot against rain, more newfangled than an ape'. She, posing as Orlando's Rosalind, will be 'more giddy in my desires than a monkey. I will weep for nothing, like Diana in the fountain, and I will do that when you are disposed to be merry; I will laugh like a hyena, and that when thou art inclined to sleep' (4.1.142–9). Her point is that Orlando will be a happier and better husband if he can begin to have a realistic understanding of what it is like for a man and a woman to live together, day after day and year after year. Rosalind is, like so many other Shakespearean heroines, more wise, more emotionally mature, more ready for the complexities of a real relationship than is Orlando. The same is true in the love tragedy of *Romeo and Juliet*.

Finally, we have Viola and Orsino in *Twelfth Night*. Like Rosalind, the resourceful Viola accepts her role as loyally obedient to her lord and master, while at the same time undertaking to educate this gentleman in all that he does not know about courtship and marriage. Orsino is infatuated at long distance with the Countess Olivia. Perhaps she senses, as we do, that his ardour for her is stereotypical; Olivia is for Orsino the unattainable goddess of a Petrarchan sonnet sequence. Being afflicted as he is with love melancholy, Orsino seems content to nurse his own exquisite suffering. His fruitless self-abasement is not unlike that of Silvius in *As You Like It*, who seems to ask nothing of his Phoebe other than that she allow him to grovel in pain; the Countess Olivia is like Phoebe, though of higher social rank, congratulating herself on the power she enjoys through withholding of her beauty. Viola has an answer for such sought-after beauties, which is to consider the costs to oneself of a frivolous denial of being truly in love. 'Lady, you are the cruel'st she alive / If you will lead these graces to the grave / And leave the world no copy', she advises Olivia (1.5.236–8). With Orsino she proceeds much as Rosalind does with Orlando, using her male guise as 'Cesario' in order that she and Orlando may talk friend to friend. 'We men may say more, swear more', she tells him, 'but indeed / Our shows are more than will; for still we prove / Much in our vows, but little in our love' (2.4.116–18). The fiction of her male identity allows Viola to generalize about male behaviour without arraigning Orsino directly.

What are we to make of this repeated configuration in the romantic comedies of the unselfknowing man and the patiently instructive woman? It is as though Shakespeare is expressing, on behalf of his fellow males, a self-critical view. Men are impossible. They need help. Without denying them the ultimate position of superiority in the conventional hierarchy of a paternalistic culture, Shakespeare presents men as generally weak and helpless without the counsel and companionship of women. The attitude toward women is correspondingly one of gratitude and admiration, along with perhaps a grudging anxiety about male dependence. Young women enable men to grow up, to achieve a kind of emotional maturity and self-understanding that would be impossible without women's help. The women do so, moreover, in a way that minimizes the hazards of male transition from immaturity to maturity. By taking on the disguise of young men, as we see in Julia, Portia, Rosalind, and Viola, these young heroines erase the barrier of gender difference that many of Shakespeare's young men discover to be so daunting. Finding themselves in the congenial atmosphere of friendship seemingly between man and man, the young males in Shakespeare's romantic comedies begin to achieve insights and intimacies they have never known before. Once this loving friendship has ripened into a genuine mutuality, then the revelation of the woman's true sexual identity is no longer threatening. The play can end, presto-change-o, with the young woman (actually a boy actor) throwing off her/his disguise.

Even after marriage, to be sure, the pattern of witty women and dithering men can continue. The title of *The Merry Wives of Windsor*

(1597–1601) lays proper stress on the self-possession and cleverness of Mistresses Ford and Page as they amusedly reflect not only on the inanities of their would-be lover, Falstaff, but on Master Ford's seemingly incurable jealousy, about which he must repeatedly be taught a lesson. Still, this is an unusual comedy for Shakespeare, with its uniquely English domestic setting and its portrayal of village life in Windsor. Shakespeare's more usual preoccupation is with the foibles of the unmarried male wooer.

Now, not all males in the romantic comedies are weak, to be sure. Even if the examples looked at thus far provide a compellingly consistent portrait of young men in love, they do not tell the whole story. Some males turn out to be remarkably self-assured, like Petruchio in *The Taming of the Shrew*. He has come from Verona 'to wive it wealthy in Padua; / If wealthily, then happily in Padua'. He is undaunted by the prospect of a shrewish wife, provided she be 'rich, / And very rich' (1.2.61–2, 74–5). The reported shrewishness of Kate is to him a challenge, not a potential hazard. Yet for all his professed interest in wealth as his uppermost consideration, Petruchio finds in Kate a worthy opponent, one whose wit deserves to be answered in kind. She in turn comes to find him more interesting by far than any of the other men she sees around her. She resists, of course, when he undertakes to tame her by putting on a grandiloquent display at their wedding and then dragging her off to his house before the wedding festivities are over. He deprives her of food and sleep, plays the tyrant with the servants, and then boasts in soliloquy of his success: 'He that knows better how to tame a shrew, / Now let him speak. 'Tis charity to show' (4.1.198–9). Whether the audience is to approve or disapprove of his behaviour as wooer and husband is today a celebratedly unsettled issue, but what can be said with confidence is that Petruchio knows what he is doing and that he succeeds in his own terms. 'I am he am born to tame you, Kate', he warns her at the start, 'And bring you from a wild Kate to a Kate / Conformable as other household Kates' (2.1.273–5). He never wavers from his plan. He justifies it as he goes along by comparing his method to the taming of a hawk (4.1.176–84). Kate learns eventually that she will be better off if she agrees with him that the sun is the moon when he says so, and that an old man may be transformed into a 'Young budding virgin' if he insists (4.5.1–48). In the concluding competition among husbands to see which of them is most contentedly married to an obedient wife, Petruchio wins hands down; Kate does as he bids her, to the point of throwing her own cap underfoot and then lecturing the other wives on the duty that every wife 'oweth to her husband', just like the duty that 'the subject owes the prince' (5.2.159–60). Perhaps, as often happens in stage productions today, she says this tongue in cheek, or even in such a way as to suggest that she has been relentlessly brainwashed, but at all events she has acceded to her husband's demands. He has won the argument.

Oberon too, in *A Midsummer Night's Dream*, carries the day in a contest of supremacy between husband and wife. He humiliates Queen Titania for her disobedience in refusing to give him the 'changeling boy' that she cherishes in memory of the boy's mother, a votaress of Titania's order (2.1.120–37). He does so by charming her into falling in love with the absurd Bottom. His method of revenge may seem strange by human standards, in that he causes her to take a lover and thus to cuckold himself, but the representation of this affair is extraordinarily delicate; Bottom's chief delight, as Titania's lover, is to eat a peck of good dry oats and to have his head scratched by Peaseblossom and Mustardseed. (This is another instance of Shakespeare's decorous expurgating of the erotic, although one would never guess as much from many a modern production, in which the implicit is often made explicit.) At any rate, Oberon is the fairy king, and all that the fairies do seems upside down from our mortal perspective. The main point here is that he succeeds entirely in teaching Titania a lesson in wifely obedience. She, like Kate in *Taming*, submits without question. When she is awakened from her trance by Oberon, and is shown her asinine lover lying by her side, her only response is one of revulsion: 'How came these things to pass? / Oh, how mine eyes do loathe his visage now!' (4.1.77–8). She offers not a word of reproof or hurt feelings. Perhaps her question, 'How came these things to pass?' is directed at Puck, whom she knows to be a mischief-maker, but she expresses no resentment toward her husband, even though he now has the child. 'When I had at my pleasure taunted her', Oberon reports to Puck, 'And she in mild terms begged my patience, / I then did ask of her her changeling child, / Which straight she gave me' (56–9). The victory is complete. And, lest we wonder if this is a dispensation taking place only in the fairy kingdom, we note that Theseus has conquered the Amazonian queen Hippolyta prior to the commencement of the play. *A Midsummer* is, among other things, a celebration of that male conquest.

The raw conflict of Petruchio and Kate in *Taming* mellows appreciably in the famous war of words between Benedick and Beatrice in *Much Ado*. Not that the exchanges are any less sharp and vehement. The difference is that a critical balance between the sexes is restored. Beatrice gives as good as she takes. During the evening revels of Act 2, she trumps Benedick so resoundingly in their battle of wits that he is genuinely hurt; she has left him with the impression that she really does regard him as 'the Prince's jester, a very dull fool', whose only gift is 'in devising impossible slanders' (2.1.131–2). It is as though Shakespeare revisits the scene of *Taming* with a view to equalizing the contest. Beatrice is not asked to submit, nor does Benedick simply win. To the contrary, when Beatrice has something momentous to ask of him, he listens seriously and agrees to try. 'Kill Claudio', she demands of him, when Claudio has slandered her dear cousin Hero and has deserted Hero at the altar (4.1.288). Claudio is Benedick's friend and fellow officer. For Benedick to challenge Claudio and thus incur the enmity of him and of their commanding officer, Don Pedro, is a heavy burden indeed. Yet Benedick, unlike these men, has seen that something is seriously askew in the accusation brought against Hero by Don John, even if that accusation is backed by the seeming proof of what they saw at Hero's window on the night before her wedding. Benedick's own admirable scepticism, combined with his respect for Beatrice's insistent faith in Hero, gives to him a complex and mature view of human relationships that sets him apart from most of the other men in the play.

Overall, then, one can see in Shakespeare's romantic comedies a debate about men and women in the serious game of courtship. Just as George Lyman Kittredge has proposed a 'Marriage Group' in Chaucer's *Canterbury Tales*, variously exploring the dimensions of romantic love from the tender to the sardonic, Shakespeare's romantic comedies look into many aspects of the question. If *Much Ado* represents something of an evolution in his thought about courtship, as compared with the earlier *Taming*, then perhaps Shakespeare is thinking his way through to a less paternalistic and less male-dominated idea about men and women. We need to be cautious about any such conclusion, since we are dealing with plays that stand by themselves as dramatic entertainments, but perhaps we have reason to expect that Shakespeare's thoughts about the relationships of the sexes should gain in complexity as he continues to revisit the subject.

A darker side of this debate about courtship concerns the propensity of men not just toward immature behaviour but toward irrational jealousy and possessiveness of women, as though a wife or sweetheart were a property to be guarded against the claims of other men. Claudio in *Much Ado* is a notable instance. His immediate instinct, when he is told at the evening revels by Don John and Borachio that Hero is being wooed by Don Pedro, is to assume that the accusation is true. As Claudio's senior officer, Don Pedro has agreed to court Hero on Claudio's behalf; now, it seems, Don Pedro is pleading for himself. ''Tis certain so', Claudio concludes. 'The Prince woos for himself. / Friendship is constant in all other things / Save in the office and affairs of love' (2.1.168–70). The proverbial nature of this observation – all's fair in love and war – should warn us that Claudio thinks in clichés about male competition for women. This particular misunderstanding is soon gotten over by Don Pedro's assuring Claudio that Hero is to be his, but Claudio does not learn from his mistake. When Don John comes forward with a more serious accusation, that Hero is sleeping with other men, even on the eve of her marriage, Claudio is once again prepared to believe the worst of her. He scarcely knows her; his suspicion is toward women in general. What is more, the other men generally second his misogynistic view. Don Pedro credits the attack on Hero's reputation. Even Hero's father is convinced at first that she is guilty. Only Benedick has the sagacity to be sceptical, as we have seen. Men have a problem this way; they are fearful that women can undo men's frail sense of pride in their masculinity. The threat of a woman's infidelity is a potential blow to the heart of a man's ego. It is to suggest that he is something less than a man. Claudio is eventually cured of his jealousy and restored to his Hero, but it is as though she has to be reborn for this to happen. Claudio is saved from his worst self by the fact that his fears are chimerical, and by Hero's charitable forgiveness.

Much Ado is in many ways an earlier study, with a happy ending, for *Othello* (c.1603–4). Desdemona is, like Hero, innocent of what her husband fears and suspects in her. She is utterly devoted to Othello and so loyal to him that she readily forgives his harsh treatment of her. Even as she lies dying at his hands, she attempts to turn the blame away from him to herself. When her lady-in-waiting, Emilia, asks her who has done this deed, she answers, 'Nobody; I myself. Farewell. / Commend me to my kind lord. Oh, farewell!' (5.2.128–9). Desdemona's last utterance is a lie intended to deflect suspicion from her abusive husband. Othello is thus, like Claudio, a victim finally of his own apprehensiveness about women. His fear that he has been scorned and rejected by the 'delicate creature' who is the very source of his life and happiness is unbearable to him:

> But there where I have garnered up my heart,
> Where either I must live or bear no life,
> The fountain from the which my current runs
> Or else dries up – to be discarded thence!
>   (4.2.59–62)

For all his calm manliness and nobility of bearing in the early scenes of the play, Othello is prone to Iago's warped insinuations about the incurable waywardness of women. Othello loves Desdemona dearly, but Iago's suggestions that her love for him is 'unnatural' because he is older than she and of a different race, and that such 'unnatural' fascinations on her part will inevitably wither into disdain, soon find their fulfillment in Othello's own reflections on who he is:

> Haply, for I am black
> And have not those soft parts of conversation
> That chamberers have, or for I am declined
> Into the vale of years – yet that's not much –
> She's gone. I am abused, and my relief
> Must be to loathe her. Oh, curse of marriage,
> That we can call these delicate creatures ours
> And not their appetites!   (3.3.279–86)

Othello's insistent belief that men have a right to 'own' women is not unlike that of Claudio, and it is a major part of Othello's undoing. To claim ownership of women is to generate a fear of what women can do to men by betraying them through womanly 'appetites'. Othello's murdering of Desdemona at Iago's prompting is a terrifying expression of his hatred for the betrayal that he has erroneously felt.

In *Much Ado*, then, and in *Othello*, as well as in *The Merry Wives*, the women are innocent, while the men are guilty of suspecting the women of infidelity; the problem lies chiefly in the recesses of the diseased male ego. Even Viola, in *Twelfth Night*, is accused falsely of inconstancy by Orsino. What happens when the male nightmare turns out to be true? Shakespeare begins to explore the dimensions of this problem in the Sonnets and in *Troilus and Cressida*.

Troilus and Cressida (1601) is about a love affair that comes to a dispiriting end when the Trojans agree to give Cressida to the Greeks in exchange for a valuable Trojan warrior (Antenor) whom the Greeks hold captive. Cressida's father, having previously gone over to the Greek side and having proved useful to them as a seer, now requests that his daughter be allowed to join him. This is only a chance incident in the long Trojan War, but it is painfully consequential to the two lovers thus separated. By the time Shakespeare came to this often-told tale, Cressida's reputation had fallen precipitously. In Chaucer's poem, *Troilus and Criseyde* (1382–6), she is resourceful, witty, and capable of insightful tenderness. By the early seventeenth century, on the other hand, her name had become virtually synonymous with that of the inconstant woman. Cressida herself, in the play, imagines what might happen: if she is false to Troilus, she insists, let everyone say, 'As false as Cressid' (3.2.195). Just as Troilus's name will become associated with male constancy ('As true as Troilus') and just as Pandarus's name will become a byword for 'all brokers-between' (181, 202–3), Cressida is aware that if she proves false to her vows in love, her name will be forever equated with falseness in women. She says this, to be sure, before she and Troilus have become lovers and before the separation occurs. Our awareness of the ironic truth of her prophecy is informed by our historical knowledge as to what will in fact happen.

Shakespeare's task, as dramatic artist, is to deal with this fallen reputation. His Cressida is a realist: sardonic, wary, and fully cognizant that her uncle is doing his best to coax her into Troilus's bed. She is attracted to Troilus, but very careful not to surrender to his importunities until she can have some reassurance that the emotional rewards of a mutual commitment will be worth the price of lost personal autonomy. Cressida is not like Rosalind or Viola or Portia. Marriage is not in question: Troilus is a prince of the royal blood. Cressida is a new kind of woman in Shakespeare, and one whose sexual mores seem to contravene those of her many predecessors. Yet Shakespeare approaches her story with remarkable sympathy. Cressida, once she has suitably tortured Troilus with delays, finally gives herself to him with deep commitment. She finds in their love relationship the emotional centre she has longed for, so much so that when the ironies of the war dictate her being turned over to the Greeks on the very next day after the first consummation of their affair, she balks at going and cannot believe that Troilus will accede to the arrangement. This new love in her life goes before all else. Such is not the case with Troilus, however. Having enjoyed Cressida sexually, he now gives priority to the military state of affairs and the demands of his brothers and fellow officers that Cressida be exchanged for Antenor. It is just as she feared: 'Men prize the thing ungained more than it is.' A man will do anything to fulfill his sexual desire; once that is obtained, the woman loses control. 'Achievement is command; ungained, beseech' (1.2.291–5). Cressida does finally yield to a new lover, Diomedes, in the Greek camp, in part at least because she will need a strong man to fend off the advances of the other sex-starved Greek officers. We are invited to wonder, nevertheless, who has deserted whom. Troilus has insisted on her return to the Greeks; he means to visit her secretly, but in effect the love affair is over. She yields to oppressive circumstance, not happy with herself or indeed with women generally, but realistically. 'Ah, poor our sex!' she laments. 'This fault in us I find: / The error of our eye directs our mind' (5.2.112–13). Shakespeare's exploration of a more 'adult' sexuality than he had presented generally in his romantic comedies of the 1590s begins around 1600, just when he was finishing his engagement with romantic comedy in *Twelfth Night*.

The Sonnets are hard to date; they were not published until 1609, and could have been written any time previously. Some are no doubt early, especially the sonnets at the beginning of the sequence possibly addressed to the Earl of Southampton, who befriended Shakespeare in 1593–4 by serving as patron for two long narrative poems, *Venus and Adonis* and *The Rape of Lucrece*. The early sonnets make a point of urging a young man to marry and bear a male child who can be his heir. Soon, however, the relationship of the poet-speaker to the young gentleman grows complicated by jealousies, absences, rivalries for the gentleman's favour, anxieties about ageing, and still more. Then, Sonnet 127 through 152, constituting the last twenty-five sonnets of the entire sequence except for the final two (153 and 154, which seem disconnected from the series), bear down relentlessly on the theme of sexual jealousy. The poet-speaker's mistress, known as the 'Dark Lady' because her eyes and brow are 'raven black' (Sonnet 127), deserts him for the gentleman friend. Earlier, too, in Sonnets 40–2, the friend is arraigned and then forgiven for having taken away the poet-speaker's mistress. The order of the Sonnet sequence used to be called into question,

especially since Shakespeare seems not to have had a hand in its publication in 1609, but that order is now generally accepted, and seems
plausibly to represent a chronological order of composition as well as
a continuous narrative line; that is, the late sonnets seem aptly suited
to time of *Troilus and Cressida* and *Hamlet*, around 1600. (Gertrude,
in *Hamlet*, offers another instance of womanly frailty.) The 'Dark
Lady', like Cressida, is alluring, sexually adventurous, and ultimately
unfaithful.

The poet-speaker's response to the Dark Lady, both before and
after her desertion of him, is distinctly unhappy. 'My love is as a fever,
longing still / For that which longer nurseth the disease', he confesses (Sonnet 147). 'Love is my sin' (142). He contrasts the two most
important persons in his life: one is a 'better angel' and a 'man right
fair', while the other is a 'worser spirit', 'a woman colored ill' (144).
He is ashamed of and disgusted by his own lust. If even the amorous
prelude leading up to sexual consummation is 'perjured, murd'rous,
bloody, full of blame, / Savage, extreme, rude, cruel, not to trust', the
achievement of orgasm can lead only to bitter disillusionment: 'Enjoyed
no sooner but despisèd straight . . . no sooner had / Past reason hated'
(129). The poet-speaker sees himself as compulsively addicted to an
illusory pleasure that makes him feel terrible each time he succumbs
to desire. The woman is tyrannous and proud, taking pleasure in
tormenting him (131). Her most unbearable cruelty is to steal away
the affections of the poet's friend. Sex is dirty.

Whether Shakespeare as a man experienced a sense of revulsion about
his own sexuality is of course impossible to tell, but he certainly knew
how to portray the symptoms and the disease. The man bears the chief
responsibility for letting himself become enslaved. Perhaps then Shakespeare's idealized portraits of women like Desdemona and Hero, whose
goodness and charitable forbearance under duress almost surpass belief,
may stem from a guilt feeling about masculine aggressiveness. Shakespeare seemingly manifests a need, as dramatic artist, to portray women
who can either save men from their worst selves (as in the case of
Hero and Claudio) or at least endure for ever in literary art as tokens
of a redemptive goodness in the human race. Such idealized women
in his plays and poems atone not only for the men, but for those women
who do sometimes prove to be inconstant.

The intense friendship portrayed in the Sonnets raises another question about Shakespeare's representation of sexuality. This friendship

is a loving one, beyond question. The poet-speaker is disconsolate when he is separated from his friend and desperate when he fears that the love he feels may not be fully returned. 'Take all my loves, my love,' he pleads, 'yea, take them all' (Sonnet 40). A bitter farewell in Sonnet 87 leaves the poet-speaker with the haunting realization that he is left with nothing but a dream. What are we to make of this emotional bonding of the male speaker to a young gentleman? Is it what today we would call homosexual? The poet-speaker denies that there is, or even could be, a physical consummation between the two: Sonnet 20 insists that the gentleman's almost feminine beauty is a thing created by Nature for woman's pleasure and for the purposes of procreation, but is not the necessary condition of the poet-speaker's love for this man. The Sonnet puts it bawdily: Nature has 'pricked' out this gentleman for woman's pleasure by 'adding one thing to my purpose nothing', i.e., the penis or prick. ('Pricked out' also means 'designated'.) 'Mine be thy love and thy love's use their treasure', he concludes, meaning that the poet-speaker will have the young gentleman's love in the Platonic sense while women (or a woman) will share sexual pleasure with him and bear him children. The Sonnets seem intent on defining a love between men that is deeply emotional in all the ways that can point toward a loving partnership, but in which physically erotic pleasure is seen as inappropriate or at least unnecessary. The idea of male-to-male physical sex is not denounced as revulsive, as it was by many Puritan preachers, but it is presented as somehow contrary to the natural order of things in the physiological makeup of men and women.

Not all critics agree with this interpretation or with its implications for male friendship as portrayed in the plays. In today's theatre, loving male friendships in Shakespeare are often depicted as overtly homosexual. In *Twelfth Night*, for example, the sea captain called Antonio who washes ashore with Viola's brother Sebastian says things that certainly attest to a very strong love. 'If you will not murder me for my love, let me be your servant', he pleads, when Sebastian suggests that considerations of safety prompt them to separate in Illyria (2.1.33–4). Antonio knows that he is in danger here as one who is confessedly Orsino's enemy (5.1.71–2), and yet he is willing to risk his very life to stay close to Sebastian: 'But come what may, I do adore thee so / That danger shall seem sport, and I will go' (2.1.45–6). Sebastian appears to feel no less of a love for Antonio. 'Antonio, O my dear Antonio!'

he greets his friend when they are reunited in Act 5. 'How have the hours racked and tortured me / Since I have lost thee!' (5.1.217–19). One can easily see how theatre directors and actors find these the words of men who are physically in love. Yet the play offers no evidence for a relationship that differs from that described by the poet-speaker in the Sonnets as lovingly Platonic. Sebastian's sexual preference is for Olivia, and Antonio raises no objection to this match.

The same is true of another Antonio, in *The Merchant of Venice*. Undoubtedly his love for young Bassanio is very deep; it is certainly one for which he is willing to risk his life. Accordingly, Antonio's sadness, with which the play begins, is often explained today (as in Michael Radford's 2004 film with Jeremy Irons as Antonio) as a result of his partially unexplored amorous feelings for Bassanio. Yet Antonio seems genuinely ready to help Bassanio woo and marry Portia, and he shares in the celebration of the marriages at the play's end. If he is left out from marriage himself, any sense of incompletion may simply be a result of the play's commitment to marriage as a form of dramatic closure; Antonio's feelings at this point are not demonstrably more homosexually oriented than those of Jaques, say, who is unpartnered at the end of *As You Like It*, or Mercutio in *Romeo and Juliet*, who mocks romantic love and who dies a confirmed bachelor. To be sure, Mercutio is sometimes also seen in performances today and in the critical literature as gay; Franco Zeffirelli's successful 1968 film and Baz Luhrmann's *Romeo + Juliet* (1996) offer lively instances. Such interpretations can be very appealing to modern audiences, and we can easily see why: they help explain in our terms certain exchanges of language between men that our culture regards as amorous. On the other hand, to the extent that we are interested in Shakespeare's ideas about sexual ambiguity, we need to be cautious about what we attribute to his own generation of playgoers. The evidence may be seen to suggest that Shakespeare expresses the emotions of love between men with the remarkable intensity and vigour he brings to other personal relationships as well. He wrote for a generation in which professions of love between men were not unusual or indecorous, and need not imply overt physical longing.

He also wrote for an acting company that assigned the roles of women on stage to pre-adolescent boys. Some of these boys appear to have performed women's role until they were sixteen or seventeen; adolescence generally came later in the early modern period than today, owing chiefly to less adequate nutrition in the diet. What was the life of these boys like? Although they could not be apprentices in the acting company as such, since it was not a London guild, many were apprenticed individually to adult actors who were themselves members of one London guild or another. The relationship was necessarily close; the boys spent their lives with adult members of the acting company, receiving from them whatever education they got. They played women on stage to the adult men with whom they were so close. Kissing between men and 'women' in the plays is generally restrained, but it does occur: Juliet and Romeo kiss briefly at the masqued ball in Act 1, and when they bid one another farewell at Juliet's window in 3.5, even though they are physically separated during their long wooing scene in 2.2 by Romeo's remaining below in the Capulets' orchard while addressing Juliet at her chamber window. We can only speculate as to what loving friendships may or may not have formed in the acting company. The adult actors themselves, all male, were presumably close to one another; actors left the company rather seldom, and were lifelong colleagues in many instances.

What we can say is that the assigning of women's parts to boy actors gave Shakespeare a rich opportunity to sport dramatically with sexual ambiguity and to interrogate gender differences. The boy-women in his comedies are often described as nearly feminine in their beauty. Orsino, in *Twelfth Night*, is struck by this feature in 'Cesario' (really Viola masquerading as a young man):

> they shall yet belie thy happy years
> That say thou art a man. Diana's lip
> Is not more smooth and rubious; thy small pipe
> Is as the maiden's organ, shrill and sound,
> And all is semblative a woman's part.
> (1.4.30–4)

Malvolio says much the same, though less sympathetically, when he reports to Olivia the 'personage and years' of the seeming young man, Cesario, who has asked to be admitted to see her:

> Not yet old enough for a man, nor young enough for a boy; as a squash is before 'tis a peascod, or a codling when 'tis almost an apple. 'Tis with him in standing water between boy and man. (1.5.153–6)

More than plot hangs on the use of gender-crossing disguise in these comedies. Gender is something that can be performed. It is constructed, like any theatrical performance, out of costume, voice, and gesture. Shakespeare's young heroines in disguise become the objects of desire by persons of both sexes. Viola/Cesario is pursued by Olivia as Cesario; as Viola, she ultimately becomes the partner of the man she loves, Orsino. Rosalind in *As You Like It* uses her disguise as Ganymede to play-act being 'Rosalind' to Orlando until the resolution of the plot allows her to become that Rosalind indeed; meantime, as Ganymede she has awakened the desire of the shepherdess, Phoebe. The name 'Ganymede', taken by Shakespeare from his source, Thomas Lodge's *Rosalynde*, has unmistakable homoerotic resonances; Ganymede was, in classical myth, Zeus's cupbearer and male favourite. Shakespeare plays with these resonances, even though he does so in a decorous way that seems consistent with the tactful expurgating we saw earlier. The seeming male-to-male friendships between Orlando and Rosalind and between Orsino and Viola are understood by the audience to be ones that will ripen into heterosexual union. Once the male disguises are thrown aside, the heroines of these plays are no longer desired by women: Phoebe consents to marry Silvius rather than marry a woman, and Olivia seems entirely happy to join in marriage with Sebastian, the male twin and look-alike of the 'Cesario' with whom she fell in love. Theatrically, to be sure, we understand that the men and the women in these delightful mixups are performed by adult and juvenile males. Metatheatrical awareness of these levels of disguise and of sexual iden-tity greatly enriches the comedy of sexual ambiguity in these plays.

Despite the difficulties of separating Shakespeare's own ideas on sex and gender from those of his London audience, we can nonetheless point to many features in the romantic comedies that are not only distinctive but also cohere together into a comprehensive view of human sexuality. Young women in Shakespearean comedy are often cleverer, more resourceful, and more knowledgeable about themselves than are their male wooers. Perhaps Shakespeare is in effect apologizing for male importunity, but in any case the men have much to learn from women. Sometimes in Shakespeare's early comedies the male is the winner, but increasingly in the comedies of the late 1590s the men come to realize that they are lucky to have won the affection of the admirable and patient young women whom they will marry. Wit and intellect provide a basis for a kind of equality that helps ameliorate the social practices giving men the upper hand. The women at their best willingly enter into a balanced and mutually beneficial companionship with men, while also accepting the norms of a patriarchal world to the extent at least of granting that men are to be lords and masters in their households. Generally, indeed, young men and women in the romantic comedies find comfort and safety in acceding to established codes of sexual behaviour. At the same time, Shakespeare finds equal worth and intellectual stimulation in loving relationships between two men or between two women, where shared friendship is everything and sex is at least nominally not involved. Sexual desire is very insistent but it can too easily become degraded, so that it needs to be relegated to a lesser status in the hierarchy of values. The struggle to control sexual feelings is rife with peril, but in a strong relationship it can add immeasurably to the complex bonds of love. In the more fraught relationships that Shakespeare begins to explore around 1600, the dark side of human sexuality exerts itself in ways that can be terrifying. These ideas, extensively developed in the 1590s, persist into Shakespeare's late work, most of all in *The Tempest*.

3

What is Honour?
Shakespeare's Ideas on Politics and Political Theory

During the decade of the 1590s, as Shakespeare was writing romantic comedies at the rate of nearly one a year (ten in all, from *The Comedy of Errors*, *The Two Gentlemen of Verona*, and *Love's Labour's Lost*, c.1589–94, down to *As You Like It* and *Twelfth Night* around the turn of the century), he also devoted extensive energies to the writing of English history plays. Some nine plays span the decade, from the early *Henry VI* plays in three parts and *Richard III* to *King John* and then a four-play sequence from *Richard II* through the two parts of *Henry IV* to *Henry V* in 1596–9. He also wrote *Titus Andronicus* some time around 1590 and *Romeo and Juliet* in mid decade, but even these seeming exceptions tend to confirm the pattern of two predominant genres, since *Romeo and Juliet* incorporates many of the ideas on sexuality and gender we explored in the previous chapter, while *Titus Andronicus* is a fanciful history play with a deep interest in the tragic consequences of civil conflict.

Throughout the 1590s, then, Shakespeare was committed chiefly to two prevailing genres. Why these two genres in particular, and what are the implications for a study of the development of Shakespeare's thought? One possible answer is that the two genres appealed to him in different but related ways as exploring the dilemmas of human existence from a relatively youthful and hopeful perspective. The comedies look at problems and potentials of sexuality and gender. The English history plays examine political conflict in an attempt to understand its origins and mode of operations. The insights to be gained from such an examination are full of potential significance for an English people only recently having emerged from a prolonged period of civil and religious conflict into the beginnings of modern nationhood. These insights also illuminate the political career of England's most successful and charismatic king, Henry V. As he approaches manhood in the Henry IV plays, Prince Henry, or Hal, is a young man facing the challenge of succeeding his father as king. The political and philosophical consequences of such a *rite de passage* are those a young author might well want to sort out on his way to encountering the darker philosophical issues that will confront him in later years. Like the romantic comedies, the English history plays, especially those in the latter half of the 1590s, are ultimately upbeat in Shakespeare's largely admiring portrait of England's hero king, Henry V. Yet problems and ambiguities are also manifest.

Shakespeare's approach as a dramatist to politics and political theory is essentially one of encouraging the play of ideas in a series of historical debates that are hugely relevant to his own culture. Whether he takes sides in the debates is often unclear. What is clear is that he genuinely tries to represent the contending issues fairly and with extraordinary insight. Shakespeare is not a political theorist as such, but his analytical skills are formidable, and so is his ability as a dramatist to bring issues alive on stage through the words and actions of unforgettably vivid characters. The result is both instructive and entertaining for his audiences. The plays are supportive of values about which his own generation of English people cared deeply, whatever their varying political persuasions, and they are values that interest us today despite the passage of roughly four hundred years.

Let us take as a central example the representation of political conflict in *Richard II* (c.1595–6) and *1 Henry IV* (1596–7), two of Shakespeare's finest history plays. The subject is civil war, at a time in the early fifteenth century when England stood on the verge of an entire century of civil strife. Since that war would end only with the coming to the throne in 1485 of Henry VII, founder of the Tudor dynasty and grandfather of the queen who ruled England during the first thirty-seven years of Shakespeare's lifetime, the conflict was profoundly meaningful to Elizabeth's subjects. They generally viewed it as a trial of fire out of which England, like the legendary phoenix, finally arose in a mystical rebirth from its own ashes. Painful though the war was, it led to the making of the early modern English nation.

What had led to that prolonged civil conflict, and who was at fault? In *Richard II*, Shakespeare distributes the responsibility with notable evenhandedness. Richard is a weak and irresponsible monarch, but he is indubitably the legitimate king of England, and he carries that office with regal charisma. Having inherited the throne at a hazardously early age (historically, Richard was ten when his father, Edward the Black Prince, died in battle in 1376), Richard has found himself surrounded by powerful and ambitious uncles. The feudal custom of primogeniture, specifying that the eldest son should inherit at his father's death, has meant that Richard is now king rather than some older and more experienced member of his family. The practical result in this instance is that John of Gaunt, Duke of Lancaster and Richard's eldest uncle, has assumed a dominant position in the affairs of state during Richard's minority, while a younger uncle, Thomas of Woodstock, the Duke of Gloucester, has been a constant source of irritation to the young king. Historically, Woodstock led a successful effort to impeach and condemn five of Richard's supporters (1385). This incident is not reported in *Richard II*, but the consequences hang heavy over the play, for when Woodstock is killed at Calais while in the custody of Thomas Mowbray, the Duke of Norfolk, Richard is widely suspected of having suborned Mowbray to do away with a troublesome uncle. Whether Richard did so or not, his political opponents have no doubt of his guilt. As Woodstock's widow says to her brother-in-law Gaunt, 'Oh, sit my husband's wrongs on Hereford's spear, / That it may enter butcher Mowbray's breast!' (1.2.47–8). 'Hereford' is Gaunt's son, Henry Bolingbroke, Duke of Hereford, who has challenged Mowbray (the Duke of Norfolk) to a trial by combat on an accusation of having plotted the Duke of Gloucester's death (1.1.100).

With that challenge, political conflict intensifies, for Richard must now preside over a trial by combat in which Mowbray is manifestly a stalking-horse for Richard himself. No love is lost between Richard and his eldest cousin, Bolingbroke, the son and heir of John of Gaunt. Yet Richard dares not proceed too openly against Bolingbroke, because Richard himself is implicated in Woodstock's death. The young king's solution is to exile both antagonists. He banishes Mowbray forever, but accedes to political pressure in sentencing Bolingbroke to ten years of banishment and then reducing the number to six (1.3.140–212). The decision is presented in the play as lawful since it is reluctantly agreed to by John of Gaunt and other members of the King's council

(124), but it is plainly also a matter of expediency if not outright desperation on Richard's part, and it bodes more trouble.

The responses of various members of the royal family to the aborted trial and banishment are interestingly varied. Woodstock's widow, as we have seen, cries out for blood. Hers is the ethic of revenge, as old at least as the demands of Aeschylus's Erinyes or Furies (in the *Eumenides*) for the death of any person guilty of a crime against the ties of blood kinship. As the Duchess of Gloucester insists to her brother-in-law,

> Ah, Gaunt, his blood was thine! That bed, that womb,
> That metal, that self mold that fashioned thee,
> Made him a man; and though thou livest and breathest,
> Yet art thou slain in him.   (1.2.22–5)

She speaks with the same appeal to the code of revenge that Hamlet's father's ghost employs in urging his son to revenge a 'foul and most unnatural murder' committed by Hamlet's uncle. The code is archaic; it always poses a problem for civil society by vesting the authority for revenge not in the state but in the murdered individual's family, leading inevitably to a cycle of vengeance and counter-vengeance. Still, the code of revenge has its own ethical rationale, and it is one that appeals strongly to those whose kinsfolk have been wronged. The desire for revenge and counter-revenge becomes a driving force of civil war in the fifteenth century, a force that Shakespeare sees in almost apocalyptic terms. We will return to this problem later in this chapter when we look at Shakespeare's earlier history plays about Henry VI.

John of Gaunt disavows his sister-in-law's call for personal vengeance. He is very clear that vengeance must proceed only through the direct intervention of God Almighty, the great judge of all things:

> God's is the quarrel, for God's substitute,
> His deputy anointed in His sight,
> Hath caused his death; the which if wrongfully
> Let heaven revenge, for I may never lift
> An angry arm against His minister.
>   (1.2.37–41)

That is to say, God's substitute, Richard, having caused the death of Woodstock, will suffer divine punishment if he did so wrongfully. Gaunt has no doubt that Richard is responsible for Woodstock's death, but

Gaunt refuses to pass judgement as to the rightness or wrongness of that action and disclaims any argument that he should act personally against Richard.

At least two great political commonplaces unite in this speech: the principle of divine right of kings, and that of passive obedience to royal authority. The first posits that a duly constituted monarch is the head, on earth, of a divinely ordered hierarchy that derives its authority from its having been created by God in His own image. Royal authority, in this view, is not derived in any way from social contract or the consent of the governed; it is the finest representation we have on earth of a dispensation handed down to us from above. Gaunt's second principle depends on the first: since the monarch is invested with divine authority and sanction, his subjects may not remove or forcefully punish him in any way. The king is God's minister, and to oppose this minister with force is to rebel against God Himself. God will know in His own good time when to punish malefactors; to doubt this is to question God's dispensing of justice in human history. As Gaunt says earlier in the same scene:

> since correction lieth in those hands
> Which made the fault that we cannot correct,
> Put we our quarrel to the will of heaven,
> Who, when they see the hours ripe on earth,
> Will rain hot vengeance on offenders' heads.
> (1.2.4–8)

We cannot hope to know all of heaven's intentions, and so we cannot know when wrongs will be avenged by the heavenly powers, but to doubt that vengeance will come eventually is to embrace heresy. To take matters into one's own hands amounts to committing the same sacrilege; it is a manifestation of impatience, pride, and arrogance, and can only make matters worse.

This is a deeply conservative political philosophy, if by 'conservative' we mean a philosophy designed to reinforce the existing power structure as sacrosanct and disavow any attempt at structural change. One can argue, to be sure, that the doctrines of divine right and passive obedience were evolved by governing elites over the ages as a kind of mythology aimed at preserving the status quo. This is an interpretation with which John of Gaunt would disagree. But what about

Shakespeare? Do his history plays invite, or at least allow, such a sceptical and secular view of history? The answer is not easy to come by, but we can at least begin by observing that John of Gaunt is not Shakespeare's mouthpiece in *Richard II.* Gaunt's political philosophy is presented lucidly and sympathetically. It is also set in debate with contrary views, not least of all by the political reasoning (or manoeuvring, at any rate) of his own son, Henry Bolingbroke.

The sympathetic side of John of Gaunt is to be found, first of all, in his magnificent rhetoric, for which Shakespeare of course deserves the credit. Gaunt's famous 'Sceptered Isle' speech in 2.1, describing England in a series of vivid images as 'this seat of Mars', a second Eden, a 'demi-paradise', a 'fortress built by Nature for herself / Against infection and the hand of war', a 'precious stone set in the silver sea', etc., and yet now 'bound in with shame, / With inky blots and rotten parchment bonds' (2.1.40–64), is deservedly one of the great speeches for actors and audiences alike. It characterizes Gaunt as a genuine patriot, caring more for his country than for his own life. It shows his noble integrity and commitment to the highest traditions of public service. No less appealing is his insistent belief that a royal counselor like himself, though denied the option of threatening the king with force, is under a sacred obligation to offer unsparing and honest advice to the throne, even if at the expense of his own political well-being. For Gaunt, honest counseling is the concomitant of the doctrine of passive obedience: one must not oppose the king through force, but as a counselor one must criticize where criticism is due. The fact that Shakespeare's Gaunt possesses considerably more integrity in these regards than the historical Duke of Lancaster, who went about manipulating anticlerical feelings for his own ends and probably aimed at the royal succession, highlights the way in which Shakespeare has been at some pains to depict Gaunt as principled and decent. Shakespeare needs an eloquent proponent of conservative political philosophy, if only so that the play can thereby demonstrate how history is moving away from the traditional ideologies of England's medieval past. Shakespeare's Gaunt is a noble representative of the old order.

Gaunt's son, Henry Bolingbroke, belongs to a new generation. He never theorizes. We never hear him defending or attacking the idea of the divine right of kings. He is a pragmatist, responding to the immediate present and never tipping his hand as to long-range plans. His first move is to challenge Mowbray on charges of treason involving the death of Thomas of Woodstock. He undertakes this as a sacred crusade, staking his life on the honour of his cause. When he is banished by the King along with Mowbray, Bolingbroke's response is that of a patriot whose native country means everything to him; 'Where'er I wander, boast of this I can: / Though banished, yet a trueborn Englishman' (1.3.308–9). Shakespeare's audience might well consider Bolingbroke to be in the right thus far. Modern historians generally concur that Mowbray was guilty of Woodstock's death. To be sure, Shakespeare speaks well of Mowbray too, with a generosity toward both sides that is characteristic. The last we hear of Mowbray is that he has scrupulously observed the terms of his banishment and has devoted his energies to fighting 'For Jesu Christ in glorious Christian field' before dying in Venice (4.1.94–9). Whatever we may think today of the Crusades, this report of Mowbray's final years depicts him as a brave soldier and loyal Christian.

Bolingbroke has also gone into banishment, according to the sentence imposed, but soon we learn things about him that invite us to wonder about his unstated aims. When, at the death of old Gaunt, King Richard seizes into the royal treasury 'The plate, coin, revenues, and movables / Whereof our uncle Gaunt did stand possessed' (2.1.161–2), doing so without any legal justification, Gaunt's son and heir is understandably outraged. So is Bolingbroke's uncle, Gaunt's younger brother, the Duke of York, who insists that Bolingbroke is entitled, by medieval law and custom, to add to his current earldom of Hereford the dukedom of Lancaster held by his father. Bolingbroke, for his part, responds to Richard's seizure of the dukedom of Lancaster by returning to England to claim his inheritance. The action is illegal, since he has been banished, but he is supported by the Earl of Northumberland and other noblemen who have been galled by Richard's highhandedness. Bolingbroke claims that he has returned to England for no other reason than to take possession of his inheritance. When asked by his uncle York why he has dared to violate the terms of his banishment, and, more seriously, to return with military might against King Richard, Bolingbroke has his answer, plain and simple: 'As I was banished, I was banished Hereford; / But as I come, I come for Lancaster' (2.3.113–14). Northumberland supports this contention: Bolingbroke has come back to England 'But for his own' (148–9). Yet we have good reason to believe that Northumberland and his allies have their own reasons for backing Bolingbroke's return, and we must wonder too if Bolingbroke can really believe that he can oppose the crown militarily without momentous consequences. York, for his part, is unimpressed by the apparent simplicity of Bolingbroke's defence of his action. 'Well, well', says York, 'I see the issue of these arms' (152). The Duke of York is a swing figure in this conflict. His political persuasions appear to be essentially those of his brother Gaunt: a firm belief in the divine right of kings and the duties of passive obedience imposed upon the king's subjects, together with a solemn obligation to offer frank advice to the crown. Gaunt expends his last breath attempting to drum some sense into his irresponsible nephew-king. York faces a still more severe challenge when Richard seizes the dukedom of Lancaster from Gaunt's son and heir. York cannot remain still; he must explain to Richard why this unlawful act on the part of the King undoes the very basis on which medieval kingship itself is founded:

> Is not Gaunt dead? And doth not Hereford live?
> Was not Gaunt just? And is not Harry true?
> Did not the one deserve to have an heir?
> Is not his heir a well-deserving son?
> Take Hereford's rights away, and take from Time
> His charters and his customary rights;
> Let not tomorrow then ensue today;
> Be not thyself; for how art thou a king
> But by fair sequence and succession?
> (2.1.191–9)

York is good at seeing the larger consequences of acts performed by both Richard and Bolingbroke. York argues logically and on the basis of coherent political theory. If medieval kingship is based on the essential idea of the integrity of property and the right of all property owners to hand on their estates to their eldest sons, and if the kingship itself is understood to be subject to the laws of inheritance, then Richard's attack on Gaunt's property rights must threaten not only Gaunt and Bolingbroke but other peers of the realm as well, and indeed the very institution of kingship. Similarly, if the concepts of divine right of kings and passive obedience are to be held sacred and inviolable, any use of military force against a king to oblige him to give back what he has taken, no matter how unwise that taking may have been, amounts to an attack on the entire structure of medieval kingship.

York, as he understands English law, is in the right on both counts. He is right also to understand that other peers share his deep concern and will not tolerate what Richard has done, even though their resistance will necessarily place them in opposition to divinely sanctioned concepts of orderly rule.

What is York himself to do? His problem is that his theories of divine right and passive obedience work well to keep a society in proper order under most circumstances, but are essentially defenceless against the extraordinary events that are now taking place. No higher appeals are possible in a kingdom governed by principles of divine right; the King is the ultimate judge. If he breaks the law, no proper recourse is available to his subjects other than the passive obedience that Gaunt has spelled out so clearly: subjects must wait for God to punish or forgive, as He will surely do in His own good time. But what if subjects are not willing to wait? Bolingbroke clearly is not. He makes no attempt to theorize in response to ideas of passive obedience; he simply acts, justifying his actions on the narrowest grounds possible of wanting back the dukedom that was unjustly and illegally taken from him.

York understands and even sympathizes with his nephew's position. Yet he also understands the frightening consequences of Bolingbroke's armed intervention. York's choice in coping with this dilemma is dictated to a great extent by expediency: he does his best to persuade Bolingbroke to desist, but York also knows that his own military might as deputy governor in England during Richard's ill-timed expedition to Ireland is not sufficient to offer effective resistance to Bolingbroke. York has no practical choice but to go along with the new order of things. Expediency is often an inglorious stance to take, and York does look a little ridiculous. Is he not inconsistent to trumpet the doctrine of divine right and then cave in to what he knows is a morally indefensible position? Yet York can also be said to exemplify a kind of pragmatism that may be able to save England for another day, at least in the short term. England's political life must go on, and if a change of regime is inevitable, so be it. York's pragmatism may not be internally consistent in theoretical terms but is at least workable.

The consequences that York has worried about do in fact take place. However much Bolingbroke may insist that his return to England has been solely for the purpose of recovering his dukedom, he must in effect take King Richard hostage if he is to achieve his aim. The showdown occurs at Flint Castle, where Bolingbroke finally catches up with Richard and surrounds him in this fortress. Bolingbroke makes a great show of submission to Richard as his king, but Bolingbroke enters the negotiations with a non-negotiable demand. He will, on both his knees, 'kiss King Richard's hand' and send 'allegiance and true faith of heart / To his most royal person', laying down his arms and power, 'Provided that my banishment repealed / And lands restored again be freely granted' (3.3.36–41). That word 'Provided' speaks volumes. If, and only if, that condition is met will Bolingbroke offer tokens of fealty. 'If not', he continues, 'I'll use the advantage of my power, / And lay the summer's dust with showers of blood / Rained from the wounds of slaughtered Englishmen' (42–4). Bolingbroke insists that this is the last thing he could wish to have happen, but if Richard gives him no alternative, then military destruction will follow.

Richard is as prescient as Bolingbroke is stubbornly unwilling to face the larger issues. Richard knows that his acceding to Bolingbroke's terms is a surrender, no matter how much it may be disguised by the political farce of Bolingbroke's kneeling in a gesture of submission. What is a king when he must obey a subject? The whole theory of kingship collapses under the weight of absurd self-contradiction. When Richard is then publicly arraigned and 'asked' to resign of his 'own good will' (4.1.178), what is this but another charade? Richard plays his own role in his trial as both protagonist and victim in a mockery of justice; he knows that he has no choice but to resign as king, but he will not do so without showing everyone what a shabby business this is. He invents a ceremony of divesting a king of his sacred crown and sceptre in a way that dramatizes the blasphemous nature of the event. He prophesies his own death, knowing what Bolingbroke should know but cannot acknowledge, that a deposed king is sure to be such a rallying point for opposition to the new regime that his elimination will become a political necessity.

King Henry, as he is now known, squirms at the prospect of such a political murder. His solution is to say aloud, within the hearing of others, 'Have I no friend will rid me of this living fear?' (5.4.2). Then, when a certain Sir Pierce of Exton acts on cue and dispatches the wretched Richard in Pomfret Castle, King Henry responds with pious protestation. 'They love not poison that do poison need, / Nor do I thee', he says to Exton. 'Though I did wish him dead, / I hate the murderer, love him murderèd' (5.6.38–40). The new king banishes

Exton, much in the way that Bolingbroke and Mowbray had earlier been banished by Richard. King Henry hopes that 'The guilt of conscience' (41) can be scapegoated onto Exton. Yet when the King compares Exton to Cain, the first murderer in human history (Genesis 4: 1–16), the guilt of that crime clearly doubles back on to Henry himself as the killer of his royal cousin.

King Henry's attempt at what today we would call 'deniability', that is, trying to arrange matters so that subordinates are held to blame for one's own crimes, is apt to strike us as craven and devious. Conversely, Richard looks better and better in our eyes as his fortunes decline. However foolishly and unjustly he has behaved as king, his attempts at thoughtful and honest self-understanding emerge in his nightmare of captivity. Confined within 'ragged prison walls', alone and unbefriended, Richard tries to come to terms with his own failures and with the teachings of the Christian gospel. Richard begins to understand what Jesus meant when he said 'Come, little ones' to the children who were brought to him, and when he said that it is as hard for a rich man to enter into the kingdom of heaven 'as for a camel / To thread the postern of a small needle's eye' (5.5.14–17; cf. Matthew 19: 14 and 24). In pondering these lessons from the Gospels, Richard strives to be a better person and to feel some contrition for the ways in which the perquisites of kingship have made him oblivious to the sufferings of his subjects. We catch here an intimation of King Lear's mad but revealing confession that he has 'ta'en / Too little care' of those who, in their 'looped and windowed raggedness', cannot defend themselves from the storms of fortune (*King Lear*, 3.4.28–33). Richard's very death is to him a moment of profound paradox in which the rewards of power and wealth on earth sink into insignificance: 'Mount, mount, my soul! Thy seat is up on high, / Whilst my gross flesh sinks downward, here to die' (111–12).

Thus the contest of power between Richard and his successor is held in delicate and antithetical balance in the play. Richard is unwise but ineffably royal, whereas Bolingbroke is canny but unprincipled. Richard embodies a beautiful but impractical ideal of medieval kingship; Bolingbroke as Henry IV is a pragmatist who never really succeeds in gathering to himself the aura and mystery of kingship. As we shall see shortly, his political philosophy significantly anticipates that of Niccolò Machiavelli. He is a de facto king; legitimacy eludes him, since he seized power by irregular means. Even the various names and titles by which he is known in the course of the play – Bolingbroke, Hereford, Lancaster, King Henry – bespeak a sense in which his political identity is in constant flux. To his supporters at the end he is King Henry, while to his opponents he is still Hereford (4.1.135), since in their view his other titles were taken from him with due process of law. Who can say what it is to be a king? Yet history must go on, and Bolingbroke is the man of the hour. Shakespeare refuses to give final judgement, even though he freely appeals to our sympathies as the story unfolds. His job as dramatist is to present opposing sides with sympathy and insight, inviting his audience to be enlightened and entertained by the clash of ideologies.

1 Henry IV proceeds along a similar course. King Henry continues to be plagued by the consequences of his irregular seizure of power. In the play's opening scene he is 'shaken' and 'wan with care' (1.1.1), yearning for a cessation of the hostilities that bedevil him in the north and the west; the Scots and the Welsh, sensing England's weakness in a time of political crisis and change of regime, are attacking on two fronts. More serious is the trouble that soon arises between Henry and the Percy clan. Henry Percy the Earl of Northumberland and his son Harry Percy, known as Hotspur, have been fending off the Scots in the north with considerable success. Edmund Mortimer, the brother of Hotspur's wife, has been doing battle in the west, though a report arrives at the English court that he has just been captured by the Welsh Glendower (38–40). Northumberland was chief among the lords who helped Henry Bolingbroke depose Richard. His son, Hotspur, has done well at the battle of Holmedon (historically Homildon Hill, 1402) and has taken some important prisoners. The trouble is that Hotspur, egged on by his uncle the Earl of Worcester, refuses to turn over his prisoners to the King with the exception of Mordake, Earl of Fife, whose royal lineage means that Hotspur cannot claim him according to the law of arms; the others 'To his own use he keeps' (92–4), meaning that he will collect the ransom money himself. One might suppose that this difficulty could be gotten over by men who have stood together against Richard, but the good will they once shared seems to have dissipated. Hotspur now insists that the King ransom Hotspur's brother-in-law Mortimer from his Welsh captivity. Again, this sounds reasonable enough on its face, but we soon learn that King Henry regards Mortimer as one who has 'betrayed / The lives of those that he did lead to fight / Against that great magician, damned Glendower'.

As evidence of Mortimer's defection, the King reports having heard that Mortimer has married Glendower's daughter (1.3.80–5).

The fact that the King calls Mortimer the 'Earl of March' (1.3.84) is significant. Historically this represents a conflation of two Mortimers, one the brother-in-law of Hotspur who did indeed marry Glendower's daughter, the other a nephew of this man who was fifth Earl of March. Shakespeare's conflation of the two, whether intentional or unintentional, has the effect of producing in this individual a serious threat to the throne occupied by Henry IV. Being childless, Richard II had named a second cousin of his, Roger Mortimer, fourth Earl of March, as his heir. When that gentleman died, the fifth Earl became the presumptive heir to the English crown, according to this Richardian line of succession. He could claim direct maternal descent from Edward III through Philippa, wife of the third Earl of March, since Philippa was the daughter of Lionel Duke of Clarence, the eldest of Edward III's sons once Edward the Black Prince and another son named William had died. Lionel was older than John of Gaunt, Henry IV's father. This is presumably why Richard had proclaimed Roger Mortimer heir; if one were to allow that his claim could trace its validity through the female in the person of Philippa, he was descended from Edward III by a genealogical line taking precedence over that to which Henry IV and his father belonged.

Small wonder, then, that King Henry should be reluctant to ransom such a man, especially one who (in Shakespeare's conflated account) has married the daughter of the very Welsh chieftain he was supposed to have been fighting. Small wonder, too, that Hotspur should react to the King's intransigence with scornful defiance. 'But, soft, I pray you, did King Richard then / Proclaim my brother Edmund Mortimer / Heir to the crown?' he asks excitedly, having just learned from his father and his uncle Worcester about Richard's naming Mortimer as 'the next of blood' (1.3.145–57). Perhaps we wonder at Hotspur's naïveté in learning now for the first time this important fact about his brother-in-law, but it goes with the character of a man who is so driven by chivalric idealism. In an instant, Hotspur sees why it is that he has been so mistrustful of the King's motives: of course, this self-styled King is refusing to have anything to do with the man he has unfairly excluded from the English throne! 'Nay, then I cannot blame his cousin king, / That wished him on the barren mountains starve', Hotspur exults (158–9). The word 'cousin' puns artfully on 'cozen', 'cheat'. How could

Hotspur's father and uncle, he wonders, being men of honour and nobility, have committed themselves 'To put down Richard, that sweet lovely rose, / And plant this thorn, this canker, Bolingbroke?' (173–6). Hotspur has changed from being a hard-fighting if cantankerous warrior against the Scots on Henry's behalf to being a true believer not only in the rightness of Mortimer's claim to the throne but also in the sacredness of Richard II's own kingship. To Hotspur, King Henry is now no better than a usurper. What's more, he is a cad.

Hotspur is an enormously attractive character because of his forthrightness, his bravery, and his idealism. Yet we are also invited to see him as young, innocent, and easily misled. His father and uncle seem ready to exploit this innocence in him. Why are they so mistrustful now of King Henry, and he of them? What has happened to the spirit of cooperation among them that led to the installation of Henry as king? One answer, seemingly, is that Henry has turned out to be not the sort of king that his erstwhile allies had expected. The Percy clan backed the insurgency of Henry Bolingbroke because they were outraged by the irresponsible taxing policies of King Richard that had endangered their welfare and independence as medieval barons. Henry, they hoped, would be more tractable and willing to leave them alone in their independent northern fiefdoms so far from the English court. Now that he is king, however, Henry appears to have a very different idea of what would be best for England and for himself as monarch. Henry wishes to centralize power in the English throne. This is Shakespeare's way, perhaps, of dramatizing what historians describe as a conflict between a waning medieval feudal order and what will become a more centralized state in the early modern era. That era is still some years away, but Henry's political instincts, as Shakespeare portrays them, are those of the Tudor monarchs under whom Shakespeare and his countrymen lived in the sixteenth century. Henry is a man of the new order. The Percys, and especially Hotspur, embody the values that we associate with medieval chivalry.

Shakespeare dramatizes the process of historical change with multiple sympathies. He allows much to be said on both sides. We can see why King Henry wishes to discipline Hotspur in the business of the prisoners' ransom: Henry likes and admires the young man's spirit but wishes to have it clearly understood who is in charge. Hotspur will have none of this, turning with personal revulsion against a king whom he now dismisses as 'this vile politician, Bolingbroke' (1.3.240).

He interprets the King's former kindness to the Percys as the kind of hypocrisy one expects from 'politicians' – meaning those who are schemers, cheaters, and scoundrels. He eagerly accepts the mantle of leadership thrust upon him by his canny uncle and father, who have been coaxing him around to a rebellious point of view because they need his charismatic leadership in the civil war they are about to initiate. The irony is that Hotspur cannot see the extent to which his uncle and father are just as cunning at political manoeuvering as is the King.

Shakespeare's fairmindedness toward both sides invites us to see further ironies. These men have common interests and political concerns, and yet the drift toward civil conflict seems unavoidable. The Percys know that the risks of war are weighty, but they also sense that, unless they put up a resistance, their future is unsafe because of the King's open animosity; he has already banished Worcester from the court. As Worcester says later, after the Percys' defeat at Shrewsbury, 'What I have done my safety urged me to' (5.5.11). It behoves the Percys to 'save our heads by raising of a head' (1.3.282), that is, by raising the standard of rebellion. The King, for his part, fears that if he gives in to these powerful barons they will drift increasingly out of his control.

War is the unavoidable consequence, and it is a war in which the ironies of a lost hope for peace become more and more insistent. Most painful of all, perhaps, is the decision of Worcester not to inform his nephew Hotspur of 'the liberal and kind offer of the King' (5.2.2), in the pre-battle negotiations, to pardon the rebels and be reconciled with them (5.1.103–8). As Worcester and Sir Richard Vernon return to the rebel camp from those negotiations, Worcester explains to Vernon his fear that the King cannot keep his word; he might indeed forgive Hotspur, but he will suspect the barons still, keeping them out of the counsels of power. No doubt Worcester is right, but his insistence that they not inform Hotspur of the King's offer, as Vernon would prefer to do, means that Hotspur goes into the battle having been lied to by his own uncle. Hotspur dies for what he takes to be a valiant and honourable cause, unaware of the political infighting and compromises with the truth that have occurred on both sides.

In his portrayal of the King's relationship with his son, Prince Henry (or Hal), and even more importantly of Hal's relationship with Falstaff, Shakespeare manifests the same evenhandedness that enables him to highlight political issues and ask hard questions without propounding dogmatic answers. Is Hal's relationship with Falstaff a healthy one, and should it be allowed to continue? Should Hal heed more the call of duty as the King's son and heir, or is he learning something invaluable about himself and about his subjects-to-be by hobnobbing with Falstaff and his raffish companions? Does the Prince realize what he is doing, or is he putting off the responsibilities of adulthood by pretending that idle dissipation can be called profitable recreation? Does he want to grow up? Directors, actors, and critics alike have opted for almost every imaginable possibility. Hal has been variously presented as a playboy, a drunkard, a youngster with a deep emotional dependency on Falstaff, a thoughtful young politician who knows exactly where he is going, and a sardonic observer of human nature who from the very start has sized Falstaff up. Falstaff, conversely, can be seen as a funny and endearing old rascal, an irresponsible alcoholic with a massive weight problem, a practising highwayman, a calculating and ambitious campaigner for the office of Lord Chief Justice, and a cynic who adopts a whimsical style in order to curry favour with the future king of England. King Henry can be played as a careworn monarch plagued by political and military difficulties, a much-put-upon parent, a student of Machiavelli whose every gesture has political intent, and an overbearing father who fails utterly to understand his son. The transparency of Shakespeare's text is such that any of these interpretations can be made to work.

The contest of allegiances among these various interpretations emerges in Hal's first scene with Falstaff. For all the liveliness of their badinage, they are discussing a weighty topic. 'Shall there be gallows standing in England when thou art king?' Falstaff asks the Prince, 'And resolution thus fubbed as it is with the rusty curb of old father Antic the law?' (1.2.57–9). Hal parries the question with a quibble, but the issue is serious enough. When Hal ascends the throne, will he keep Falstaff at his side, and will justice then be perverted to personal ends? Is Falstaff capable of 'amendment' (100)? Hal's decision in this same scene to go on a robbing expedition with Falstaff and his cronies hardly gives us reason to hope that law and order will prevail under his kingship. Yet Shakespeare is at pains to end the scene with a soliloquy by the Prince, who assures us and perhaps himself that he will eventually 'imitate the sun' by 'breaking through the foul and ugly mists / Of vapors that did seem to strangle him' (191–7). By associating himself with the conventional image of king-to-be as sun and also (in this case) son of his father, Hal disparages Falstaff and crew as 'foul and ugly mists'. These companions are useful to him, he claims, only to provide contrast with his greatness when he emerges as England's king. 'My reformation, glitt'ring o'er my fault', he says, 'Shall show more goodly and attract more eyes / Than that which hath no foil to set it off', like a jewel set before a 'foil' sheet of metal to enhance its beauty (206–9). The soliloquy thus seems to characterize the Prince as fully aware of how he can use Falstaff and the rest for ulterior political purposes. Yet lest we write him down as a cynical and heartless manipulator, we must recognize that this soliloquy can be read in a number of different ways, from self-aware calculation to whistling in the dark. Hal does seem to be enjoying Falstaff's company immensely; the play of wits is keenly enjoyable, presumably for him as for us. We need too to consider that Shakespeare may have his own purposes as dramatist in ending the scene with this soliloquy: to reassure us as audience that Hal is not unredeemable.

In the great tavern scene of 2.4, Falstaff is at his best as an engaging companion. His comically outrageous narrative of the robbery at Gad's Hill deftly inflates two rogues in buckram suits into eleven opponents, whom he claims to have slain singlehanded. Hal and Poins exult in catching Falstaff out in this lying. But who is fooling whom? If, as seems most probable, Falstaff has figured out how Hal and Poins left the robbing party shortly before the robbery took place and then came down on the robbers to take away the booty from them, Falstaff's lie must be his way of setting himself up as the comic butt of Hal's joke of discovery. Such an interpretation makes him out to be not simply an outrageous liar but one who wishes to endear himself to the Prince by being funny. When the two of them take turns playing King Henry and the Prince in anticipation of Hal's having to face his father the next morning, Falstaff again offers himself up as the gross subject of their conversation: he is, in Hal's affectionately insulting language, 'that trunk of humors, that bolting-hutch of beastliness, that swollen parcel of dropsies, that huge bombard of sack', and still more (2.4.444–6). The charade they are improvising suddenly takes a more sombre turn as Falstaff uses the moment to sum up the case for the Prince's holding on to Falstaff's endearing company. 'If sack and sugar be a fault, God help the wicked! If to be old and merry be a sin, then many an old host that I know is damned.' The Prince, pleaded with thus directly to 'banish not him thy Harry's company', acknowledges that he must: 'I do, I will' (465–76). Whether he says so wistfully or mockingly or curtly depends on the actor. The debate continues as to what to do about Falstaff, but the issues are clarified.

At the battle of Shrewsbury Falstaff is at once supremely irresponsible and an incisive critic of the senselessness of this war. On the one hand, he corrupts the process of recruitment for his own ends, sends his poorly equipped men to their death with blithe unconcern, hands Prince Henry a bottle of sack (wine) when the Prince has asked for a sword, plays possum to avoid being killed by the Scottish Douglas, and claims credit for having slain the dead Hotspur by stabbing the corpse in the groin and then swearing to the Prince, 'I'll take it upon my death I gave him this wound in the thigh' (5.4.148–9). This is craven, even if it is funny. Given the exigencies of battle, the practical joking is ill-timed. On the other hand, Falstaff's catechism on honour, asking if honour can take away the 'grief' or pain of a wound, and concluding sardonically that honour must be 'air' or reputation that provides no comfort for the dead and will not even stay with the living since 'Detraction' or slander will not allow it (5.1.127–40), is the play's finest commentary of the absurdity of a battle in which so many deaths are brought about by misunderstandings and deceptions among proud men. Falstaff's very preference for life over death seems, in its way, admirable. One has so many more options when one is alive than when one is dead. 'The better part of valor is discretion', he triumphantly concludes, 'in which better part I have saved my life' (5.4.119–21).

Shakespeare invites us to consider whether some wars might be avoidable through better understanding, especially when the contestants are all from the same country. He depicts honour and chivalry as exemplified in Hotspur as inspirational, and yet he interrogates what 'honour' too often can come to mean. He understands the need of a prince for companionship and entertaining diversions, and yet seems sensitive too to the way in which the education of a future king necessarily sets him apart from his fellow mortals. The phenomenon of political rebellion he regards with great wariness: he understands its motives and complexities, while at the same time never minimizing the threat it poses to public order. Prince Henry makes this point when he addresses his opposite number in battle, Harry Percy, as 'A very valiant rebel of the name' (5.4.62). 'I am the Prince of Wales', he insists.

Two young men named Henry or Harry must do battle to determine the political future of England. Prince Henry asserts legitimacy as his own best claim against rebellion. Shakespeare does not let us forget the massive irony that Hal is himself the son of a former rebel and regicide. At all events, Hal is the winner, and in that respect he is very much his father's son. The future belongs not to Hotspur but to Hal.

The realization that Hal is the son of a rebel never leaves him. On the eve of what will be his great victory over the French at Agincourt, he implores God to forgive that circumstance over which this young king has no control: 'Not today, O Lord, / Oh, not today, think not upon the fault / My father made in compassing the crown!' (*Henry V*, 4.1.290–2). Can time and the succession of generations erase such a guilt? The new King Henry V has re-interred King Richard's body with many contrite tears, and has built two chantries 'where the sad and solemn priests / Sing still for Richard's soul' (293–300). He has shown himself to be a loyal son of the church, seeking ecclesiastical endorsement of his war against the French. In the wake of his great victory he issues a proclamation throughout the army that death will be meted out to any soldier so brazen as 'To boast of this or take that praise from God / Which is his only' (4.8.114–16). He orders that 'all holy rites' be performed and that '*Non nobis*' and '*Te Deum*' are to be sung, the first of these (a verse from Psalm 115) underscoring King Henry's point that God's alone is the victory: 'Not unto us, O Lord, not unto us, but unto thy name give glory.' The Chorus extols the piety of a king who, when petitioned that his helmet and sword be carried before him on his triumphant entry into London, 'forbids it, / Being free from vainness and self-glorious pride' (5.0.19–20). This king is presented, then, not just as God-fearing, but as a firm believer in a providential view of history. He sees his victory as confirmation that God has indeed forgiven his father's act of regicide.

Such, at least, is King Henry's self-presentation. He is certainly not above using piety as an essential part of his image as Christian king. In the opening of *Henry V* (1599) he masterfully orchestrates support for the impending war. By means of a proposed bill in Parliament that would strip the church of many of its lands, he prompts his bishops to volunteer as a counter-offer 'a greater sum / Than ever at one time the clergy yet / Did to his predecessors part withal' (1.1.80–2). He receives vociferous backing from his nobles before calling in the French ambassador. The justification of the war, as recited by the Archbishop of Canterbury, seems like an intricate piece of nonsense (often hilarious in performance) about the Salic law and whether it applies to France, but Henry's intent in having the issue publicly aired is clear enough. 'May I with right and conscience make this claim?' he asks the Archbishop, and gets back precisely the answer he wants: 'The sin upon my head, dread sovereign!' (1.2.96–7). The church has assumed moral responsibility, as Henry wished it to; the war is proclaimed a just war.

The young King Henry has learned much from his father, despite their wariness toward one another. The son has shown, by saving his father's life at the battle of Shrewsbury (*1 Henry IV*, 5.4.39–57), that he cares deeply for his father, and regrets bitterly that the old king seems to have suspected Hal of wanting his predecessor dead and out of the way. When father and son effect one last and tearful reconciliation as Henry IV lies dying, the old man has one last crucial piece of advice to offer his successor: 'busy giddy minds / With foreign quarrels' (*2 Henry IV*, 4.5.212–13). In other words, find a foreign enemy to attack as the surest way of uniting the English people behind their leader. Henry IV himself had hoped to conduct a crusade to the Holy Land for just this purpose at the start of *1 Henry IV*, so that he and his subjects could 'March all one way and be no more opposed / Against acquaintance, kindred, and allies' (1.1.15–16), but was prevented from doing so by the exigencies of Scottish and Welsh invasion. His timeless counsel to his son is Machiavellian in the truest sense in that it proposes to seek war less for inherent reasons than as a means to solidify political support at home. War should be an instrument of royal policy. Whether or not Shakespeare actually read Nicolò Machiavelli to study his lessons in political pragmatism we cannot be sure, since the writings of that hated statesman were banned in England as the utterances of an atheist and moral relativist, but Shakespeare must have had some awareness of what those writings were all about. Henry IV and especially his son Henry V represent a new kind of kingship in Shakespeare. Both men seem adept at practising the kind of ruthless pragmatism and concern for image-making as a means of consolidating power that goes with the name of Machiavellism. Nothing ignites patriotic feeling more effectively than does a war against a foreign enemy, and in England's case that means the French above all. Does the young King Henry V go to war largely for this reason? Does such a motive enhance his personal rivalry with the French Dauphin? He never says so, and the Chorus provides an incessant drum-beat of enthusiasm for the war, but Shakespeare does allow us to see behind the scenes in a most telling way.

Whether Shakespeare approves or disapproves of Henry V's pragmatic warring against the French (and, by extension, whether he disapproved or disapproved of what he understood to be the principles of Machiavellian statecraft) is not really the point. Positive and negative interpretations of Henry V have been strongly advocated in productions and in critical analyses. Liberals like George Bernard Shaw and William Hazlitt generally deplore Henry's warmongering. The Chorus of the play, on the other hand, is an unabashed booster, even if we allow that the Chorus need not be identified entirely with the author's view of the subject. Undoubtedly Henry V was regarded by many English people in Shakespeare's time as a model king, probably more so than any other king in English history, but even that large truism does little to establish Shakespeare's position as for or against the consensus view. His history plays were very popular in their own day, and *Henry V* especially has been used in recent years to enhance national patriotism during periods of military crisis, notably in Laurence Olivier's 1944 film version funded in part by the British government to bolster morale during World War II. Yet the same play has been filmed in a more disillusioning way by Kenneth Branagh in 1989 under the weight of public anger over the Vietnam War and the Falklands engagement of 1982.

What we can perhaps say is that Shakespeare is fascinated by the complexity of the political process. He sees what manipulation of public opinion can do for a ruler. He studies the arts of governing and of military leadership in all their pragmatic details. Undoubtedly we find in these plays a considerable admiration for Henry V's skill at getting what he wants. History is on Henry's side, whether one regards this as a good or a bad thing. Henry is a successful king, whatever one thinks of kingship or of success. Concomitantly, the view of history that emerges from these plays is that the quality of individual leadership matters crucially. Being born into royal power is not enough, as Richard II abundantly illustrates by his failure. Being flexible and smart, on the other hand, can enable some persons to overcome formidable obstacles, such as being the son of a rebel king whose enemies are now the son's enemies and whose guilt may now devolve upon the son. History has its ups and downs. Much depends on the man of the hour.

Nowhere is this point more clearly illustrated than in Henry V's being succeeded by his infant son, Henry VI.

Henry VI was less than a year old when he came to the English throne. He proved to be unlike the father in every way: indecisive, improvident, and so deeply committed to a life of pious devotion that he cared little for the arts of governing. During his long minority, the country was run by powerful members of the royal family, whose factionalism was greatly increased by the shadow of illegality that still hung over Henry IV's seizure of the throne from Richard II. The claim of the fifth Earl of March, named presumptive heir by Richard, was reinforced by the marriage of his sister Anne to Richard, Earl of Cambridge, the son of the Duke of Aumerle who was son to the Duke of York in *Richard II* and who had conspired against the Lancastrian dynasty of Henry IV. The Earl of Cambridge and his Percy-connected wife Anne's son was Richard Plantagenet, later Duke of York, who founded the Yorkist dynasty. Plantagenet and his sons mounted a military challenge to the kingship of Henry VI in what is known as the War of the Roses, white rose of York versus red rose of Lancaster. Eventually the Yorkists prevailed, seating Edward (the eldest son of Richard Plantagenet) on the English throne in 1461 as Edward IV. The fighting continued, see-sawing back and forth (Henry VI was actually restored to the throne in 1470 for six months) until the Yorkists gained decisive control. When Edward IV died in 1483 he was succeeded, in a series of canny manoeuvres, by his youngest brother Richard as Richard III. Edward's two young sons, Edward and Richard, were thus denied the royal succession by their uncle, and were perhaps secretly murdered on his orders in the Tower of London. Richard III ruled until 1485, when he was overthrown by Henry Tudor, whose slender dynastic claim to the throne as Henry VII depended on his mother's having been descended from a line of Beauforts who had been barred from the royal succession (since John Beaufort had been born out of wedlock to John of Gaunt and his mistress, Catherine Swynford). On his father's side, Henry Tudor had an equally tenuous claim to the throne: he was grandson of the Owen Tudor who had married Katherine of Valois after her husband, Henry V, died in 1422.

This is the story that Shakespeare chose to dramatize in his first four-play historical series, the three parts of *Henry VI* and *Richard III* (c.1589–94). He wrote these before writing *King John* (c.1594–6) and before turning to the plays we have already discussed, from *Richard II* to *Henry V* (c.1595–9).

For a number of reasons, the political object-lessons seem more sharply etched in the earlier-written historical plays about Henry VI than in the later-written series. The events of the fifteenth century leading up to 1485 were closer in time to Elizabeth's subjects, and more anguishing in their account of the atrocities of civil war. Moreover, those years had culminated in the accession to the throne of Henry VII, Elizabeth's grandfather and founder of the Tudor dynasty. That event needed to be presented as a celebration of England's emergence at long last from nearly a century of civil war. By the same token, the civil wars themselves had to be told as a horror story of brother against brother and family against family. Shakespeare's *Henry VI* plays make no attempt to minimize the butchery that took place and the anarchy that insistently threatened. The best that could be said for the civil war was that it eventually brought forth the Tudor dynasty.

One manifestation of the fear of anarchy that so pervades these plays is to be seen in Shakespeare's account of the Cade Rebellion of 1450. Historically, the event was a spontaneous protest of Kentishmen against the incompetence of Henry VI's government; it was England's most widespread popular uprising since the so-called Peasants' Revolt of 1381. Shakespeare's *2 Henry VI* depicts the event in the most pejorative ways possible. Jack Cade, the leader, is a buffoon making absurd pretensions of ancestral descent from Lionel Duke of Clarence, older brother of John of Gaunt (3.1.359, 4.2.38–41), in a fatuous parody of the genealogical title put forward by Richard Plantagenet of the house of York. Cade is surrounded by Dick the butcher, Smith the weaver, a Sawyer, and other handicraftsmen whose pretensions to expertise in matters of governance are ludicrous. Even they laugh privately at Cade's puffed-up ancestry: when Cade proclaims that he is 'descended of the Lacys', Dick's sotto voce pun is that 'She was, indeed, a peddler's daughter, and sold many laces' (4.2.43–5). Cade's 'field' or coat of arms, Dick assures us privately, suggests a 'field' in an absurdly mundane sense: Cade was born in a field, 'under a hedge' (48–50). Cade promises his followers a world of cheap prices and plentiful goods to be had without labour: 'There shall be in England seven halfpenny loaves sold for a penny, the three-hooped pot shall have ten hoops, and I will make it a felony to drink small beer' (meaning that everyone will drink strong beer instead). There is to be no money.

Instead, all persons are to eat and drink at Cade's expense, and dress all in one livery 'that they may agree like brothers and worship me their lord' (63–74). The so-called Pissing Conduit in Cheapside is to 'run nothing be claret wine this first year of our reign' (4.6.3–4). Like many a radical reformer in parodic Utopian literature, Cade will eliminate wealth and rank in his communal state while arrogating all wealth and royal rank to himself.

For all his foolishness, Cade is a dangerous threat, especially to London's commercial class and to the country's ruling elite. In what today has become this play's best-known line, Cade and his followers plan to 'kill all the lawyers' (4.2.75). A soldier is summarily slain for addressing their great leader as 'Jack Cade' instead of 'Lord Mortimer'; the offending soldier has had no time to hear the proclamation of this prohibition, but no matter (4.6.7–8). A clerk of Chartham (i.e., Chatham, near Rochester) is hanged simply because 'He can write and read and cast account' (4.2.83–4). The damage to London, to its palaces, its shops, and its legal institutions, is extensive. 'Pull down the Savoy', Cade orders; 'others to th' Inns of Court' (4.7.1–2). 'Up Fish Street! Down Saint Magnus' Corner! Kill and knock down! Throw them into Thames!' (4.8.1–2). Shakespeare's appeal is to his own London audiences, doubtless containing many shopkeepers, merchants, lawyers, scriveners, and the like for whom popular revolt was anathema.

Shakespeare is wary generally of popular movements. Aristocrats are often to blame for starting the trouble, to be sure. Richard Plantagenet boasts in soliloquy that his plan is to unleash widespread violence through Cade: 'This devil here shall be my substitute' (*2 Henry VI*, 3.1.371). Plantagenet joins in conspiracy with the Duke of Suffolk to snuff out the life of 'the good Duke Humphrey' (1.1.160), the Duke of Gloucester, King Henry's uncle and Lord Protector, because, in their cynical view, Humphrey is too much loved of the commoners and thus inclined to deal justly with their grievances. Once this mediating figure is out of the way, these opportunists and their allies (including Cardinal Beaufort, a great-uncle of the King) hope that anarchy will enable them to seize power. Yet even if popular unrest is stirred up by unprincipled manoeuvrings of this sort, and even when that unrest appears to have grievances with which we can sympathize, the resulting inversions of authority are presented by Shakespeare as unnerving. When the commons hear rumours of the murder of Duke Humphrey

'By Suffolk and the Cardinal Beaufort's means' (3.2.124), they demand that the King execute or banish Suffolk. If not, they say, 'They will by violence tear him from your palace / And torture him with grievous ling'ring death' (246–7). To these non-negotiable demands the weak King accedes, protesting feebly that 'had I not been cited so by them, / Yet did I purpose as they do entreat' (281–2). The commons are for the moment pacified, but when the banished Suffolk is subsequently taken at sea and is identified as the hated architect of Duke Humphrey's death and also as the cuckolder of the King (by having become the lover of Queen Margaret), ransom is denied and Suffolk is summarily slain. However much his end may seem to be a suitable reward for his villainies, this is posse justice. Shakespeare's alarm is undisguised. This anarchy is the baleful fruit of civil conflict.

In *Richard III* as well, the role of the populace in political decision-making is a matter of grave concern, though here the Londoners are more cautious and less easily prevailed upon. In a scene of choric wisdom, various unnamed citizens utter their worries about a land 'that's governed by a child'. They see clearly that 'full of danger is the Duke of Gloucester'. They are wisely prepared to stay out of trouble if they can and 'leave it all to God' (2.3.12–46). When Richard sends his chief lieutenant, the Duke of Buckingham, to 'play the orator' (3.5.95) with the citizens in Guildhall and thereby win their support for Richard's intent to have himself named king after the death of Edward IV in lieu of Edward's eldest son, Buckingham meets with passive resistance. The citizens say nothing, as though stalling for time. When some followers of Buckingham, on cue, shout out 'God save King Richard!', Buckingham cannily interprets the silence of the rest as consent (3.7.34–41). With the Lord Mayor and his fellow aldermen and some citizens, Richard himself has better success: as counseled by Buckingham, he adopts a pose of intense piety, standing between two clergymen with a prayer book in his hand and protesting that he has no wish to assume the heavy burdens of kingship. The Mayor and citizens are taken in by this show of reluctance, and, coached in what they say by Buckingham and Catesby, endorse Richard's new royal title as 'Richard, England's worthy king' (3.7.45–241). Thus the citizens and civic officials of London, as well-intentioned as they are, allow themselves to be manipulated into sanctioning a devastating violation of English law and custom. As a collective force they are unstable.

In other plays too, Shakespeare's citizens are generally sensible and patient when left to themselves, but they are apt to become worrisomely irrational in moments of political crisis. The tradesmen of Rome in *Julius Caesar* (1599) are good-natured and even amusingly witty at first, but, being naïve in their hero-worship of Caesar, they are putty in the hands of the canny orator, Mark Antony, in the wake of the assassination. The crowd in *Coriolanus* (c.1608) has many just complaints against the aristocracy: grain is being withheld in a time of famine, and Coriolanus is insufferable in his arrogant contempt for the citizens. They are forbearing in spite of his disdain for them, and willing to elect him to the consulship. Yet they are moved to violence by their spokesmen, the Tribunes. Once again, we see that Shakespeare is ready to show sympathy for both sides of a political conflict. As in *2 Henry VI*, political leaders bear the first responsibility for stirring up popular unrest. Shakespeare's plays show understanding for the causes of popular unrest, while at the same time taking a dim view of collective political action.

An associated worry in the *Henry VI* plays is that civil war quickly spirals downward into uncontrolled reciprocal violence and counterviolence. *3 Henry VI* especially is structured antithetically to represent on stage the baleful concept of an eye for an eye. To avenge the death of the Lancastrian old Clifford at the end of *2 Henry VI*, young Clifford slaughters the Earl of Rutland, youngest son of Richard Plantagenet (*3 Henry VI*, 1.3.48), and then assists the remorseless Lancastrian Queen Margaret in stabbing the captured Plantagenet himself (1.4.61–178), setting that man's severed head above the gates of his city of York (2.2.1–3). In return for these atrocities, young Clifford is the next to suffer retribution: the sons of Plantagenet take Clifford prisoner in the fighting, torment him for his crimes, and then erect his head on York's battlements in place of their father's (2.6.58–86). And so it goes. The very names of the main contestants underscore the dismal business of reciprocity. As the widow Queen Margaret sums up the grisly account in *Richard III*, in the aftermath of the fighting:

> I had an Edward, till a Richard killed him;
> I had a Harry, till a Richard killed him;
> Thou hadst an Edward, till a Richard killed him;
> Thou hadst a Richard, till a Richard killed him.
> (4.4.40–3)

That is to say, Queen Margaret's son Edward, the Lancastrian crown prince, was killed by Richard of Gloucester, and so was her husband Henry (Harry) VI, whereas the widow Queen Elizabeth, to whom Margaret is speaking, has lost her two sons, Edward (Edward V) and Richard, at the hands of Richard of Gloucester. The Duchess of York adds to this grim list that she too had a Richard, namely, her husband Plantagenet, and also a Rutland, her youngest son, both of them slain, as we have seen, by Margaret and her Lancastrian supporters (44–5). Queen Margaret sees a necessary justice of revenge in all these deaths:

> Thy Edward he is dead that killed my Edward;
> Thy other Edward dead, to quit my Edward.
>   (4.4.63–4)

In other words, King Edward IV has justly died for having killed the Edward who was Lancastrian crown prince, whereas Edward V (the 'other Edward') has paid with his life to even the tally for the death of Margaret's son Edward.

Such direful reciprocity is clearly presented as insane in these plays. The Richard who becomes Richard III is personally responsible for many of these deaths, and indeed stands before us as the epitome of civil violence. He is the kind of evil ruler that England has brought upon itself through internecine conflict. Yet his role in this carnage is at last paradoxical and ironic. Although Richard does what he does out of monstrous self-interest, and seems to be succeeding brilliantly as he manoeuvres toward the throne, his murderous acts have the effect of punishing those who for the most part are guilty of punishable offences. Even those who die innocently, like Edward IV's two young sons, can be seen as sacrificial victims who must pay for the collective guilt of a country that has temporarily lost its sanity. Moreover, the violence that Richard embodies is a way of clearing out the competition for the English throne, so that when the Earl of Richmond (i.e., Henry Tudor) emerges as a claimant to the throne and to the hand in marriage of Edward IV's daughter Elizabeth, almost no one other than Richard III is standing in his way. Without his knowing or intending it, every accomplishment of Richard III turns out to be a necessary step to the coming to power of Henry VII.

Historically, Richard III was a more worthy king than Shakespeare portrays him to be; conversely, Henry VII used some of the same rough expedients as did Richard to do away with troublesome rivals to his disputed possession of the crown. Shakespeare's maligning of Richard III and his near sanctifying of Henry VII smack today of propagandistic rewriting of history. However uncomfortable it may make us to attribute such party-line work to England's greatest author, we need to consider why the issue of legitimacy in the great change of regime from Richard III to Henry VII in 1485 was of such burning importance to Queen Elizabeth I and her government a century or so later. Elizabeth loathed the very idea of forcible resistance to any monarch, no matter how incapable or troublesome that monarch may have been. Elizabeth's reluctance to consent to the execution of her cousin Mary Queen of Scots in 1587 grew out of Elizabeth's fear of countenancing any regicide. Mary was a rallying point for Catholics as long as she lived and was therefore a constant threat to Elizabeth, but she was still a duly constituted monarch. A homily 'Against Disobedience and Wilful Rebellion', read obligatorily from English pulpits, hammered away at the perils of sedition and the virtues of passive obedience to divine-right rule. Elizabeth could allow no exceptions. Yet there was the example of her own grandfather, Henry Tudor, who, with only the slenderest of dynastic pretensions to the English throne, had landed on England's shores from abroad and had defeated in battle an anointed king. Whatever one thought of the rival dynastic claims of the Lancastrians and the Yorkists, Richard III had a pedigree in comparison with which that of Henry Tudor was laughable.

The only way out of this embarrassment for Elizabeth's government was to cover up historical evidence under a smokescreen of rhetoric. The Tudor monarchs were quick to employ revisionist historians retailing stories about Richard's hunched back and his having been born with teeth in his head; as Richard himself is made to say, in *3 Henry VI*, 'The midwife wondered and the women cried, / "Oh, Jesus bless us, he is born with teeth!" / And so I was, which plainly signified / That I should snarl and bite and play the dog' (5.6.74–7). Some of the things that the historical Richard had done in finagling his elevation to the kingship in place of his nephew, including quite possibly the killing his two young nephews in order to eliminate dangerous rivals to power, made him fair game for some of the blackening of character that took place. Thomas More's *Life of Richard III*, incorporated into Holinshed's *Chronicles*, based some of its account on information personally derived by More from the Cardinal Morton in whose house More was brought up and who had been present at some of the events thus narrated. The distortions of historical truth are more patent in the Tudor-sponsored presentation of Henry VII. His hands were no more clean than those of his predecessor. The great reason for the historical vindication that followed his coming to power is simply that he succeeded where Richard had failed. The Tudors had every reason to whitewash this coup d'état. The event itself came to be seen as a kind of spontaneous rising up of the English nation for which Henry was not the chief designer. His agency needed to be downplayed so that he would not be cast in the role of regicide – the very precedent that Elizabeth feared most. Henry Tudor himself needed to be represented as wholesome, God-fearing, incorruptible, and capable of inspirational leadership. This is precisely the portrait of him we get in *Richard III*.

Artistically, the ending of *Richard III* fulfills a dramatic design, not only for this play but for the four-play series as a whole. The ironies of history serve well in fashioning closure for the entire narrative. Civil war is a nightmare; anarchy is a constant threat; selfish personal ambitions can overwhelm a state when it is weakly led; revenge is a double-edged sword that turns on itself in the form of endlessly reciprocal violence. How is a dramatist like Shakespeare to make artistic sense of what could so easily become an endless litany of barbarous deeds? Shakespeare needs to find meaning in history and in his art, and he does so by showing, belatedly but surely, how all the carnage of the Wars of the Roses has a meaningful purpose of which its perpetrators and victims are ironically unaware. The carnage produces a Richard III and then it disposes of him once the job of destructive punishment has been finished.

In providential terms, Richard III can be characterized as a scourge of God – that is, the unwitting agent of Providence, carrying out its long-range intentions of which he himself is unaware. This reading provides a neat answer to the question as to why so much evil and suffering occurred in the first place. If one adopts a providential reading of history, much evil and suffering can be seen as the deserved punishment for a people who have lost their way spiritually. Many examples were available to Shakespeare and his contemporaries from Old Testament history, as for example by way of explaining why even God's chosen people, when they worshipped golden images, incurred divine punishment (Exodus 32). The concept reinforces the idea of passive obedience: those who flout divine command by forcibly opposing a legitimate monarch invite and deserve divine wrath. Such is the story of the English nation, as related in the *Henry VI* plays and *Richard III*. Those who suffer at the hands of Richard III freely confess the sins that have led them to their suffering and punishment. They see purpose in their own tragedies, and respond with contrition.

Yet Shakespeare's reading of history is not as massively providential as was once assumed. To trace the horrors of civil war back to Henry Bolingbroke's defiance of Richard II and to argue that all that follows is a form of divine vengeance for that act is to impose too coherent a pattern on the whole series. True enough, that idea does find expression at key points. The Bishop of Carlisle in *Richard II*, aghast at the sacrilege of deposing 'the figure of God's majesty, / His captain, steward, deputy elect, / Anointed, crownèd, planted many years', prophesies eloquently that 'The blood of English shall manure the ground / And future ages groan for this foul act' (4.1.126–39). He is of course right: much blood is to be spilled. He is right even in the sense that if Bolingbroke had not deposed Richard II, history would have taken a different turn; this is a truth so self-evident and at the same time so hypothetical in its predictive powers as to be essentially useless. Bolingbroke did depose Richard, and what followed was what we call history. Shakespeare seems comfortable with the existential and secular dimensions of this idea of history, while at the same time allowing that a providential reading is also plausible. The providential reading suits his own artistic purposes, even while it also conforms handily to the official Tudor line.

To the extent that history seems to swing back and forth between strong and weak kings, another explanation becomes available. This explanation would appear to embrace the matter-of-fact, the existential: sometimes, under a good ruler, things go well; at other times, when an inept or corrupt ruler occupies the throne, things can go very badly. Shakespeare tends to sidestep this issue in his English history plays, letting history speak for itself. In his Roman plays, on the other hand, in which Christian providential ideas no longer have any say, the up-and-down vicissitudes of political rule seem more exposed. *Julius Caesar* is filled with ironies, but not of the benignly providential sort that rescues England at last from its nightmare of civil war in *Richard III*. In *Julius Caesar*, Brutus's public-spirited intentions all backfire on him and his cause. He takes part in the assassination of Caesar to free

Rome from tyranny. The result is uncontrolled mob violence in Rome and a sharp diminution under Antony and Octavius Caesar of the very liberties for which Brutus did what he did. Caesar himself is no less a victim of ironies: he thinks himself as constant as the North Star, 'Unshaked of motion' (3.1.71), and yet his susceptibility to flattery and superstition prompts him to go to the Capitol on the very day when his death has been prophesied. The wry endings of *Coriolanus* and of *Timon of Athens* give us a similar impression of events that wind down without hope of recovery. Men are sometimes their own worst enemies. It is as though Shakespeare anticipates Karl Marx's maxim that men make their own history, but not under circumstances of their own choosing (*The Eighteenth Brumaire of Louis Bonaparte*, Chapter 1). As Shakespeare moves away from writing history plays and romantic comedies, in the time around 1599–1600, he seems more and more bemused with the ironies of history that may take place under neither human nor divine control.

Overall, then, the political philosophy embedded in Shakespeare's plays is complex. Shakespeare dwells on political ironies and impasses that will yield to no easy solution. (If we had time, we could observe the same configuration in *King John*, the one English history play of the 1590s that, isolated chronologically as an account of early thirteenth-century politics, is not part of either of Shakespeare's four-play series.) He fairmindedly reports the political arguments of all sides, lending his impressive powers as a poet to the expression of conflicting ideologies. No doubt as a result, his allegiance has been claimed ever since by proponents of contending political stripes. Is he what we might call a conservative? He voices strong arguments for established monarchy, yet he also sees with great clarity the rationale of a coup d'état against an incapable or tyrannical ruler. Is he a defender or critic of war? He allows the Chorus of *Henry V* to laud Henry's great defeat of the French at the battle of Agincourt, and yet he is not afraid to show us the matter-of-fact political machinations that go into Henry's decision to go to war, and elsewhere, especially in the *Henry VI* plays, he devastatingly portrays the terrors of civil conflict. Is he a social elitist or a democrat? He dramatizes the harmful consequences of crowd hysteria, but also shows us ordinary citizens who seem to have better political instincts than their supposed social superiors. Does he think Prince Hal of the *Henry IV* plays benefits from his association with Falstaff? Yes, perhaps, up to a point. Is

Shakespeare's philosophy of history providential or Machiavellian, even Marxist? Rival ideologies are abundantly in play.

This does not mean that a comprehensive political view is indiscernible. One approach may be to consider the shifts of emphasis that manifest themselves as we move from the early 1590s to later work. The *Henry VI* plays and *Richard III* are more open to providential interpretation than are later plays, even if the providential view of history is by no means the only way to understand the Wars of the Roses. The justification of Henry VII's coming to power in *Richard III* offers an implicit defence of Tudor monarchy that seems, on the whole, less qualified than the ironies of history we find in the later sequence known as the Henriad. When Shakespeare pursues these same ironies of history in *Julius Caesar* and other plays set in classical times, the absence of a Christian providential view enables him to see more clearly than before how history can be understood in secular and existential terms. Even in the Henriad, pragmatic statecraft tends to win out over chivalric and outmoded ideas of honour. Shakespeare need not be perceived as endorsing such a seismic shift in the very nature of history, and indeed *Hamlet* (c.1599–1601) can be read in part as a lament for the passing of the old order, but we can at least see the enlarged consciousness about history in his Henriad as integral to what we mean when we attempt to define Shakespeare's political philosophy. The pragmatic and sceptical nature of the inquiry will be expanded in plays to come, as Shakespeare turns more and more to issues of religious controversy and philosophical doubt.

4

Hold the Mirror Up to Nature
Shakespeare's Ideas on Writing and Acting

One set of ideas that Shakespeare needed to consider, as he ventured with increasing daring into philosophical issues of scepticism and doubt, has to do with the nature of poetry and drama. What are the artistic and moral purposes of poetry and drama, and how does the poet or dramatist go about his task as purveyor of moral wisdom? Shakespeare's utterances about his craft as writer, both implicit and explicit, take it for granted that poetry and drama alike serve as important guides to human conduct. In this assumption Shakespeare was following the line of ancient and Renaissance theorists from Aristotle and Horace to Philip Sidney and Ben Jonson, The idea is at the heart of Sidney's *Defence of Poesy* (1595): poetry surpasses both history and philosophy, in Sidney's view, because it so powerfully illuminates great truths with piquant example, thus avoiding the disabling particularity of history on the one hand and the dry abstractions of philosophy on the other.

For Shakespeare, the power of art is just as important to the playwright and actor as it is to the poet. What does it mean to say that acting is an imitation of nature? Why is imitation of this sort so important to us that it can affect people's lives, for better or for worse? What styles of acting can best achieve theatre's function of holding the mirror up to nature? These things seem to matter greatly to Shakespeare, and particularly so when he wrote his Sonnets and *Hamlet* (c.1599–1601). Implicit notions about the nature of dramatic art are to be found throughout the canon, of course, but explicit verbalizing is especially in evidence around the turn of the century. The Sonnets are hard to date individually, but some key ones are plausibly from the end of the 1590s or early 1600s, and then too we can assume that Shakespeare has been thinking about his art for some time. It is as though Shakespeare takes stock of his artistic method as he turns from the writing of romantic comedies and English histories to plays of more problematic genre like *Troilus and Cressida* (1601) and to the great tragedies. At any rate, this seems like an appropriate time for us to look at Shakespeare's view of his own craft.

Even though Shakespeare never wrote a literary essay or a preface to a play or poem expressing his views on what it means to be a poet and dramatist, and even though we have no preserved correspondence of his or records of literary conversation, we can intuit quite a lot from passages in his poems and plays where the topics of writing and acting come up. As always, we have to be careful not to attribute to Shakespeare the thoughts of his characters, but we can identify positions that are put in debate. Then, too, certain themes stand out in such a way as to suggest that they are of some importance to their author.

The Sonnets seem deeply interested in the phenomenon of fame achieved through writing, and fame achieved through being written about. These are commonplace ideas going back to the ancient classical world, so that one must not place too much emphasis on individuality of view, but they do insistently present themselves as among the central themes of the Sonnets. A well-known example is Sonnet 55:

> Not marble nor the gilded monuments
> Of princes shall outlive this powerful rhyme,
> But you shall shine more bright in these contents
> Than unswept stone besmeared with sluttish time.

The best protection against the ravages of time, oblivion, and war, the poet goes on to assure us, is literary remembrance: 'your praise shall still find room / Even in the eyes of all posterity / That wear this world out to the ending doom'. 'Your' here can mean the young gentleman to whom the Sonnets are addressed generally and us as readers.

Several features of this sonnet are noteworthy. The poet lauds the merits of poetry over stone monuments that might seem durable but are in fact subject to decay and neglect. A problem with marble monuments is that they are too soon forgotten, 'besmeared with sluttish time', 'unswept', or they are overturned and rooted out. Poetry, on the other hand, will endure not just for centuries but for ever. War is emblematic of the processes through which wasting Time will inevitably 'burn / The living record of your memory' unless it is redeemed by poetry. The poet stresses repeatedly the advantages of poetry to the person thus commemorated: such a person will 'live in this' until 'the judgment that yourself arise', that is, until the Judgement Day at the very end of time itself. Concurrently, the sonnet implies that poetry will also immortalize the author. The sonnet is reflexively about itself: as we read it, we remember the words of William Shakespeare and see in this sonnet a demonstration of how indeed poetry can achieve a special kind of immortality for the maker. The sonneteer is also implicitly proud of a fellowship among poets and lovers of poetry who can scorn 'the gilded monuments / Of princes'. The achievements of proud and powerful men (like Alexander, say, or Julius Caesar) inevitably decay, as do all the things of this mundane world. Poetry is of a higher order. It shares with religion a timeless truth that can laugh with gentle scorn at mere worldliness.

Poetry is a defence against ageing, not in the sense of slowing down the biological process but of teaching us to put our trust in the eternal values of true love and friendship. To guard against the fast-approaching time when the poet's dear friend will be, as the poet is already, 'With Time's injurious hand crushed and o'erworn' and his brow filled 'With lines and wrinkles', the poet fortifies himself by the assurance that Time 'shall never cut from memory / My sweet love's beauty': 'His beauty shall in these black lines be seen, / And they shall live, and he in them still green' (Sonnet 63). Poetry can eternize beauty of the sort that cannot decay. Again, in Sonnet 65, the answer to the awesome challenge posed by 'sad mortality', against which 'brass, nor stone, nor earth, nor boundless sea' can hold out long, is poetry, and poetry alone. Nothing can hold back the 'swift foot' of time, 'unless this miracle have might, / That in black ink my love may still shine bright'. The emphasis on 'black ink' in both sonnets makes its point paradoxically: poetry is immortal, and yet it is created by a mere mortal who writes in a fluid substance that seems almost dirty. The physical act of writing, and the paper on which words appear, are ephemeral, but the ideas and images contained in those words are not.

For all the poet-speaker's characteristic modesty about his own abilities as a poet, he is unapologetic about the power of poetry itself and its ability to bestow fame through writing. 'Your name from hence immortal life shall have', he assures his friend, 'Though I, once gone, to all the world must die.' 'You still shall live – such virtue hath my pen – / Where breath most breathes, even in the mouths of men' (Sonnet 81). When the poet feels that his genius is flagging or that he is wasting his efforts on 'some worthless song', he implores the Muse to come to his assistance for the higher purpose of commemorating the friend. The poet speaks to his Muse as though he, the poet, is simply an instrument whose humble pen is taught both 'skill and argument' by the power and 'fury' of inspiration. Only the Muse, then, can do what poetry must do: 'Give my love fame faster than Time wastes life; / So thou prevent'st his scythe and crooked knife' (Sonnet 100).

The poet-speaker of the Sonnets is sensitive to the complex relationship between art and mere artifice. Like Sir Philip Sidney, in his sonnet sequence called *Astrophel and Stella*, the speaker of Shakespeare's sonnets insistently refuses to follow the lame conventions of sonneteering – which, by the 1590s, had attracted many followers and imitators. 'My mistress' eyes are nothing like the sun', he proclaims, alluding to the way in which far too many sonnets reiterate that clichéd comparison. 'Coral is far more red than her lips' red.' Her breasts are not snow-white, her hair is wiry and black, her cheeks do not resemble damask roses, her breath is not perfumed, her speech is not music, and her manner of walking is more earthbound than godlike. Shakespeare is here satirizing not only the parade of lifeless and predictable images but also the sonnet convention of the blazon, or catalogue of a lady's charms, set forth as though they were heraldic insignia. 'And yet, by heaven, I think my love as rare / As any she belied with false compare', he concludes (Sonnet 130). Poetry must avoid clichés because they cheapen the subject, substituting the trite and expected for images that are fresh and compelling.

The advice here is close to that of Rosalind in *As You Like It* when she counsels Orlando to eschew the empty formulas of wooing, as for example to say that he will die for love if his passion is not requited. 'No, faith, die by attorney', she advises him. 'The poor world is almost six thousand years old, and in all this time there was not any man died in his own person, videlicet, in a love cause.' Her examples include Troilus, who 'did what he could to die' of love without succeeding in doing so, even though he is 'one of the patterns of love', and Leander, who died not because he was lovesick (as the 'foolish chroniclers of that age' keep insisting) but because he caught a cramp while swimming the Hellespont to reach his beloved Hero of Sestos. 'These are all lies', Rosalind concludes (4.1.89–102). Orlando would be well advised to avoid the hoary vow of loving 'For ever and a day'. 'Say "a day," without the "ever"', Rosalind insists (138–9). Love needs to be realistic in its expectations; so does love poetry. Juliet is much of the same mind in *Romeo and Juliet* when she begs Romeo not to swear 'by the moon, th'inconstant moon, / That monthly changes in her circled orb, / Lest that thy love prove likewise variable' (2.2.109–11). As in Sonnet 130, the idea points to the need for sincerity both in human relationships and in art. At the same time, we are constantly aware, as we read this sonnet or any other, of how studiously artificial are the conventions of sonnet-writing, with its highly structured stanzaic form and rhyming pattern. Writing must learn to create the aura of genuineness through the inventive use of poetic convention.

At times, the poet-speaker of the Sonnets is capable of painful self-abasement in his art, or at least in his profession. Sonnet 111 begins as follows:

> Oh, for my sake do you with Fortune chide,
> The guilty goddess of my harmful deeds,
> That did not better for my life provide
> Than public means which public manners breeds.
> Thence comes it that my name receives a brand,
> And almost thence my nature is subdued
> To what it works in, like the dyer's hand.

If this is at least partly autobiographical, it seems to suggest that the poet-speaker regrets the circumstances that have left him with little choice other than to put himself on view to the public in such a way as to breed 'public manners' in himself and to incur disgrace for something shameful and dirtying, like the dyer whose hand is stained by the dye it handles. This could refer to acting, which is necessarily public, and which bears with it (then as now) a reputation for a bohemian life style. Acting, in this view, is at once adventuresome and brazen. The actor inspires his audience with his skill at representation while at the same time making a display of himself. Do these painful contradictions apply to the dramatist as well? Is the writer's very nature in danger of being darkened by the medium in which he works, namely, the language of poetry and the world of commercial theatre? When the poet-speaker complains to his friend, 'Alas, 'tis true, I have gone here and there / And made myself a motley to the view' (Sonnet 110), he sounds again the note of self-deprecation or even self-loathing for a profession in which the speaker has 'Gored mine own thoughts, sold cheap what is most dear'.

Yet elsewhere Shakespeare sounds as though he regards acting and playwriting as the noblest of professions, and the most able to minister to a world in need of art's perspectives. Nowhere is this admiration more eloquently expressed than in Hamlet's advice to the players who have visited Elsinor and are about to put on a play at Hamlet's behest. Avoid overacting, he cautions them: 'o'erstep not the modesty of nature. For anything so o'erdone is from the purpose of playing, whose end, both at the first and now, was and is to hold as 'twere the mirror up to nature, to show virtue her feature, scorn her own image, and the very age and body of the time his form and pressure' (*Hamlet*, 3.2.19–24). These are high moral aims. The very purpose of mimesis, Hamlet seems to argue, is to instruct through illustration and example. The mirror of art shows us what we are: it warns us away from negative models and encourages virtuous conduct. Actors are 'the abstract and brief chronicles of the time' (2.2.524). This is not a reductive or utilitarian view of art, because art needs to be eloquent and beautiful in order to inspire rightminded behaviour, but this view seems quite unembarrassed by the proposition that at its very best, art has a didactic function.

Indeed, it proves so in the present instance. Hamlet's purpose in putting on 'The Murder of Gonzago' is to test the conscience of King Claudius by showing him a representation of the murderous act that Hamlet believes Claudius to have committed. He has heard 'That guilty creatures sitting at a play / Have by the very cunning of the scene / Been struck so to the soul that presently / They have proclaimed their malefactions' (2.2.590–3). Claudius responds as though on cue. When the performance of 'The Murder of Gonzago' reaches the critical point at which the King's nephew, Lucianus, is about to pour poison into the ear of his sleeping uncle, Claudius can take no more. He rises and makes a hasty departure, much to the consternation of all present except Horatio and Hamlet. The latter, having prepared this 'Mousetrap', is now ready to 'take the ghost's word for a thousand pound' (3.2.235, 258–85). Hamlet has tested and verified the truth of what his father's ghost has told him about the murder of old Hamlet by his brother.

The sequence has also confirmed in action Hamlet's theory about the efficacy of dramatic art in awakening conscience. 'The Murder of Gonzago' shows precisely what Hamlet means by holding 'the mirror up to nature'. The idea is profoundly idealistic in its view of writing: just as art can eternize fame, it also can change our hearts and help us to grapple with our own sinful natures.

This high moral purpose explains why, in Hamlet's view, acting must 'acquire and beget a temperance that may give it smoothness'. Hamlet goes on at some length in his insistence that actors must not 'mouth' their speeches as if they were the town crier, or saw the air with their hands, or 'tear a passion to tatters, to very rags, to split the ears of the groundlings, who for the most part are capable of nothing but inexplicable dumb shows and noise'. They must take care not to out-Herod Herod in rant, or crack some ill-timed joke to make 'the unskillful laugh' – a fault that 'cannot but make the judicious grieve, the censure of the which one must in your allowance o'erweigh a whole theater of others' (3.2.1–28). Clowns especially must avoid the temptation to ad-lib some frivolous matter and then laugh at their own witticism 'to set on some quantity of barren spectators to laugh too, though in the meantime some necessary question of the play be then to be considered' (39–43). Good acting aims at representing what one sees in a true mirror, without distortion. Reform of acting style (36–8) is necessary to avoid the abuses of unskilful acting, which are generally the combined result of bad taste on the part of some spectators and willingness on the part of too many actors to cater to an appetite for triviality and 'whirlwind' passions.

Hamlet's highminded view of dramatic art, then, goes hand in hand with an intellectually patrician view of what constitutes a properly educated viewer. Shakespeare dares to allow Hamlet to refer to his spectators as 'groundlings' – a term first employed by Shakespeare in this sense (and still current today) to describe those who stood in the 'yard' on three sides of the Elizabethan public theatre stage. Many of those who heard Hamlet's speech in the original production some time around 1600 must have been groundlings themselves, at least in the practical sense. Is Hamlet insulting them? More likely, he is appealing to their best critical instincts by bidding them to join the select ranks of those who have a mature grasp of what drama should be all about. At all events, he appeals to drama as high art. Drama should 'Suit the action to the word, the word to the action' (3.2.17–18). This advice applies to the dramatist as much as it does to the actors whom Hamlet is addressing.

In a similarly rarefied vein, Hamlet describes to the players a dramatic speech he heard once. It had never been acted, 'or if it was, not above once, for the play, I remember, pleased not the million; 'twas caviar to the general' – that is, it was a choice dish too elegant for coarse plebeian tastes (2.2.434–7). Again, Hamlet is bearding his spectators standing close to the stage, or is he asking them to measure and elevate their own tastes in dramatic literature by this high standard? At all events, the play was, in Hamlet's own view and in that of others 'whose judgments in such matters cried in the top of mine', an excellent play, 'well digested in the scenes, set down with as much modesty as cunning', and with 'no sallets in the lines to make the matter savory' or 'matter in the phrase that might indict the author of affectation' (437–43). Hamlet seems intent on lauding a work that was too sophisticated for ordinary viewers; his praise is directed toward the chosen few whose impeccable taste entitles them to be judges of literary merit. The play Hamlet remembers was so highbrow, in fact, that it failed on stage if it ever was acted at all – a description that uncannily fits the early history of Shakespeare's *Troilus and Cressida*, with its publisher's blurb in 1609 advertising the work as 'never staled with the stage, never clapper-clawed with the palms of the vulgar, and yet passing full of the palm comical' (even though another version of the play's 1609 quarto title page did declare it to have been 'acted by the King's Majesty's Servants at the Globe'). Why this insistence on intellectual refinement at the expense of popular theatrical entertainment? The report that Hamlet has just received from Rosencrantz and Guildenstern about a poets' war in which the adult acting companies are losing ground to companies of boy actors, seemingly with reference to the London theatrical scene around 1600–1 and appearing only in the Folio text of *Hamlet* (2.2.338–62), adds to Hamlet's sense that the theatre has a serious obligation to maintain the very highest standards of artistic excellence.

Hamlet's sample of high dramatic art is about the slaying of King Priam of Troy by the Greek Pyrrhus (or Neoptolemus), son of Achilles, and the passionate cries of Queen Hecuba 'When she saw Pyrrhus make malicious sport / In mincing with his sword her husband's limbs' (2.2.450–518). The passage is studiously classical, being derived in the main from Virgil's description of the burning of Troy in the *Aeneid*,

Book II. It may also pay a wry homage to *Dido, Queen of Carthage*, a play written by Christopher Marlowe in collaboration with Thomas Nashe some time before Marlowe died in 1593. The piece evokes nostalgia for a past world of classical tragedy, in its dramatization of an often-told myth, its poetic diction and carefully controlled blank verse, its Senecan long phrases and sententious moralizations, its focus on moments of intense tragic passion, its stoic pronouncements about Fortune, and its acknowledgement of the presence of the gods. Its recital on this present occasion displeases Polonius as 'too long', thereby providing Hamlet with still another opportunity to express his preference for auditors of educated taste; as he says about Polonius to the players, 'He's for a jig or a tale of bawdry, or he sleeps' (2.2.498–501). The archaic style used to describe Priam's and Hecuba's tragic misfortune is not Shakespeare's usual idiom, in fact, but it adroitly serves a dramatic purpose here of defining Hamlet's tastes as anything but lowbrow.

Can we hear Shakespeare's own voice lurking behind that of Hamlet? The spirited commitment to theatre reform, the solid advice about suiting the action to the word, etc., do sound so unexceptionably and importantly true that we are tempted to view Hamlet as a kind of mouthpiece for the author. The appeal to sophisticated audiences is perhaps consistent with the aims of Shakespeare's acting company, who valued invitations to perform at court and who, as the first decade of the seventeenth century wore on, chose more and more to act indoors at their Blackfriars Theatre before courtly and sophisticated audiences. At the same time, part of Shakespeare's genius was, and is, that he knows how to appeal to kings and clowns. The discourse in *Hamlet* about the purposes and artistic styles of dramatic art should perhaps be regarded in the light of a debate in which Hamlet is one particularly eloquent speaker.

Generally, Shakespeare has had the reputation in his own day and in succeeding generations of being a writer in a popular and romantic vein more than in the style favoured by neoclassicists in England and on the Continent, especially in France and Italy. Although Shakespeare does not voice his own preferences in so many words, his literary practice confirms that general impression. He shows no consistent regard for the so-called unities of time, place, and action that were so essential a part of neo-Aristotelean critical tradition. *The Comedy of Errors* (c.1589–94), to be sure, follows a five-act structure like that of its chief source, Plautus's *Menaechmi*, or *Twins*. Its action takes place chiefly in or near the house of Antipholus of Ephesus, as well as the street and a nearby priory. The Courtesan dwells in the vicinity. An entrance '*from the bay*' (4.1.84) and exits '*to the priory*' and '*to the Abbess*' (5.1.37, 282) reinforce the impression of a single street location in the town of Ephesus. The action lasts only one day; the plot is a single plot. Shakespeare evidently apprenticed himself to classical tradition in this early play. He certainly knew what the unities were. He followed them as well in *The Tempest*, the capstone of his career as a dramatist in 1611 or so. Its action is limited to the island and to something less than the 'two days' in which Prospero promises to free Ariel (1.2.301–2, 424–5); apparently, the entire story unfolds in about 'three hours' (5.1.136, 188, and 225; see also 1.2.241 and 5.1.4–5). The story of what took place some 'twelve years' ago in Milan (1.2.53), when Miranda was a baby, is told in proper neoclassical fashion as a flashback. Granted, *The Tempest* uses multiple plotting, especially in its ludicrously comic subplot of the conspiracy of Caliban, Stephano, and Trinculo, but the whole is still gracefully unified.

On the other hand, *Antony and Cleopatra* (1606–7) moves all over the middle and eastern Mediterranean, from Rome to Egypt and back again, as well as to Messina in Sicily (2.1), Misenum near Naples in southern Italy (2.6), a location in the Middle East not far from northeast modern-day Iran (3.1), Athens (3.4), and Actium, on the northwestern coast of Greece (3.7–10). Not all of these locations are specifically named in the play, but the large geographical movements are essential to the story. The passage of time, though not registered in specific dates, extends from the meeting of Antony and Cleopatra on the River Cydnus in southeast modern-day Turkey in 41 BC down to their defeat at the battle of Actium in 31 BC and their deaths in Egypt the following year. The play is made up of forty-three separate scenes, if by 'scenes' we mean sequences of action marked off by a bare stage. A few, during the fighting at Actium, are brief. Some of Shakespeare's history plays are no less epic in their chronological sweep. The three *Henry VI* plays extend cumulatively from the death of Henry V in 1422 to that of Henry VI in 1471, and move all over England and France; in *1 Henry VI* alone, action occurs in Orleans, Auvergne, Rouen, Paris, Bordeaux, Angiers, and Anjou, as well as in London and Westminster. Multiplicity of action is a trademark of the history plays.

Even in the more tightly organized tragedies, time and location do not obey neoclassical restriction. The plot of *Hamlet* must allow time for Hamlet to be put on a ship bound for England, evade his escorts by boarding a pirate vessel during the melee of the pirates' attack, and make his way back to the Danish court after having exchanged the instructions in the diplomatic packet of Rosencrantz and Guildenstern, who proceed on their way to England (4.6.15–29, 5.2.12–25). *Othello* shifts location from Venice in Act 1 to Cyprus for the remainder of the action – a dramatic solecism according to neoclassical practice that Giuseppe Verdi solved in his *Otello* (1887) by beginning his opera in Cyprus, much as John Dryden had classicized his version of *Antony and Cleopatra*, entitled *All for Love* (1678), by locating the entire play in Egypt and telling all the previous history through the characters' recollections. *King Lear* moves from the British court to Scotland (Albany) and thence to Gloucestershire and Dover, over a period of some months at least, and with the employment (unusual in tragedy) of a double plot. The action of *Macbeth* must allow time, following the murder of Duncan, for disaffection to grow under Macbeth's increasingly tyrannical reign and for an army of resistance to organize itself with English support.

A common geographical motif of the romantic comedies is a journey, usually from some centre of civilization to a sylvan or magical world where strange transformations can occur. The young lovers of *A Midsummer Night's Dream* escape from the harsh Athenian law into the forest or wood, where they remain in the grip of fairy magic until the closing action at the court of Duke Theseus. *The Two Gentlemen of Verona* shuttles back and forth between Verona, Milan, and a forest in Mantua replete with brigands. Rosalind and Celia, in *As You Like It*, choose banishment from the unfriendly court of Duke Frederick into the friendlier Forest of Arden, which may be located in France (Ardenne), or in Warwickshire, or in the world of the artist's imagination. Bassanio, in *The Merchant of Venice*, journeys from the legalistic world of Venice to Belmont, the very name of which betokens quiet beauty and a retreat from the Venetian world of commercial conflict. These are journeys to what Northrop Frye has dubbed the 'green world' of Shakespearean romantic comedy. The geographic relocations bring with them a visionary glimpse into a world of fairies, shepherds, goblins, even monsters. Shakespeare's late romances return emphatically to the motif of the imaginative journey: *Pericles* wanders all over the

Mediterranean, *Cymbeline* travels from England to Rome and mountainous Wales, and *The Winter's Tale* moves from Sicilia to the make-believe pastoral world of Bohemia. Even *The Tempest*, though located throughout on the island, embodies this same journey in a narrative that juxtaposes the dark political world of Milan and Naples with an uninhabited island existing only in the artist's imagination and in this play.

One way to gain a perspective on Shakespeare's blithe disregard for the neoclassical unities is to compare him with Ben Jonson, and with what Jonson has to say about Shakespeare. Though Shakespeare says nothing for the record, Jonson is hardly silent about Shakespeare. Can we reconstruct a conversation between these two men out of Jonson's various remarks and the unstated but implied literary persuasions of Shakespeare as seen in his work? Jonson was the younger of the two, having been born in 1572, eight years after Shakespeare. Jonson outlived Shakespeare by twenty-one years, dying in 1637. Jonson thus had ample opportunity to reflect on Shakespeare's achievement as a dramatist and poet. Moreover, Jonson arrogated to himself the role of England's chief literary critic and scholar. His conversations with William Drummond of Hawthornden in 1618 are peppered with pronouncements about writers in England, including Sir Philip Sidney, Edmund Spenser, Samuel Daniel, Michael Drayton, John Donne, and Shakespeare. In the prefatory materials to his own plays and in other writings, Jonson enunciated a comprehensive neoclassical theory through which to judge the literary achievements of his generation. He was himself well schooled in Latin and only to a lesser extent in Greek.

Jonson's most generous estimate of Shakespeare as a writer is in his tribute 'To the memory of my beloved, the author, Mr. William Shakespeare, and what he hath left us', published in the first complete edition of Shakespeare's plays, the so-called First Folio, in 1623. Jonson freely confesses Shakespeare's writings 'to be such / As neither man nor muse can praise too much'. Shakespeare is the 'soul of the age', 'The applause, delight, the wonder of our stage'. Jonson will not lodge Shakespeare even by England's greatest poets, namely, Chaucer, Spenser, and Francis Beaumont; Shakespeare is in a category all by himself. He is 'a monument without a tomb', that is, needing no funeral monument to guarantee his immortality, for his greatness will endure 'while thy book doth live / And we have wits to read and praise to give'. In his writings Shakespeare far outshines John Lyly or 'sporting Kyd' or 'Marlowe's mighty line'. To raise the standard of comparison still higher, Jonson compares Shakespeare favourably as a writer of tragedies with the Greek tragedians Aeschylus, Euripides, and Sophocles, and also with the Roman tragedians Marcus Pacuvius (c.220–130 BC), Lucius Accius (170–c.86 BC, a younger contemporary of Pacuvius), and 'him of Cordova dead', i.e., Seneca the Younger (c.4 BC to AD 65), the best known of Latin tragic dramatists in the English Renaissance. For comedy, Jonson has still higher praise; Shakespeare is a nonpareil. 'Leave thee alone, for the comparison / Of all that insolent Greece or haughty Rome / Sent forth, or since did from their ashes come.' Even the best of the ancient comic writers, the Greek Aristophanes and the Roman Terence and Plautus, no longer please audiences, but lie 'antiquated and deserted' in the wake of Shakespeare's phenomenal success. Jonson's Shakespeare is thus 'not of an age, but for all time', the 'Sweet swan of Avon' who will be apotheosized as a heavenly constellation, shining as the 'star of poets', beaming down 'influence' to 'chide or cheer the drooping stage'.

For all its warmth of praise, and its note of hyperbole that is appropriate to a poem commemorating one who is now dead and definitively published, this appraisal by Jonson is written from a neoclassical and at times critical point of view. Jonson himself is extraordinarily present in the poem as literary dictator. He accepts as his due the task of sizing up Shakespeare in the roster of the great writers of antiquity and the present. The canon is highbrow and classical. Implicitly, Jonson appears to wonder at the phenomenon of a writer from Stratford-upon-Avon, the 'Swan of Avon', who has not merely broken into the ranks of the immortals but has topped them all, at least in comedy. The observation is at once a mark of pride in England's accomplishment in rivalling the ancients ('Triumph, my Britain, thou hast one to show / To whom all scenes of Europe homage show') and an acknowledgement that England has had a lot of catching up to do. Jonson parades his own learning by citing ancient dramatists that only the learned would know anything about. Even the Greek tragic writers were little known or translated in Renaissance England, and Shakespeare almost certainly did not read them. Nor does he ever refer to Pacuvius or Accius. Even the better-known Seneca may have reached him chiefly through the plays of Thomas Kyd and other dramatists of the popular stage; the only mention of Seneca in all Shakespeare is to be found in the fatuous utterance of Polonius that 'Seneca cannot be too heavy, nor Plautus too light' (*Hamlet*, 2.2.400–1). Shakespeare's two passing references to Aristotle refer to the writings on ethics and moral philosophy (*The Taming of the Shrew*, 1.1.32, and *Troilus and Cressida*, 2.2.166–7); no evidence points to his having read the *Poetics*.

Jonson's commemorative poem is thus directed by a man of immense learning at one who was somehow self-taught, without classical training. Jonson cannot refrain from observing that Shakespeare had 'small Latin and less Greek'; that fact makes his accomplishment as a poet and dramatist all the more astonishing. The remark also calls attention to the fact that Jonson himself had plenty of Latin and Greek. Even Jonson's allowance that Shakespeare was no mere child of Nature underscores the point that Shakespeare had to learn his craft by diligent application, as every good writer must do: 'he / Who casts to write a living line must sweat' in order to 'strike the second heat / Upon the Muses' anvil'. Jonson insists that 'a good poet's made, as well as born'. Jonson was sensitive to the charge that he laboured too diligently in his writing; that is why his Prologue to *Volpone* (1605–6) is quick to observe, ''Tis known that five weeks fully penned it / From his own hand' (16–17). Shakespeare, conversely, had a reputation for the easy flow of his writing (see below). Accordingly, Jonson makes a conscious effort in the Folio commemorative poem to refashion Shakespeare as much as he can into Jonson's own model of the true poet.

Jonson's poem acknowledges only two kinds of drama: tragedy and comedy. The tragic actor treads the stage in his 'buskin' (the 'cothornus') or laced boot reaching halfway or more to the knee, symbolizing the high seriousness of a drama that draws its story lines from mythic legends about the misfortunes of princes. The comic actor wears the 'sock', a low shoe or slipper symbolizing the lower status of comedy in its engagement with the day-to-day antics of commoners. (The genre known as the Satyr play occupies no place in this dual classification.) Historically, the distinction between the two genres of drama was sharply delineated on the ancient classical stage: comedies, with choruses of perhaps twenty-four members and a characteristically episodic structure, were performed in Athens on the festivals of the greater Dionysia and the Lenaea, whereas tragedies employed a smaller chorus and a more tightly organized structure for performance also on the greater Dionysia and the Lenaea but as a separate event. Prizes went for the best comedy and for the best tragedy. This codification of categories continued into the writings of Aristotle and Aristotelean tradition. Jonson measures and praises Shakespeare's achievement in these dual terms. The division into two genres was common in the Renaissance. Francis Meres, in his *Palladis Tamia*, 1598, praises Shakespeare as follows: 'As Plautus and Seneca are accounted the best for comedy and tragedy among the Latins, so Shakespeare among the English is the most excellent in both kinds for the stage.'

But does this classificatory system suit the Shakespeare canon? In Meres's taxonomy the *Henry IV* plays are listed as tragedies, along with *Richard II, Richard III*, and *King John*. A case can be made for these last three plays as tragedies, to be sure: *Richard II* was called '*The Tragedy of King Richard the second*' on its 1597 title page and *Richard III* was similarly titled when it was first published in the same year, though we also encounter titles in the Folio like '*The Life and Death of Richard the Second*' and '*The Life and Death of King John*' that lay more stress on the openended nature of history. *Richard II* is about the downfall of Richard, but it is also about the rise of Henry Bolingbroke, King Henry IV. The *Henry IV* plays challenge the bipartite classification of classical tradition even more searchingly. In quarto they were known as '*The History of Henry the Fourth*' and '*The Second Part of Henry the Fourth*' in 1598 and 1600; in the 1623 Folio the first part is called '*The First Part of King Henry the Fourth*'. Hotspur does of course die in that play, but on the whole the story is one of success for Henry IV and for his son, the future Henry V. Even Falstaff is riding high at the conclusion of *1 Henry IV*, and the play itself contains some of Shakespeare's best comic writing.

The Folio of 1623 is divided into three groups: not comedies and tragedies, but comedies, histories, and tragedies. Ten plays out of a total of thirty-six belong to the group called histories. Cumulatively, they dramatize the history of England during the reign of King John in the early thirteenth century and then continuously from the reign of Richard II in the late fourteenth century through to Henry VIII's reign and the birth of the future Queen Elizabeth in 1533. What is the history play as a type of genre? In one sense its meaning seems plain enough in the Folio's 'Catalogue' or table of contents: these ten plays are all about English history. King John, the monarch least connected to the others chronologically, presumably captured Shakespeare's attention because of the ambiguity of John's claim to the English throne and because of his struggles with the Catholic church; the other nine plays tell the story of England during the civil wars that eventually led to the establishment of the Tudor dynasty. But what does this say about genre? What is the history play structurally and formally? Why are *Macbeth* and *King Lear* not classified as history plays? Both deal with kings from British history or legendary history. What does it mean that some English history plays can be classified as comedies and others as tragedies?

The English history play, then, is an anomaly in terms of classical definitions of dramatic genres. It also represents one of Shakespeare's major achievements. He had an important role in devising the genre, though he did know and make use of a few early experiments by other dramatists, including the anonymous *The Famous Victories of Henry V* (1583–8) and *The Troublesome Reign of King John* (c.1587–91). He was clearly the leading practitioner in the writing of English history plays throughout the 1590s. His approach to what constitutes an English history play is entirely pragmatic. He wrote these plays as sequels; the form and content developed as he went along. When he began writing about Henry IV and his son, he may have planned a single play reaching down to the death of the father; if so, he changed his mind as he wrote, discovering that he had much to say about Falstaff and Hal, and so we have the story of Henry IV in two parts. Tradition has it that he took time off to write a play (*The Merry Wives of Windsor*) about Falstaff in love, at the behest of Queen Elizabeth; of this we cannot be certain, but it speaks to the reputation Shakespeare enjoyed as an improviser. He seems to have felt under no compulsion to observe the genres of classical tradition, any more than he felt constrained by the so-called unities of time, place, and action. A successful play for him appears to have been whatever works on stage for an audience.

When Polonius announces to Hamlet that actors have just arrived at Elsinor, he praises them for the many dramatic genres in which they excel. They are, Polonius says, 'The best actors the world, either for tragedy, comedy, history, pastoral, pastoral-comical, historical-pastoral, tragical-historical, tragical-comical-historical-pastoral, scene individable, or poem unlimited' (*Hamlet*, 2.2.396–400). Is Shakespeare laughing at himself? We note that the list begins with 'tragedy, comedy, history', the three categories that would later be employed in publishing the 1623 Folio. Both 'pastoral' and 'pastoral-comical' are terms that could be applied to *As You Like It* or *The Winter's Tale*. 'Tragical-historical' aptly describes plays like *Julius Caesar* and *Antony and Cleopatra* that fashion great tragedy out of history. If 'scene individable' means a play that observes the unity of place, then *The Comedy of Errors* and *The Tempest*, among others, fit the description. If 'poem unlimited' refers to plays that disregard the unities of time and place, the instances in the Shakespeare canon are almost – well – unlimited. Polonius is a bad literary critic on whom to rely for insightful commentary, but his mingle-mangle of dramatic categories does seem instructive when we think about types of Shakespearean drama.

The label 'comedy' covers a multitude of blessings. Romantic comedy about young lovers and their strange misadventures is a staple of the plays Shakespeare was writing in the 1590s; but then, around the time of *Hamlet*, we encounter a set of plays so strikingly at variance with the norms of romantic comedy that critics have sought out new labels. The most prevalent name for these new forms of comedy today is 'problem comedy' or 'problem play'. *Measure for Measure* (1603–4) describes for us a Vienna so adrift in sexual permissiveness that the Duke absents himself from town, leaving in charge a deputy, Angelo, who soon discovers that his own raging lust for a young woman bent on joining a convent (Isabella) is so ungovernable that he threatens her with the execution of her brother Claudio on a charge of fornication unless she consents to have sex with the deputy. Her seeming compliance takes the form of substituting in her place a woman whom Angelo has jilted some years ago. This 'bed trick' saves the day, but at the cost of an ethically dubious means. Several scenes of the play take place in prison. Among the play's liveliest characters are the pimps, madams, and customers of the criminal demimonde of Vienna. Even the marriages at the end are bizarre.

Such is the case also in *All's Well That Ends Well* (c.1601–5). This play features a young aristocrat, Bertram, who, disdainfully reluctant to obey the King's behest that he marry a young woman of lower social station (Helena) who has saved the King's life, runs off to the wars in the company of an engaging rascal named Parolles. Helena, like Isabella in *Measure for Measure*, is driven to the ethically dubious expedient of the bed trick: when Bertram pursues a widow's daughter during his military campaigning in Florence, Helena arranges with the widow to have Helena take the place of the daughter (Diana) at night in the planned sexual assignation. Bertram learns a lesson about the obligation that men should feel to acknowledge the consequences of their sexual aggressions, and all ends well, as the play's title promises, but not without having raised troublesome questions about human failure. As a comedy the play is unusual for the sympathetic attention it gives to older figures like Bertram's mother and 'an old lord' named Lafew, who repeatedly voice their disappointment in young people and especially in young males. This is not a comedy about the heady pleasures and risks of young love.

Both *Measure for Measure* and *All's Well* are included among the comedies in the 1623 Folio, thereby expanding our understanding of what Shakespeare may have included under that flexible term. *Troilus and Cressida* breaks the mold entirely. Its place in the 1623 Folio is entirely anomalous: it stands between the histories and the tragedies, almost entirely without page numbers, and is not listed in the 'Catalogue' or table of contents. Evidently its inclusion in the printing came late, following an abortive attempt to print it after *Romeo and Juliet*, which would have placed it among the tragedies. The play is arguably comedy or history or tragedy, or all of the above. It is a dark comedy in the spirit of its fellow 'problem plays', featuring a pair of lovers whose brief affair is brought to an abrupt end by a senseless war between Greeks and Trojans and by the failures of the lovers themselves. It is a history play in that it chronicles the most famous – and infamous – war in history. It is a tragedy in its dramatization of the deaths of Patroclus and especially Hector. Most of all, perhaps, it is a satire. Its choric voices, especially those of Pandarus and Thersites, point out for us in leering tones how 'lechery eats itself' (5.4.35). As Thersites says by way of sardonic characterization of the war, 'All the argument is a whore and a cuckold, a good quarrel to draw emulous factions and bleed to death upon' (2.3.71–3). *Troilus and Cressida* seems not to have been a success on stage in its own day, quite possibly because it was perceived as too avant-garde.

Shakespeare's late comedies further stretch the boundaries of what the term can mean. *Pericles* (c.1606–8) was not included in the 1623 Folio at all, perhaps because the editors sensibly regarded it as only partly by Shakespeare. At all events it can perhaps be classified as part romance and part tragicomedy: 'romance' in the sense that it takes its hero on many 'romantic' adventures of the sort found in many a marvel-filled narrative of travel to far-off lands ending at last in reunion with loved ones, and 'tragicomedy' in the sense of blending tragic and comic elements. On the tragic side are the apparent death of Pericles's wife Thaisa and his daughter Marina's threatening encounters with wicked stepmothers, pirates, and bawds; on the comic side are the amusing bordello scenes and the moments of tender joy when father, daughter, and wife finally are together again.

Cymbeline (c.1608) is arguably another tragicomedy, so very close to tragedy, in fact, that the 1623 Folio editors decided to print it among the tragedies as the last play in the volume. One can see why the editors put it here. Not only is it a very long play, third only to *Hamlet* and *Richard III*, it is set in a mythical pre-historical Britain in the vein of *King Lear*. Like *Othello*, it dwells at length on the agonies of sexual jealousy. Posthumus Leonatus's jealous fury at the apparent faithlessness of his wife Imogen, and then his suicidal remorse in supposing that he has succeeded in having her killed, are the stuff of tragic drama from which he is saved only by the providential ministrations of tragicomic romance. The grotesque death by beheading of Imogen's unwelcome wooer, Cloten, and the horror-filled deathbed confession of Cloten's mother, the Queen, are the sorts of things one expects to find in a tragedy. Yet here they are.

Leontes's jealous rages against his innocent queen, Hermione, in *The Winter's Tale* (c.1609–11), are similarly tragic in their intensity, and with baleful effect. Once again we are confronted with death in a play published among the comedies. The young prince, Mamillius, is so devastated by the public trial of his mother for adultery that he dies of grief and shock. Hermione too appears to die from her ordeal, and indeed we as audience are led to believe that she is truly dead. Leontes is stricken inconsolably with guilty shame when he realizes too late what he has done. The result is that the first half of this play would be unrelievedly tragic, were it not for some few hints that all will eventually be well. The break between the play's two halves is especially marked. Time as Chorus takes us forward over sixteen years and to the pastoral world of Bohemia where Perdita, having been abandoned by her royal father to a cruel fate of being left on a distant shore, grows up among shepherds and shepherdesses. The springtime festive atmosphere of Bohemia could not be more different from the fallen world of Leontes's Sicilia. Here in Bohemia romance flourishes between Perdita and the princely son (Florizel) of Leontes's estranged friend, Polixenes. Eventually the young lovers make their way to Sicilia and to a reunion between father and daughter, and then, in one of Shakespeare's greatest theatrical surprises, to a reunion with the supposedly dead Queen Hermione.

The Winter's Tale is thus a hallmark illustration of what is meant by 'tragicomedy'. It embodies a dramaturgy that Shakespeare shared with other London dramatists in the latter half of the first decade of the seventeenth century, notably John Fletcher. Audiences in public and indoor theatres alike seem to have been calling for the kind of metatheatrical tours de force we find in these plays. *The Winter's Tale*'s leaping over an entire generation of time, so characteristic of the genre, recalls a similar handling of time in *Pericles* (in which Marina must be allowed to grow from a newborn babe to a young woman of marriageable age) and in *The Tempest*, where the gap of twelve years since Miranda's infancy is presented through narrative recollection rather than in sequential staging, so that in this respect *The Tempest* is more of a romantic comedy in the vein of *The Merchant of Venice* or *Much Ado About Nothing*. Even in these romantic comedies we find elements of the tragicomic: in *The Merchant*, Antonio's very life is seemingly at risk from Shylock's vengeful knife, and in *Much Ado* the false accusation of sexual profligacy levelled against Hero is serious enough to threaten her with being committed for life to a religious convent. The late so-called tragicomedies are different in degree from the earlier romantic comedies, not really in kind. *All's Well*, though usually classified as a problem play, contains tragicomic elements in its lament for the fallen state of human nature and its riddling and almost magical resolution. As a comic writer, Shakespeare defies easy classification according to any classical 'rules'.

Shakespeare's ideas about comedy, then, seem as varied as the colours of the rainbow. What about tragedy? Here again we find a resolute refusal on Shakespeare's part to toe any sort of party line. One instance of his seemingly intentional irregularity is the inclusion of comedy in his tragedies. According to classical standards, this is a breach of decorum, and as a result Shakespeare has often been lambasted by classically trained scholars when, for instance, he brings on stage in *Othello* a bunch of clownish musicians who tastelessly compare the 'wind' of their wind instruments to flatulence, and the like, just when Iago has put us on warning that he is going to poison Othello's mind with jealous thoughts about his wife (3.1.1–31). In a similar vein, many critics have questioned the wisdom of introducing a drunken porter in *Macbeth* to jest about greedy farmers, dishonest English tailors, and so on, only moments after Macbeth has murdered his royal guest (2.3.1–20). The clownish fellow who brings an asp concealed in a basket of figs to Cleopatra as she prepares to die (*Antony and Cleopatra*, 5.2.241–79) is another instance. Clichés about 'comic relief' will hardly answer serious objections: why should tragedy need comic relief? Why break the mood of hysterical anxiety and guilt? Yet an artistic purpose can usually be intuited. Macbeth's porter jests about serious subjects of devilish 'equivocation' (a Jesuit practice of justifying a lie by keeping in one's mind a secret reservation about some sense in which the utterance might be true) and hellfire, all of which reminds us of Macbeth's destined fate to 'go the primrose way to th'everlasting bonfire' (18–19). Cleopatra's talk about 'the pretty worm of Nilus' that 'kills and pains not' is highly informative of her state of mind as she prepares to commit suicide in the least painful way possible. Whether or not such arguments of relevance in such comic passages are always convincing, the point here is that Shakespeare seems to find no problem with blending comedy with tragedy.

Then, too, *Romeo and Juliet* contains some of the most delightfully funny scenes that Shakespeare ever wrote. Perhaps the play is a 'comi-tragedy'; its ending is very sad. Hamlet is brilliantly funny in his satirical barbs directed at Polonius as a fishmonger, or at the ironic fates of lawyers and great landowners whose skulls will, in time, end up in the gravedigger's clutches. 'Why may not that be the skull of a lawyer? Where be his quiddities now, his quillities, his cases, his tenures, and his tricks?' (*Hamlet*, 5.1.98–100). Cleopatra in *Antony and Cleopatra* vies with Falstaff as one of Shakespeare's most fascinatingly comic creations. The scenes in which, during Antony's long absence, she consoles herself languidly by torturing poor Mardian about being a eunuch, or raunchily imagines what it would be like to be a horse and thus 'bear the weight of Antony' (1.5.22), or flies into a frenzy against the messenger who has brought her news of Antony's marriage to Octavia and then listens complacently as the wised-up messenger reports to her the unattractive features of her rival, are simply delicious. If Shakespeare is unhesitant about introducing tragic elements into his romantic comedies and tragicomedies, the same is true in reverse about the use of comic elements in tragedy. His remarkably inventive punning, which Dr Johnson once called the 'fatal Cleopatra' tempting Shakespeare away from high art, is perhaps another instance of his inclusive view of the interconnectedness of dramatic genres that could find an occasional purpose for laughter in tragedy.

Purist classical approaches to Shakespearean tragedy have sought diligently for the tragic flaw in Shakespeare's tragic heroes. After all, Aristotle's *Poetics* defines the highest sort of tragedy as that in which a noble and worthy protagonist is brought low not simply by misfortune but by a *hamartia*, variously defined as tragic flaw or, more appropriately, tragic mistake. (The word in ancient Greek comes from *hamartanien*, meaning to miss the mark, to err.) Aristotle is thinking above all else of Sophocles's *Oedipus the King* as a perfect example of what he meant. Even here critical disagreement persists as to what Oedipus's *hamartia* might be – pride, anger, blasphemy, or the fatal mistake of killing his father and marrying his mother, acts decreed by fate as unavoidable. At all events, the consequence for neo-Aristotelean critical tradition is that *hamartia* has loomed large as an essential component of the tragic hero. Aristotelean interpreters in Western Europe are apt to see *hamartia* from a Christian perspective as something quite close to sinfulness. This is almost surely a misreading of *hamartia*, which has to do with pollution or defilement in ways that are offensive to the gods rather than with sinful guilt, but Western European ways of reading Aristotle in the Middle Ages were bound to look for cultural equivalents, and Western Europe was, and still is, by and large, a guilt culture.

Outwardly at least, *Othello* and *Macbeth* appear to incorporate a structural device resembling *hamartia*. Othello is a noble Moor of extraordinary bearing, and he is devotedly in love with Desdemona as she is with him. His tragic flaw would appear to be a jealousy not easily aroused but terrifying in its power once awakened. He comes at last to accept fully his responsibility for having killed an innocent wife out of jealous rage; he was goaded into it by a resourcefully cunning tempter, Iago, but Othello knows that the guilt rests fundamentally with him. He is, in his own final estimate, 'one that loved not wisely but too well', 'one not easily jealous but, being wrought, / Perplexed in the extreme' (5.2.354–6). He asks only that devils may whip him 'From the possession of this heavenly sight', blowing him 'about in winds', roasting him 'in sulfur' and washing him 'in steep-down gulfs of liquid fire' (286–9). The meaning of his tragedy seems intelligible, and it is indeed close to Aristotle's idea that tragedy is most meaningful when it finds a link between cause and effect, between misfortune and suffering. Othello deserves at least the punishment of having lost Desdemona for ever through his own benighted agency. The idea is suffused with Christian values here; Othello and Emilia both regard Iago as a kind of 'devil' (5.2.135, 294–5) who has prevailed over Othello through insidious temptation and has destroyed for a time his faith in the goodness of Desdemona. That Othello recovers his faith in her goodness also gives meaning to this tragedy; Othello has destroyed his own happiness and sees that he must suffer justly for it, but also sees that Desdemona's goodness is eternally true. She is, as Emilia has said, 'the more angel' (134).

Macbeth is similarly eloquent on the momentous spiritual consequences of the murder he contemplates and then commits, and on his own overwhelming burden of guilt. Even if this translation into Christian terms loses sight of the Greek meaning of *hamartia*, the linkage of cause and effect is no less prominent. 'This evenhanded justice / Commends th'ingredience of our poisoned chalice / To our own lips' (1.7.10–12), he considers in soliloquy as the time for him to murder King Duncan fast approaches. Duncan is in Macbeth's castle in double trust: as the king to whom Macbeth owes fealty and a guest to whom Macbeth owes a sacred duty as host and guardian.

> Besides, this Duncan
> Hath borne his faculties so meek, hath been
> So clear in his great office, that his virtues
> Will plead like angels, trumpet-tongued, against
> The deep damnation of his taking-off;
> And Pity, like a naked newborn babe
> Striding the blast, or heaven's cherubin, horsed
> Upon the sightless couriers of the air,
> Shall blow the horrid deed in every eye,
> That tears shall drown the wind.
> (*Macbeth*, 1.7.16–25)

Macbeth is thus fully conscious that what he is about to do is a heinous sin, against human decency, against the heavens. The only things propelling him to go ahead are his 'Vaulting ambition' (27) and the promptings of the Weird Sisters and his wife. His *hamartia* is easy to identify and to name in Christian terms: it is sinful ambition, the besetting evil of Satan himself. For all its wondrous poetic complexity, *Macbeth* seems like a case of crime and punishment.

Other Shakespearean tragedies, however, are not so open to neo-Aristotelean analysis, and suggest that Shakespeare often thought of tragedy in strikingly different terms. Hamlet is often (too often) analyzed as victimized by his indecisiveness: his alleged *hamartia* is a propensity for delay. True enough, Hamlet berates himself for not acting more quickly and decisively in response to his father's ghost's command to 'Revenge his foul and most unnatural murder'. 'Haste me to know't', Hamlet replies, 'that I, with wings as swift / As meditation or the thoughts of love, / May sweep to my revenge' (*Hamlet*, 1.5.26–32). Yet a more comprehensive reading of the play urges us to consider that swift action is often rashly inappropriate, as when Hamlet kills Polonius in his mother's chambers, logically assuming that Claudius must be lurking behind the arras when in fact he was not. The result is a needless death that sends Hamlet packing to England and sets in motion the whole tragic ending of the play, including the return of a furious Laertes to avenge his father's death. Laertes does not hesitate, and accordingly ends up being the slayer of Hamlet by underhanded means because Laertes has not known enough to realize that the real villain in the case is Claudius. Conversely, Hamlet's final decision to leave matters in the hands of Providence brings about a more satisfactory ending than Hamlet or anyone else could have devised: the slaying of Claudius, and a noble death for Prince Hamlet, reconciled with his dying mother and relieved of the burden of living in such a troubled world. Here indeed is 'a consummation / Devoutly to be wished' (3.1.64–5).

If a propensity for delay is not a very satisfactory answer to a search for Hamlet's *hamartia*, then what is a good answer? Perhaps the best idea is to set aside the question entirely, and to think of Hamlet instead as a good man who must pay the price of the world's manifest corruptions. He is too honest for this world. When he is impatient and difficult, as he often is, he is so with those he regards as fools, like Polonius, or timeservers, like Rosencrantz and Guildenstern, or villains, like Claudius. With his mother he is tough, but that is because he truly wants to save her from what he sees as the spiritually deadening effects of her sinful life with Claudius. He is deeply regretful about Ophelia's unhappy death, and he readily exchanges forgiveness with her brother. With Horatio he is a loving and loyal friend. Hamlet ultimately accomplishes what his father commanded him to do, yet in a way that absolves him of coldblooded murder. He dies, and is to be buried with all the funeral rites belonging to a soldier, since, as Fortinbras says, he is a man who was likely, had be become king, 'To have proved most royal'

(5.2.398–400). Horatio bids his dying friend a long 'Good night', adding, 'And flights of angels sing thee to thy rest!' (361–2). Hamlet is a tragic hero in a world that does not know what to do with such heroes until it is too late, until the corruptions of this world have taken their toll.

Romeo and Juliet is another tragedy that does not yield well to a categorical insistence on tragic flaw. Romeo and Juliet are not even tragic protagonists in the normal Aristotelean sense: they are not of heroic or mythic stature, like Oedipus or Medea, but instead are nice, ordinary young people falling in love like the central characters of romantic comedy. Although they are desperately eager to be united as husband and wife, any attempt to find the meaning of their tragedy in undue haste is surely inadequate. Their problem is that a world of bitter family rivalries will not let them be happy together. Even when their parents might be disposed to forget the Capulet–Montague feud, the spirit of vendetta is just too strong. Misunderstanding contributes to the disaster: we can understand why Juliet cannot tell her parents she has married Romeo. Bad luck and unfortunate timing play a part when Friar Laurence's note to the banished Romeo miscarries. At a crucial moment, Romeo does bear some responsibility for the tragedy because of his rash decision to kill Tybalt in vengeance for the death of Mercutio; Romeo succumbs to the macho instincts of the vendetta in a way that he quickly regrets. Yet even here, one can hardly build a case for this play as centred on *hamartia*. Instead, as Capulet says, Romeo and Juliet are 'Poor sacrifices of our enmity' (5.3.304).

More instances could be cited. King Lear and Gloucester in *King Lear* are both foolish old men who make disastrous choices, but to judge them as the authors of their own unhappiness is to choose sides with Goneril, Regan, and Edmund. The old men are, as Lear says of himself, 'More sinned against than sinning' (3.2.60). *Julius Caesar* makes a certain amount of sense in Aristotelean terms, not surprisingly, since it is drawn from ancient classical history, but even here the dramatic emphasis is more on ironic waste than on regarding Caesar and Brutus and Cassius as punished for hubris. *Antony and Cleopatra* reverses the strictures of classical tragic definition by its triumphant finale in which Cleopatra takes away from Octavius Caesar the opportunity to put her on display in Rome as his captive. Shakespeare's ideas about tragedy are as pragmatically derived and as varied as the plays for which they are designed.

The criticisms levelled at Shakespeare by Ben Jonson are again a useful way of assessing Shakespeare's literary ideas from the opposite perspective of a self-proclaimed neoclassical writer and theorist. Along with the praise we have already examined, Jonson had many adverse comments to offer. He complained to William Drummond of Hawthornden in 1618 that Shakespeare 'wanted art', as could be seen in his having 'brought in a number of men saying they had suffered shipwreck in Bohemia, where there is no sea near by some hundred miles'. Jonson presumably had in mind *The Winter's Tale*, where Bohemia is mentioned numerous times (and nowhere else in Shakespeare), and where indeed the babe Perdita is left in a deserted region on the coast. Shakespeare is following his source, Robert Greene's *Pandosto*, in giving a seacoast to a country that is traditionally located in central Europe. Jonson's impatience here with inaccuracy is of a piece with his lampooning Shakespeare for the perceived anachronisms in *Julius Caesar* of outfitting the city streets of Rome with 'walls and battlements', 'towers and windows', and even 'chimney tops' (1.1.38–9) as though ancient Rome were sixteenth-century London, and of providing a striking clock (2.1.192) in blithe disregard for the fact that the mechanical clock was not invented until about 1300. Jonson's larger point is that Shakespeare wrote too quickly. 'The players have often mentioned it as an honour to Shakespeare, that in his writing, whatsoever he penned he never blotted out [a] line', Jonson noted in *Timber, or Discoveries*. 'My answer hath been, would he had blotted a thousand.'

Jonson also objected strenuously to Shakespeare's free and easy way with probability on stage and with the unities of time, place, and action. In the prologue to the 1616 edition of his *Every Man in His Humour*, Jonson inveighed against English history plays in which the combatants, 'with three rusty swords, / And help of some few foot-and-half-foot words, / Fight over York and Lancaster's long jars, / And in the tiring-house bring wounds to scars'. This same preface goes on to prefer plays 'Where neither Chorus wafts you o'er the seas, / Nor creaking throne comes down, the boys to please, / Nor nimble squib is seen to make afeard / The gentlewomen, nor rolled bullet heard / To say it thunders, nor tempestuous drum / Rumbles to tell you when the storm doth come'. The Induction to *Bartholomew Fair* (1631 edition) compares Jonson's own stage world with the improbable fantasies of romantic drama: 'If there be never a servant-monster i' the fair, who can help it, he [Jonson] says, nor a nest of antics? He is loath to make Nature afraid in his plays, like those that beget tales, tempests, and suchlike drolleries, to mix his head with other men's heels.'

All these criticisms point to Shakespeare as the chief offender among London's dramatists, even when Shakespeare is not specifically mentioned by name. The fighting over 'York and Lancaster's long jars' can have no other serious target, since Shakespeare had written eight history plays on the subject. The Chorus wafting audiences overseas sounds a lot like the Chorus in *Henry V*, who promises the audience 'thence to France shall we convey you safe, / And bring you back' (2 Chorus, 37–8), albeit other playwrights also sometimes employed the same tactic. Thunder announcing the approach of a storm marks the opening scene of *The Tempest*: '*A tempestuous noise of thunder and lightning heard*', to be followed shortly by '*Enter Mariners, wet.*' The 'creaking throne' descending by means of winches and ropes from a trapdoor in the 'heavens' above the stage is a prominent feature in *Cymbeline*: '*Jupiter descends in thunder and lightning, sitting upon an eagle*' (5.4.92). In Act 4 of *The Tempest*, '*Juno descends*' (72) to grace the betrothal of Miranda and Ferdinand. '*Thunder and lightning*' (1.3) frighten the inhabitants of Rome on the eve of the assassination of Julius Caesar. '*Storm still*' is repeatedly sounded in *King Lear* as the old king ventures out into the 'foul weather' of Act 3, scenes 1 and 2. Squibs or fireworks may have proved useful when, at the siege of Harfleur in *Henry V*, 'the nimble gunner / With linstock now the devilish cannon touches, / And down goes all before them', to the accompaniment of a stage direction, '*Alarum, and chambers go off*' (3 Chorus, 32–4). Other battle scenes provide similar opportunities. Shakespeare himself apologizes, through his Chorus, for giving such a fearfully inadequate representation of Henry V's great victory at Agincourt, 'Where – oh, for pity! – we shall much disgrace / With four or five most vile and ragged foils, / Right ill-disposed in brawl ridiculous, / The name of Agincourt' (4 Chorus, 49–52). Jonson couldn't have said it better. And as for servant-monsters, 'tales, tempests, and suchlike drolleries', we need look no further than *The Tempest*; Jonson's very use of the word 'tempests' makes plain the object of his critical ire.

Shakespeare's own literary credo, though never enunciated in so many words, seems abundantly clear in practice: he disagrees with Jonson point by point. *The Tempest* observes the unities of time, place, and action, as though Shakespeare were saying to Jonson and likeminded critics, in his farewell to the stage, You see, I can perfectly well observe the dramatic unities when I want to. Yet even here, Shakespeare brings on a 'servant-monster' in the person of Caliban, and such 'drolleries' as '*several strange shapes bringing in a banquet*' while '*Solemn and strange music*' issues from some presumably hidden location. Prospero appears '*on the top, invisible*' (3.3.17–19), meaning high up in the theatre, wearing an 'invisible' garment like that of Puck and Oberon in *A Midsummer Night's Dream*. One can imagine Jonson's scorn for 'invisible' garments. How can one see an 'invisible' person? Yet Shakespeare impenitently brings on ghosts, spirits, witches or weird sisters, etc., who are capable of appearing to some humans while not to others. Hamlet's father's ghost visits Hamlet in his mother's chambers without wishing to be seen by Gertrude (*Hamlet*, 3.4). Banquo's ghost shows himself to Macbeth without being seen by any other person at the banqueting table (*Macbeth*, 3.4). Furniture can seem to fly through the air: when in *The Tempest* Ariel appears '*like a harpy*' to lecture Alonso, Antonio, and Sebastian on their perfidies, he '*claps his wings upon the table, and with a quaint device the banquet vanishes*' (3.3.52). This is the banquet table that the '*strange shapes*' have brought in shortly before to tease the forlorn Italians with disturbing visions, prompting even the villains to acknowledge, 'Now I will believe / That there are unicorns; that in Arabia / There is one tree, the phoenix' throne, one phoenix / At this hour reigning there' (3.3.21–4). Shakespeare revels in the magic of theatre, and has no hesitation in calling attention to his own claptrap theatrical devices. Jonson presumably hates every minute of this sort of thing.

Shakespeare engages most extensively with Jonsonian literary theory in Act 2, scene 7 of *As You Like It*. The malcontent satirist of the play, Jaques, has just encountered a fool (Touchstone) in the forest, and is bursting with desire to tell Duke Senior and the Duke's followers what the meeting with Touchstone has inspired Jaques to think about. Jaques wants the licence of an 'allowed fool' (*Twelfth Night*, 1.5.91) to speak out against human folly. 'I must have liberty / Withal', he insists, 'as large a charter as the wind, / To blow on whom I please' (*As You Like It*, 2.7.47–9). He warns his intended targets that they would do well to act unperturbed by his barbs, lest they betray their own foolishness by reacting angrily and personally; if they can pretend to seem 'senseless of the bob' (55), observers may suppose that they are not tainted by the accusation. Jaques wants, as satirist, to join forces with the professional fool, because the fool is so free to say whatever he thinks. 'Invest me in my motley', Jaques proclaims, 'give me leave / To speak my mind, and I will through and through / Cleanse the foul body of th'infected world, / If they will patiently receive my medicine' (58–61). This is the manifesto of the Roman satirist; the ideas are recognizably those of Horace, Juvenal, and Persius. Shakespeare, through Jaques, adroitly summarizes the ancient and timeless defence of literary satire: it performs a socially usefully function by exposing human folly. It is a 'medicine' designed to 'cleanse' the 'infected world'.

Jaques's defence of satire is that it is a moral art, not only because it acts on behalf of society generally but because it attacks abuses that are sinful. Jaques offers examples. He will cry out against pride, especially extravagance in dress: he will inveigh against any 'city woman' or wife of some civic dignitary who presumes to bear 'The cost of princes on unworthy shoulders' (70–6), that is, squanders money on finery as though she were an aristocrat. The observation is icily edged with social snobbism: city wives should not dress above their station. Their husbands are not exempt, of course. Jaques has equally in mind any person of 'basest function' (low social rank) who protests that his 'bravery' or sartorial splendour 'is not on my cost' (i.e., has not been bought at my expense and is therefore none of my business as satirist), but who then behaves in such a way as to make clear that what the satirist has said is true: he 'suits / His folly to the mettle of my speech' (79–82). Part of Jaques's self-justification, in other words, is that when the targets of his satire behave in such a way as to proclaim their guilt, they can have no logical answer to those who criticize. Let the shoe fit the wearer.

Jaques's last and perhaps most important defence of his art as satirist is that he does not attack individuals. He fashions a generic portrait of human folly and then lets his reader or listener determine the fitness of any hypothetical case. 'What then?' he asks, when he has made a generic character sketch of 'the city woman' or him 'of basest function', having named no names. 'Let me see wherein / My tongue hath wronged him', he continues. 'If I do him right, / Then he hath wronged himself. If he be free, / Why then my taxing like a wild goose flies, / Unclaimed of any man' (83–7). True satire afflicts only those whose own behaviour conforms to the satiric type. Conversely, anyone who is 'free' of the folly in question is by that very fact untouched.

This, again, is classic theory about satire. It appears in Horace and on down to later satirists as well, including Alexander Pope in the eighteenth century. Shakespeare's genius and fairmindedness as a writer enable him to condense the complexities of classical literary critical thinking into some densely worded but elegantly lucid verse.

At the same time, Shakespeare does not pass up the opportunity for a thoughtful riposte. Duke Senior likes and even admires Jaques, but he has an entirely different explanation of what it is that motivates the satirist: satire can be a way of getting back at personal enemies, and is too often the expression of one who has himself been guilty of the moral lapses which he now fastens on others as a way of vindicating himself. 'Fie on thee!' Duke Senior scolds Jaques, perhaps good-humouredly, but with vigour nonetheless. 'I can tell what thou wouldst do', he continues:

> Most mischievous foul sin, in chiding sin.
> For thou thyself hast been a libertine,
> As sensual as the brutish sting itself;
> And all th'embossèd sores and headed evils
> That thou with license of free foot hast caught
> Wouldst thou disgorge into the general world.
> (2.7.62–9)

The fact that Jaques gives no evidence in the play of libertine behaviour may suggest that Shakespeare's vignette of 'the satirist' here is generic. In Duke Senior's view, satirists are motivated by an uneasy awareness of their own licentious ways and thereby are all the more eager to see and condemn licentious behaviour in others. The devil loves company.

The debate in *As You Like It* ends in a draw, as is usually the case elsewhere with Shakespeare's dialectical treatment of controversial issues. Satire was certainly a controversial issue when this play was first performed in 1599. A rash of Roman satirical poems hit the book-sellers' stalls about this time, including Joseph Hall's *Virgidemiae* (1597) and John Marston's *The Metamorphosis of Pygmalion's Image* (1598), along with satirical plays that included Jonson's *Every Man in His Humour* (quarto version, 1598) and *Every Man Out of His Humour* (quarto, 1599). Jonson's *Poetaster* and Thomas Dekker and John Marston's *Satiromastix, or The Untrussing of the Humorous Poet* were soon to follow in 1601. Some of these were highly and unabashedly personal. Jonson was at the centre of the hubbub. Shakespeare may have implied some criticism of Jonson in the depictions of Achilles and Ajax in *Troilus and Cressida*, but in general Shakespeare steered away from outspoken satire. What did he think of it as a literary and dramatic genre?

As You Like It may offer clues. Shakespeare, as we have seen, presents both the defence of satire and the critique of it insightfully and sympathetically. At the same time, he sets the debate between Jaques and Duke Senior in the larger context of Act 2, scene 7, in the Forest of Arden. Much is happening. The debate on satire is immediately followed by the sudden appearance of young Orlando, famished and desperate to save the life of his old servant, Adam, who is close to death. With sword in hand, Orlando is prepared to use violence to achieve his ends. Yet his hostility is met with compassion and generosity. 'What would you have?' Duke Senior asks him. 'Your gentleness shall force / More than your force move us to gentleness' (2.7.101–2). Orlando and Adam receive the care they need, and become a part of the forest community. Moreover, the incident prompts Duke Senior to think more broadly of why it is that human beings need to care for one another. Duke Senior and his comrades have known what it is to suffer. That knowledge breeds in them a hope for a better world of shared communal values:

> True is it that we have seen better days,
> And have with holy bell been knolled to church,
> And sat at good men's feasts, and wiped our eyes
> Of drops that sacred pity hath engendered.
> And therefore sit you down in gentleness,
> And take upon command what help we have
> That to your wanting may be ministered.
>   (2.7.119–25)

Jaques, for his part, uses the occasion to meditate on the Seven Ages of Man from infancy and childhood to old age and senility, taking a more satirical view that life is ultimately little more than an existential process of ageing. The debate continues. Yet the ideas of compassion, forgiveness, and community ultimately prevail in the world of Shakespearean romantic comedy. This is by no means Shakespeare's final answer, for some strongly pessimistic views still need to be dealt with in the great tragedies of the next few years. Still, at this point in 1599, the attractions of a satirical point of view ultimately yield to the consolations of a more charitable philosophy.

Even though he is reluctant to put himself on display as a literary theorist, then, Shakespeare presents cumulatively in his work a comprehensive critical view of his art. Poetry and drama can and should serve a high moral purpose, not through dogmatic sermonizing but through the presentation of living dramatic examples. Art of this exalted kind can ameliorate the many heartaches and imperfections of life, and can outlive the ravages of time. Accordingly, drama and acting must eschew cheap appeals to popular taste. They must woo even the 'groundlings' who delight in 'inexplicable dumb shows and noise' to set their sights higher when they come to see plays. The truest dramatic art is that which seeks and wins the approval of those who really understand what art is all about. Presumably, Shakespeare does not mean that the artist should write only for the court and for those who are university-trained; he himself had not attended one of the universities, and implicitly stands as living proof that one can be a person of the highest artistic seriousness through self-education.

Indeed, Shakespeare shows little sympathy for the classical 'rules' of time, place, and action that were the darlings of classically trained scholars and playwrights. To be sure, he can follow the rules effortlessly and brilliantly when the story seems to call for them, but he is above all a practitioner of flexible and non-doctrinaire approaches to dramatic structure. Similarly, he pays scant attention to Aristotle and neo-Aristotelean traditions of critical interpretation. He approaches genre in a protean fashion, mixing comedy and tragedy as appropriate and using (even helping to invent) generic forms like the English history play and tragicomedy that defy neo-Aristotelean limitations of dramatic genre to comedy and tragedy. His tragedies sometimes lend themselves to Aristotle's idea of *hamartia* in the tragic hero, but just as often they do not. Although not himself what we would call a satirical writer, Shakespeare certainly knows how to use satire, and he gives a respectful hearing to Horatian defences of it. Above all, he is a fairminded pragmatist, given to setting rival ideas about art in debate one against the other. These are perhaps some of the ideas about art with which Shakespeare consciously armed himself as he prepared to engage with the sceptical issues that will emerge with increasing forcefulness in the second half of his writing career.

5

What Form of Prayer Can Serve My Turn?

Shakespeare's Ideas on Religious Controversy and Issues of Faith

Was Shakespeare a Catholic, privately subscribing to a faith that could have put him in danger of arrest and persecution? Some recent scholars, including Stephen Greenblatt, have wondered whether Shakespeare's father was a Catholic and whether Shakespeare himself may have had some residual Catholic loyalties. Or was he a practising Anglican communicant? If so, did he prefer a formal and traditional mode of worship, or was he sympathetic to the Puritans' call for simplicity of dress and forms of worship? Did he subscribe to the thirty-nine articles of faith adopted by the English church in 1563, establishing a Catholic-like episcopal hierarchy of bishops and archbishops and a conservative liturgy in English, or did he side with the dissenters? Theologically, was he attuned to the teachings of Martin Luther and especially John Calvin insisting that salvation was possible through faith alone rather than through works? Or was Shakespeare none of the above, pondering instead the intellectual appeals of agnosticism?

These questions about 'Shakespeare's ideas' are by their nature intensely personal. If we could answer them, they would tell us much about Shakespeare as a person and as a writer. Moreover, the issues seem to become intensely important in his work at about the time he wrote *Hamlet* (c.1599–1601). These years, as we have seen, witnessed a turning point in his career as dramatist, as he shifted from the writing of romantic comedies and English histories to problem plays and tragedies. Religiously and politically, England was also at a point of potential crisis. Queen Elizabeth was old and without an heir to the throne. The Earl of Essex's abortive rebellion in 1601 was symptomatic of widespread uneasiness and disaffection. When Elizabeth died in 1603 and her cousin, James VI of Scotland, came to the throne as James I of England, he was a Protestant, thus calming fears of a return to Catholicism, but he was temperamentally a very different sort of ruler, and he soon quarreled with the reformers. The infamous Gunpowder Plot of 1605, aimed at blowing up the Houses of Parliament, inflamed public opinion against Catholic priests and indeed all Catholic worshippers. Not surprisingly, perhaps, issues of faith and doubt assume a new urgency in the plays that Shakespeare wrote in these years and those that followed.

No controversy loomed larger in the Renaissance than that of religious differences. The Reformation begun by Martin Luther's break with the Roman Catholic church in 1517 divided country against country and neighbor against neighbor throughout Western Europe. In England, the struggle between reformers and traditionalists see-sawed back and forth, with many martyrdoms on both sides. Henry VIII declared himself supreme head of a national English church with the Act of Supremacy in 1534, as a consequence of the papacy's refusal to countenance his divorcing of Katharine of Aragon and his marriage with Anne Boleyn. At first the differences in dogma and liturgy were few; the break with Rome was, for Henry, more personal and political than ideological. A Statute of the Six Articles in 1539 defined heresy as including any denial of transubstantiation (the miracle of the holy sacrament becoming the body and blood of Christ while keeping only the appearance of bread and wine), celibacy for the priesthood, the necessity of auricular or private confession to a priest, and other points of doctrine retained from Catholic practice. When Henry died in 1547, on the other hand, leaving the crown to his ten-year-old sickly son Edward VI, the young king's uncle, Edward Seymour – the first Earl of Hertford and now Duke of Somerset – used his authority as Protector to instigate reforms. The Six Articles were quickly repealed. In their place came a newly established uniformity of service encoded in a new and more distinctly Protestant prayer-book. After Somerset fell from power and was replaced by John Dudley, Lord Warwick and then Duke of Northumberland, in 1550, reformation proceeded apace. The forty-two articles of religion promulgated by Archbishop

Thomas Cranmer in 1551 became the basis of the thirty-nine articles under Elizabeth in 1563, thereby providing the compromise basis for the Church of England. Meantime, from 1553 to 1558, England had returned to Catholicism under Mary, the daughter of Henry VIII and Katharine of Aragon, who inherited the crown when Edward VI died as Henry's only male heir. Mary did her best to restore England to the ancient faith, and many martyrdoms took place, including those of Cranmer, Hugh Latimer, and Nicholas Ridley, but recovery of the vast church lands that had been distributed to powerful political figures proved impossible. When, after an uncertain struggle over the royal succession in 1558, Elizabeth became queen, the Catholic legislation passed during Mary's reign was repealed in favour of re-enacted acts of supremacy and uniformity. A revised prayer-book, codifying religious practices in the state church, was to remain in force for the rest of the sixteenth century.

When Shakespeare began writing his plays in about 1590, England had generally prospered under Elizabeth's governance for thirty-two years, and was to continue to flourish under her rule for thirteen more years. By and large, she enjoyed loyal and enthusiastic support from her Protestant subjects. Having toyed with various marital prospects, even that of joining in marriage with Philip II of Spain (the Catholic widower of Elizabeth's older sister Mary), Elizabeth chose finally to remain single. Philip's plan to invade England with the Great Armada of 1588 was turned back, ultimately to be sure by a great storm off the western coast of Ireland, but also by the intrepidity of Elizabeth's naval commanders, Lord Thomas Howard, Francis Drake, and John Hawkins, in the English Channel. Shakespeare's history plays (see Chapter 3) capitalized on that event and its aftermath by chronicling the birth of a nation under perilous circumstances. A prima facie case can be made, then, for Shakespeare as the leading dramatist of a popular London theatre, beating the drum for Tudor ascendancy over the Catholic powers of the Continent. During the late 1580s, despite her reluctance to become involved in costly and divisive wars, Elizabeth did agree to send troops under her favourite, the Earl of Leicester, to aid the Dutch in fending off Philip's incursions on that Protestant nation. She also agreed reluctantly to the execution of her Catholic cousin, Mary Queen of Scots, in 1587. Sir Francis Drake and other seafaring captains raided Spanish holdings in the West Indies. Patriotic fervour was at its height.

Shakespeare's *Henry V* can be read as an appeal to the patriotic sentiment of the age, even if the foe in this instance is France and not Spain. Relations with France were uneasy throughout this period; the hated Duke of Guise, who had taken Calais away from the English in 1558 and was the chief architect of the slaughter of many French Protestants in the Massacre of St Bartholomew, 23–4 August 1572, was suspected of harbouring plans to return England to the Catholic fold. *Henry V* also celebrates the military achievements of 'the General of our gracious Empress', hoping that 'in good time he may, from Ireland coming' bring 'rebellion broachèd on his sword' (Chorus 5, 30–2). This appears to be a reference to the Earl of Essex, another of Elizabeth's favourites, who had been dispatched in 1597 to quell the rebellion in Ireland of Hugh O'Neill, Earl of Tyrone. Essex failed dismally and had to be replaced by Lord Mountjoy, but at the moment when *Henry V* was written Essex was riding high, and appears to have been much beloved by London and its theatre-loving population. With its ringing rhetorical appeal to a 'band of brothers' who are prepared to die for England, and its humorous depiction of Britain as a place of rich cultural diversity (Scots, Irish, Welsh, and English), *Henry V* seems on the whole to revel in the image of a small British country capable of defeating the might of France and of the Spanish-Hapsburg empire. Given the context of the Spanish Armada and England's continued struggle against militant Catholicism throughout the 1590s, the war fever of *Henry V* translates plausibly enough into patriotic anti-Catholicism. Whether Shakespeare was privately of a different mind is, to be sure, another question. We have already seen, in Chapter 3, how the play interrogates the rationale of a war fought for political and personal reasons as much as for any more idealistic cause.

Acceptance of the Reformation settlement in England had of course not been uniform or smooth. On the one hand, even before 1517 England and Europe had witnessed many reform movements. In late-fourteenth-century England, the so-called Lollards under the leadership of John Wycliffe had advocated a property-less spiritual church, direct access of the individual to God, and English translation of the Bible. Savagely suppressed under Henry V for their radicalism, the Lollards were regarded as early martyrs by the reformers of sixteenth-century England. Some of these reformers were impatient with the pace of change in the Church of England. On the other hand, resistance to the break with Rome was widespread in England, all the more intensely in outlying regions to the north and west. The so-called Northern Rebellion of 1569 in the name of Mary Queen of Scots, led by Thomas Percy, seventh Earl of Northumberland, and Charles Neville, sixth Earl of Westmorland, had to be put down by military force, and led to repressive counter-measures. (Shakespeare may be glancing at this civil conflict in his *1 Henry IV*, prominently featuring as it does the names and titles of Percy, Northumberland, and Westmorland.) The excommunication of Elizabeth by Pope Pius V in 1570 only made matters worse for Elizabeth's Catholic subjects. Conspiracies aimed at putting Mary Queen of Scots on the English throne in place of her Protestant cousin erupted on a number of occasions after Mary abdicated the Scottish throne in 1567 and took refuge – her cause having suffered a military defeat – in England, where she was placed under house arrest. Plots against Elizabeth's life variously involving Roberto Ridolfi and Thomas Howard, the fourth Duke of Norfolk (1570–1), Edward Arden (1583), Francis Throckmorton (1584), and William Parry and Edmund Neville (1584–5) culminated in the Babington conspiracy of 1588 (involving a Derbyshire gentleman, Anthony Babington, and a Catholic priest, John Ballard, among others) that was uncovered by Secretary of State Francis Walsingham and resulted in the execution of all the conspirators. As the threat of the Spanish Armada grew more and more intense during 1587 and 1588, English Catholics found themselves under deep suspicion: would they defect to Philip of Spain once the invasion began? Philip and his generals plainly were counting on just such a turn of events. English subjects who were practising Catholics, or were thought to be sympathetic to the Catholic cause, like Edward de Vere, seventeenth Earl of Oxford, Lord Burghley's son-in-law, had a lot of explaining to do. Feelings were intense because these became matters not simply of personal faith but of national security.

Shakespeare grew up in Stratford-upon-Avon, a town to the northwest of London by what was a considerable distance of travel in those days. Catholic loyalties persisted in many communities of this sort. Church authorities were busy ousting clergymen from their parish offices in favour of reform candidates, not always to the liking of the parishioners. Religious drama of the late medieval period, popular in northern and western locales like York, Wakefield, and Chester, was suppressed by the government. Wall paintings and other visual artifacts that were deemed unacceptable to the new religion were whitewashed or otherwise obscured from view. Among the generation of Shakespeare's parents, some may well have held Catholic sympathies. Members of his mother's Warwickshire family in particular seemed to have remained loyal to the old faith. Indeed, if one were to go back only a few years, the situation could hardly have been otherwise. His father, John Shakespeare, underwent financial difficulties in 1577–8: he was forced to mortgage his wife's property, became involved in serious litigation, and was assessed heavy fines for his failure to attend meetings of the corporation council until finally he was replaced as alderman. Some scholars have speculated that these adversities were the result of persecution for clinging to the Catholic faith, though such business difficulties obviously could have a more mundane commercial explanation.

What about Shakespeare himself? The possibility that he had Catholic connections and perhaps sympathies has aroused a fair amount of interest in recent years. (See the suggested Further Reading in the back of this book.) The biographical evidence remains slender, however. As with our approach to the subject of Shakespeare's ideas in other areas, in matters of religion we are left essentially with his plays and poems. Shakespeare never speaks personally about himself. What impressions do we get from things that are said by his dramatic characters?

Undoubtedly, Shakespeare was familiar with some Catholic practices and theology. When, in *Hamlet*, the Ghost of Hamlet's father describes to his son the unimaginable horrors of his sojourn in the afterlife, he uses the technical language of theology to make his point:

> Thus was I, sleeping, by a brother's hand
> Of life, of crown, of queen at once dispatched,
> Cut off even in the blossoms of my sin,
> Unhousled, disappointed, unaneled,
> No reck'ning made, but sent to my account
> With all my imperfections on my head.
>
> (1.5.75–80)

'Unhousled' means 'without having received the holy sacrament'; the 'housel' is a name for the consecrated elements in the mass, to be kept in a housel-box. 'Disappointed' here means unprepared and unfurnished spiritually for the last journey into death. 'Unaneled' means 'without having received the sacrament of extreme unction'; to 'anele' is to administer the last anointing or extreme unction to the dying. Even when we grant that the distinctions between Catholic and Anglican liturgy were sometimes blurred, and that some communicants in the English church (including Queen Elizabeth) inclined to long-established practices, these terms used by the Ghost have a distinctly Catholic flavour.

Extreme unction is, in Roman Catholic practice, a sacrament in which the priest anoints the body of any person in imminent danger of dying, while reciting a set text from the liturgy and administering the holy sacrament of consecrated bread and wine if physically possible, to ensure the soul's health as the dying person prepares for Judgement. It is one of the religious rites that was removed by the Anglican church, like other Protestant churches, from the list of sacraments. Roman Catholicism recognized seven sacraments: baptism, confirmation (a confirming or strengthening of the recipient in the practice of the Christian faith), the eucharist or mass, penance (in four stages of contrition, confession to a priest, satisfaction or the performance of penal and meritorious acts enjoined by the confessor as payment for sin, and absolution or forgiveness of sin), extreme unction, order (the conferring of holy orders or rite of ordination), and matrimony. The English church reduced this list of seven to two, namely, baptism and the eucharist. The others were recognized in some cases as religious rites, but not 'sacraments' in the sense of bestowing supernatural grace; Christ himself, in this view, had expressly commanded the spiritual obligations of baptism and the Last Supper, but had made no such unequivocal statements about the other so-called sacraments. Some English Puritans and non-conformists, regarding the whole idea of sacrament as superstitious, preferred to refer to baptism and the Lord's Supper as 'ordinances'. Protestants generally disapproved of personal or aural confession; the Anglican Prayer Book instituted instead a prayer of general confession for congregations to recite in unison. Protestants were no less unhappy with the idea of meritorious acts like the saying of the rosary with prayer beads as a presumed means of 'earning' salvation; to Lutherans and Calvinists and many others, salvation was the gift of God alone, to be bestowed as he chose on the Faithful.

Thus, the sacrament of extreme unction denied to the Ghost of Hamlet's father was not just a sacrament of the Catholic church; it was one that had been proscribed in Protestant practice. Moreover, the Ghost appears to have spent the time since his untimely death in a place known in Roman Catholic belief as Purgatory. The Ghost identifies himself to Hamlet as follows:

> I am thy father's spirit,
> Doomed for a certain term to walk the night,
> And for the day confined to fast in fires,
> Till the foul crimes done in my days of nature
> Are burned and purged away.   (1.5.10–14)

Purgatory is indeed a place of spiritual purging and purification. Though it is not named here, Shakespeare does refer to it elsewhere in this theological sense. 'I should venture Purgatory for't', says Emilia to Desdemona, playfully suggesting that she would be willing to risk anything short of outright damnation if she were offered a vast amount of wealth in return for her agreeing to an adulterous affair (*Othello*, 4.3.79–80). To the banished Romeo, 'There is no world without Verona's walls / But purgatory, torture, hell itself' (*Romeo and Juliet*, 3.3.17–18). Clearly Romeo understands that Purgatory is something akin to, but lesser than, hell.

The Ghost in *Hamlet* makes a similar distinction. He is doomed to his 'prison house' 'for a certain term', until the 'foul crimes' done in his 'days of nature' are 'burned and purged away'. The scene he describes is so horrible that he dare not tell Hamlet the secrets of the place lest they would freeze Hamlet's blood and make his hair stand on end, and the Ghost is forbidden to talk about such matters in any case, but at least the punishment is not of limitless duration. Purgatory is, by definition, a place where souls departing this life in a state of grace generally must nevertheless suffer for a time in order to be cleansed from venial (as opposed to mortal) sin, or to pay the temporal punishment due to mortal sins for which eternal punishment has been remitted. Venial sins are of a lesser kind; mortal sins are fatal to the soul unless forgiven through the sacrament of penance. The concept of Purgatory became established in medieval Catholic theology as a way of explaining how God might choose to deal with essentially worthy people caught in a situation where formal absolution by the church might prove impossible, as in the case of sudden death. The concept was similar in ways to that of Limbo, another place of confinement existing on the borders of hell, designed in this instance for those who had died before Christ's coming or had died in childbirth before baptism had been administered. Since the sacraments of baptism and the eucharist were unconditionally necessary for salvation, theologians reasoned, even such persons as Adam and Eve, Noah, Moses, and Virgil could not ascend to heaven without the Incarnation. No more could unbaptized infants, since they had not yet been received into the church.

These theological distinctions are needed to understand what the Ghost in *Hamlet* is telling his son. What then are we to make of the 'foul crimes' done in Hamlet Senior's 'days of nature', that is, while he was still alive on earth? What did he do to deserve Purgatory? Hamlet Senior is represented in the play as an exemplary king and person: gentle, kind, and so solicitous of his wife 'That he might not beteem the winds of heaven / Visit her face too roughly' (1.2.141–2). This is, to be sure, the fond recollection of a grieving son, but it nevertheless seems confirmed by everything else that we are shown. The Player King, as a stand-in for Hamlet Senior in 'The Murder of Gonzago', is wise and thoughtful to an extraordinary degree. Old Hamlet was a warrior who, 'in an angry parle', 'smote the sledded Polacks on the ice' (1.1.66–7), and who therefore had blood on his hands, but surely in the world of *Hamlet* this is to be regarded as a token of chivalric bravery befitting a king rather than as a crime meriting divine punishment. Roman Catholic theology has a simpler answer as to why Hamlet Senior suffers the torments of Purgatory: his 'foul crimes' are the things we humans all do every day of our lives. We are proud, angry, envious, covetous, gluttonous, slothful, and lustful; we blaspheme, we forget to honour our parents, we worship false gods, and so on. None of the Seven Deadly Sins or the Ten Commandments escapes our depraved attention. Humankind fell into sin with the disobedience of Adam and Eve, and can be rescued only by Christ's salvation as administered through the sacraments of the church. Any person like Hamlet Senior, no matter how virtuous, who dies without the absolutely necessary sacrament of extreme unction must spend some time in Purgatory. Protestants were no less insistent on the sinful state of humankind since the Fall, but took a very different view of the role of the sacraments in offering guidance toward salvation.

This passage in *Hamlet* demonstrates that Shakespeare was thoroughly conversant with the Catholic doctrine of Purgatory. Much harder to determine, however, is whether Shakespeare personally believed all of this about Purgatory, or some of it, or none. The concept proves vitally useful here in *Hamlet* to establish the circumstances of old

Hamlet's sudden death, to dramatize for his son the horror of it all, and to link a medieval Christian idea of the afterlife with the pagan concept of revenge. Part of what is so damnable about Claudius's act of murder, and hence what prompts Hamlet to revenge, is that Claudius has condemned his brother's soul to unspeakable torments that are hell-like in their devastating effect even if Claudius cannot send Old Hamlet's soul for ever to hell. This is perhaps the chief consideration that prompts Hamlet, when he later finds opportunity to kill Claudius at prayer, to save the murderer for a worse fate than if he were to die on his knees imploring God for help:

> Now I might do it pat, now 'a is a-praying,
> And now I'll do't. [*He draws his sword.*] And so 'a goes to heaven,
> And so am I revenged. That would be scanned:
> A villain kills my father, and for that,
> I, his sole son, do this same villain send
> To heaven.
> Why, this is hire and salary, not revenge.
> 'A took my father grossly, full of bread,
> With all his crimes broad blown, as flush as May;
> And how his audit stands who knows save heaven? (3.3.73–82)

This again posits the existence of Purgatory, and seems to say clearly that, in Hamlet's understanding at least, his father's 'crimes' deserving the torments of Purgatory were those of any frail mortal unfairly denied the blessing of remission of those venial sins through last rites. But because this business is so integral to the story that Shakespeare is dramatizing, we cannot be sure of Shakespeare's own personal view.

This interpretive difficulty attends our attempts to evaluate other moments where Catholic practice looms into view. King Henry V seeks to atone for his father's usurpation of the English crown by devotional acts that many Protestants would view as superstitious. He has reinterred Richard II's body. He provides 'yearly pay' to 'Five hundred poor' who 'twice a day their withered hands hold up / Toward heaven, to pardon blood'. He has built 'Two chantries, where the sad and solemn priests / Sing still for Richard's soul' (*Henry V*, 4.1.293–300). ('Still' means 'perpetually'.) Chantries were endowments for the chanting of masses, in chapels commonly built inside large churches or cathedrals. These endowments offered financial support in perpetuity for clergymen to chant masses for the spiritual welfare of the departed soul, in this case Richard II. The practice was abolished by Protestant churches, in good part because it smacked of attempting to earn one's way into heaven by 'good works', as though one could presume to merit salvation. Martin Luther and John Calvin were both vehement on this subject. Henry's retaining five hundred poor to pray for pardon on behalf of the King is suspect in the same way from a Protestant point of view. Yet Shakespeare seems unafraid to present Henry V as a 'good' Catholic. Henry was, of course, king of England in the early fifteenth century, long before the Reformation. He vigorously prosecuted the Wycliffite reformers – a fact that Shakespeare does not choose to emphasize.

At the same time, Shakespeare's King Henry expresses himself in ways that Protestants would find comforting and wise. Having established two chantries and all the rest, Henry concedes that such good works are not in themselves sufficient. 'More will I do', he vows, 'Though all that I can do is nothing worth, / Since that my penitence comes after all, / Imploring pardon' (300–2). As he says these words he is on his knees, praying to God. The implicit theology is broadly inclusive. Good works are holy, but they are not enough without personal prayer and sincere contrition. Henry heeds the advice of church authorities, though he also manages to extract from them a very large contribution for his war against the French. He bids his soldiers sing '*Non nobis*' and '*Te Deum*' in celebration of the victory at Agincourt. The '*Te Deum*' was a Catholic hymn of praise also incorporated after the Reformation into Anglican practice. Henry is a good son of the church, but not in a polemical way that might offend most Protestants. He is unmistakably an English hero, even though he has no quarrel with Rome. Perhaps we can see in this portraiture a way of minimizing differences in an era of Reformation, and thus of stressing elements of continuity in Western Christendom.

Shakespeare's portrayal of clerical figures is generally consistent with such a moderate and inclusive position. His friars are usually genial, even if sometimes slightly comical. Friar Laurence in *Romeo and Juliet* is a Franciscan, as is his associate, Friar John. The story is, after all, Italian in its ultimate sources and in its setting. Friar Laurence spends no time expounding Catholic doctrine. He is instead a counselor to Romeo and then to Juliet, a wise old man given to sententious moralisms that are at times poignantly relevant to the tragic story of the two young lovers. 'Two such opposèd kings encamp them still / In man as well as herbs', he soliloquizes, 'grace and rude will; / And where the worser is predominant, / Full soon the canker death eats up that plant' (2.3.27–30). When his well-intentioned efforts to remedy the banishment of Romeo are foiled by bad luck and unfortunate timing, Laurence is generously willing to accept his share of the blame. The Prince is quick to exculpate Laurence: 'We still have known thee for a holy man', he says (5.3.270). That epithet fits nicely: Laurence is a holy man, an older friend, a wise counselor, one who can sympathize with youth.

Friar Francis in *Much Ado About Nothing* is no less decent and worthy. At the intended wedding of Claudio to Hero, his role is importantly one of judging the young lady to be innocent of the terrible charge of promiscuity levelled against her. He makes this judgement on the basis of his observations of her from his vantage as an experienced clerical adviser and confessor. Having noted 'A thousand blushing apparitions / To start into her face, a thousand innocent shames / In angel whiteness beat away those blushes' (4.1.159–61), Friar Francis simply cannot believe what Claudio and Don Pedro and Don John allege against Hero.

> Call me a fool;
> Trust not my reading nor my observations,
> Which with experimental seal does warrant
> The tenor of my book; trust not my age,
> My reverence, calling, nor divinity,
> If this sweet lady lie not guiltless here
> Under some biting error.   (4.1.164–70)

Friar Francis and Benedick alone, among the men who are present, have the strength of conviction to believe in Hero's innocence. Even her father caves in for a time to suspicious fears. Friar Francis has no 'evidence' to refute the seemingly physical proof of an assignation at Hero's window the night before; his belief in Hero is based on faith and observation. Like Beatrice, who is also incredulous about the accusation, Francis simply knows that Hero could do no such thing. Once again, Shakespeare has no compunction in presenting a friar as an essentially good man. At the same time, he is like Friar Laurence in having no liturgical or doctrinal function other than that of officiating at the wedding.

The same is true, in a more wry and ironic sense, of the pretend friar (really Duke Vincentio) in *Measure for Measure*. However enigmatic his role as absent ruler observing the corruptions of Vienna from the vantage of his disguise, the Duke does act in ways that reinforce the generic portrait of a kindly friar in Shakespeare's plays. He counsels Claudio to prepare for death in a deeply moving speech about the vanity of human wishes, even while he is simultaneously manoeuvring to ensure that Claudio will be kept alive. He looks out for Isabella with genuine solicitude. His choric observations in soliloquy call upon the sort of sententious wisdom we hear elsewhere from Friar Laurence and Friar Francis. 'He who the sword of heaven will bear / Should be as holy as severe', he intones (3.2.254–5). Then, too, the friars in this play who are genuine members of their holy order are unfailingly loyal and courageous on the side of right. Friar Thomas sensibly quizzes the Duke about his motives in wishing to disguise himself in a friar's gown (1.3). Friar Peter is instrumental in the play's denouement by means of which Angelo is exposed (and then pardoned), Claudio is reunited with his sister, and the Duke is restored to his office as ruler of Vienna. Nowhere is the Catholicism of these friars seen as meddling on behalf of Rome. In a similar vein, Shakespeare presents Isabella's intent to become a nun as worthily sincere: she has good reason to renounce the world. As she explains to the nun Francisca, Isabella desires more rather than less restraint as she prepares to enter into the sisterhood of Saint Clare (1.4). Even though the oddly comic form of *Measure for Measure* does ultimately provide for Isabella a way back from renunciation of the world to the prospect of marriage (which, depending on one's interpretation, she may or may not choose to embrace), Catholic beliefs and practices are presented as matters of sincere conscience and not as menacing to the state.

The portraiture of clergymen elsewhere in Shakespeare is, on the whole, similarly tolerant and free of polemical animosity. Anticlericalism was a staple in Elizabethan and Jacobean drama, and at times it could be sharply satirical. The two friars in Christopher Marlowe's *The Jew of Malta* (1589–90) are so comically venal that one imagines Elizabethan audiences laughing in delight when one (Bernardine) is strangled by Barabas and Ithamore, whereupon the other (Jacomo) is then tricked into attacking the dead body of his fellow friar and is turned over to the authorities for murder. More ominous are the powerful and corrupt Cardinals in John Webster's *The Duchess of Malfi* (1613–14) and Thomas Middleton's *Women Beware Women* (1620–4). Many other instances could be cited. Shakespeare's anticlericalism, on the other hand, is more apt to be content with portraying a mix of interfering schemers and bunglers, along with some clergymen of integrity. The Bishop of Winchester, later Cardinal, in *1* and *2 Henry VI* is a troublemaker at court and an enemy of the king's uncle and Protector, Humphrey Duke of Gloucester, but so are the Duke of York, the Earl of Suffolk, and other secular political figures striving for precedence. The insulting epithets hurled at Winchester as 'Peeled priest', 'haughty prelate', etc., as he parades in his 'broad cardinal's hat' and 'scarlet robes' (*1 Henry VI*, 1.3.23–42), are presumably intended to excite anticlerical and anti-Catholic sentiment among London spectators, but do not unequivocally identify the villains as distinguished from the virtuous. King Henry VI's own piety is presented as no doubt excessive for one who must also rule the country, but not because such piety is ridiculous. The Bishop of Carlisle in *Richard II* is willing to risk his life for his principled belief in the sanctity of the institution of kingship (4.1.115–50). Cardinal Bourchier, in *Richard III*, tries ineffectually to uphold 'the holy privilege / Of blessèd sanctuary' when the widowed Queen Elizabeth and her two sons (one the heir presumptive to the throne) seek refuge in the church (3.1.37–43). In the play's final military sequences, the future Henry VII is supported by Sir Christopher Urswick, a priest; 'Sir' is here the honorific title used in addressing clergymen (4.5.1–20). Otherwise, the clergy are given no role in Shakespeare's account of the battle of Bosworth Field. The Archbishop of York in *2 Henry IV* joins in rebellion against Henry IV, but does so for principled reasons (4.1.53–87); he behaves more honourably than his opposite number, Prince John of Lancaster, son of the King. Presumably, all of these church figures are Catholics, but that connection is seldom emphasized.

Among Shakespeare's history plays, the only two that grapple directly with the Catholic question are *King John* (c.1594–6) and *Henry VIII* (1613). In both instances, Shakespeare approaches the question circumspectly. King John was a controversial figure in the English Renaissance. Catholic historians of the fifteenth and sixteenth centuries, such as Polydore Vergil, were strongly condemnatory of a ruler who had, in their view, abused the rights of the Catholic church in England. Protestant reformers, on the other hand, saluted King John as a flawed hero – flawed in that his standing up to the papacy had ultimately failed, but a hero in his having made the attempt. Catholics and Protestants alike were not interested in Magna Carta; what they cared about was the religious question. John Foxe lauded King John as an early

martyr in *The Acts and Monuments of the Church* (1563), known pop-
ularly as *The Book of Martyrs*. In a two-part play by John Bale, *King John*
(1538, later revised), the title figure is a champion of the cause of reform.
An anonymous play of 1587–91 called *The Troublesome Reign of King
John*, which Shakespeare appears to have known and used, sees the
King as a dauntless enemy of church corruption. Unabashedly pro-
English and anti-foreign, the play justifies Philip the Bastard's plun-
dering of church wealth and argues that John's defiance of the papacy
would have succeeded had it not been for the nefarious Catholic
loyalties of the English nobility.

Given the predominance of this anti-Catholic view of King John
among Protestant readers and playgoers in London in the early 1590s,
Shakespeare's handling of this touchy material is notably generous and
mild. John is indeed a less than admirable king: he has withheld the
kingdom from his nephew Arthur, who has a better genealogical claim
to the throne than does John himself, and John does sanction the
putting to death of Arthur when that unfortunate lad is his political
prisoner. At the same time, John enjoys the support of the intrepid
Philip the Bastard, who, as choric figure and sturdy English patriot,
makes a strong case for continuity of rule under the de facto admin-
istration of King John. The nobles who revolt against John are easily
hoodwinked into playing right into the hands of the French Dauphin,
Lewis. The Pope's legate, Cardinal Pandulph, is a practised machiavel,
but even he is outmanoeuvred by Lewis. Disloyalty to the crown is
a losing game. The Catholic church is undeniably trying to stir up
trouble in England, and succeeds in persuading John to yield up his
crown to the Pope and receive it back in such a way that John now
possesses 'sovereign greatness and authority' as 'holding of the Pope'
(5.1.1–4), but the real enemy is the French Dauphin. Shakespeare does
not put much stress on the King's ordering the Bastard to 'shake the
bags / Of hoarding abbots' (3.3.7–8); this is said in passing by way
of explaining how the King is to obtain money for his wars. Similarly,
Shakespeare reports the rumour that the King 'is poisoned by a
monk' (5.6.24), but makes no attempt to substantiate the allegation
or to exploit its potential for anti-Catholic feeling; it is simply one
explanation of the King's unexpected and painful death. Given the
prevailing Protestant view of King John in chronicles and plays that
Shakespeare consulted, his estimate is balanced and free of polemical
rancour.

Writing *Henry VIII* (seemingly in collaboration with John Fletcher) required of Shakespeare an unusual degree of circumspection. Henry VIII was, after all, Queen Elizabeth I's grandfather. Even though Elizabeth had been dead for a decade when the play was staged in 1613, she was still remembered as a popular Protestant monarch; her successor in 1603, the Protestant James I, was her first cousin twice removed. The play gives a detailed representation of Henry's divorcing of his Spanish wife, Katharine of Aragon, and his courting of Anne Bullen or Boleyn, who is to be the mother of Elizabeth. The portrayal of Henry is studiously ambivalent. He seems all too ready to engage in an extravagant display of wealth and power at the Field of the Cloth of Gold in 1520; this meeting with Francis I of France near Calais is not staged directly in the play, but is reported at length by the Duke of Norfolk in terms that stress the incorrigible vanity of striving for earthly glory (1.1.13–38). Henry finds the Duke of Buckingham guilty of high treason on the flimsiest of hearsay allegations, not heeding the plausible evidence that Buckingham's downfall has been engineered by means of perjury and bribery (1.1.198–226). Henry's meeting with Anne takes place in a highly seductive atmosphere at Cardinal Wolsey's palatial establishment in Westminster (1.4). Knowledgeable courtiers suspect that, for all the 'mincing' and 'spice' of Anne's 'hypocrisy' in holding out for marriage with Henry before giving herself to him sexually, she has 'a woman's heart, which ever yet / Affected eminence, wealth, sovereignty'; she is ready, in other words, to 'stretch' her 'soft cheveril conscience' in a high-stakes bargaining for the rank of Queen (2.3.24–33). Henry's divorce proceedings against Katharine cast him in the sanctimonious role of one who professes deep regret at having to put aside a wife who is 'alone' among women for her 'rare qualities' of 'sweet gentleness', 'meekness saintlike', and 'wifelike government', when we are given good reason to believe that his worries about 'Scruple' and the 'prick' of 'conscience' are the result of his having become infatuated with Anne (2.4.134–69). For an agonizingly long time, Henry seems oblivious of the plotting of religious conservatives like Stephen Gardiner (later Bishop of Winchester) against Thomas Cranmer, the Protestant-minded Archbishop of Canterbury.

At the same time, Shakespeare employs a number of dramaturgic strategies to minimize the effect of such an implicit criticism of Queen Elizabeth's father. Little is made of the epic confrontation between the Catholic and Protestant faiths at the time of the break with Rome;

in fact, Shakespeare never uses these words 'Catholic' and 'Protestant' in any of his writings. Nor does he use 'Anglican' or 'Calvinist'. He does use 'Papist' once, though not in this play; it is part of a quixotic witticism by Lavatch, the clownish fool in *All's Well That Ends Well*, when he contrasts 'young Charbon the Puritan' with 'old Poysam the Papist' (1.3.51–2). The term 'Lutheran' occurs once in all of Shakespeare, when Cardinal Wolsey refers to Anne Bullen in *Henry VIII* as 'a spleeny Lutheran' (3.2.100); Wolsey is speaking from his position as Cardinal. English audiences in 1613 would of course know that Henry's marriage to the Protestant Anne and his divorce of the Catholic Katharine were the motivating events of Henry's break with Rome. One reason for the downfall of Wolsey in *Henry VIII* is that he has been in secret communication with 'Rome' (i.e., the papacy) in an attempt to secure for himself the rank of papal legate (3.2.312–14). The beginning of the Reformation is implicitly part of the scene in *Henry VIII*, but it is consistently downplayed. Katharine proudly identifies herself as daughter of Ferdinand, 'King of Spain', insisting that he 'was reckoned one / The wisest prince that there had reigned by many / A year before' (2.4.45–8), and she does appeal 'unto the Pope, / To bring my whole cause 'fore His Holiness, / To be judged by him' (117–19), but she is not presented in the play as a religious zealot and certainly not as a Catholic who might be a source of political and religious disaffection in her adopted country; she is instead a loyal, decent wife whose death in the play is attended by an angelic vision (4.2.82ff.). Her dealings with Capuchius, ambassador from the Emperor Charles V, are not at all conspiratorial; her only hope is that Capuchius can deliver to King Henry her loving greetings (124–30).

Much of the implicit criticism of Henry VIII is deflected in this play onto Cardinal Wolsey. Ruthless in his ambition, proud, enamoured of worldly things, he is the quintessential corrupt priest. Yet he too is made partly sympathetic by the seeming sincerity of his penance when he is exposed, and by his belatedly seeking the consolations of renunciation. His arrogance may seem characteristic of Catholicism in this play, but it is countered by the ambivalent characterization of Anne and of Henry. The only untarnished hero, perhaps, is Archbishop Cranmer, who is both Protestant and virtuous. Nearly martyred by Gardiner and other conservatives for being 'A most arch heretic, a pestilence / That does infect the land' (5.1.45–6), Cranmer is at last rescued by royal interposition into the deliberations of the Privy Council. Henry VIII is finally instrumental in saving the English Reformation. Everything leads forward to the birth of Elizabeth, the future Queen of England. The circumstances that have resulted in this blessed event are strange and unpredictable; corrupted motives and uncertain political compromises have somehow led to the birth of this child, as though by the operation of some mysterious overseeing power. Following her eventual death, moreover, another heir will arise 'As great in admiration as herself' (5.5.42–3), that is to say, King James I. These are all 'wonders' demonstrating the will of Providence in blessing and protecting the English nation. *Henry VIII* is thus part patriotic celebration and part mystery play. It sees the great spiritual Reformation of the English church as having been brought about, paradoxically, through the actions of self-interested men and women. Polemical loyalties in the battle of Catholics versus Protestants are set aside in favour of an inclusive and forgiving view of religious harmony. With the guidance of divine providence, all somehow turns out for the best.

Shakespeare's presentation of radical Protestantism tends to be more critical. To be sure, the objections are less vehement than in many plays written by Shakespeare's contemporaries. We find no satirical portraits as polemically edged as those of Tribulation Wholesome and Ananias in Ben Jonson's *The Alchemist* (1610), for instance, or Zeal-of-the-Land Busy in Jonson's *Bartholomew Fair* (1614), whose very names betray the unmitigated scorn of the dramatist. Shakespeare is characteristically more willing to sympathize even with those he subjects to a degree of comic ridicule. Yet the fact that many extreme Puritans were enemies of theatre and all its works made for a confrontation of unusual severity. The most notable instance occurs in *Twelfth Night*.

'Marry, sir, sometimes he is a kind of Puritan', says Maria to Sir Toby as she sums up her view of Malvolio, the Countess's sanctimonious steward (2.3.139). The term awakens Sir Andrew's ire. 'Oh, if I thought that, I'd beat him like a dog', Sir Andrew avows. 'What, for being a Puritan?' Toby counters. 'Thy exquisite reason, dear knight?' When Sir Andrew confesses that he has nothing much to say on the subject other than to affirm that he has 'reason good enough' (140–5), Maria intervenes in the conversation to clarify what she meant by bringing up the term 'Puritan' in the first place:

The devil a Puritan that he is, or anything constantly, but a time-pleaser, an affectioned ass, that cons state without book and utters it by great swaths; the best persuaded of himself, so crammed, as he thinks, with excellencies, that it is his grounds of faith that all that look on him love him; and on that vice in him will my revenge find notable cause to work. (2.3.146–52)

Shakespeare uses the word 'Puritan' only rarely; apart from this passage, where it occurs thrice, and one already mentioned above in *All's Well That Ends Well*, the word turns up only in *The Winter's Tale* (4.3.44–5) and *Pericles* (4.6.9). These last two references are both satirical. In the first, the clownish Shepherd observes of the forthcoming sheep-shearing festival that there will be 'but one Puritan' among the singers, and he will sing 'psalms to hornpipes', as Huguenot immigrants from the Continent were typically thought of as doing. In the second instance, the Bawd in the Mytilene brothel of *Pericles* complains of the unassailably virtuous Marina that 'she would make a Puritan of the devil if he should cheapen [i.e., bargain for] a kiss of her'. These instances are incidental, simply reflecting the way in which the word 'Puritan' could elicit a laugh from London audiences in much the same way that anti-Catholic jokes were a staple of stage clowning. Maria's engagement with the term is more studied. She offers careful qualifications: at first she says that Malvolio is 'a kind of Puritan', not just 'a Puritan', and then goes on to indicate that the term doesn't apply well after all, since Malvolio is in reality a self-infatuated ass.

What kind of Puritan is Malvolio, then, if at all, and what is Maria saying about Puritans? The passage suggests that Puritans may be like Malvolio, or Malvolio like the Puritans, but only to the extent that they may share common characteristics. If Puritans tend to be self-important and complacently proud of themselves, then they and Malvolio deserve whatever scorn is directed at them. The 'If' issues a warning, however, about drawing easy analogies. Not all Puritans are stuffy and self-important; one must allow distinctions. At the same time, the 'If' may be a warning to Puritans as well: behave like Malvolio, and you will not be spared by the satirist critic.

This second warning is especially pertinent, because Malvolio does behave in ways that are commonly associated with Puritanism. He seems to enjoy putting down other people's revelry. He is strait-laced in his manner of dress. When he criticizes the Countess Olivia for taking 'delight in such a barren rascal' as Feste, she counters that Malvolio is 'sick of self-love' and tastes 'with a distempered appetite', instead of taking for 'bird-bolts' those things which he deems 'cannon bullets' (1.5.80–90). Evidently the Countess likes to have in her household both this apostle of sobriety and the free-spirited Feste who counsels her that 'Present mirth hath present laughter' (2.3.48); the two balance each other. Malvolio's gravity is useful to her in a time of mourning for her dead brother; presumably he is one who can keep the midnight revelry of her uncle Toby Belch and his companions down to a decorous level. Malvolio invokes her authority when he tries to break up a noisy late-night party in her house. 'My lady bade me tell you that though she harbors you as her kinsman, she's nothing allied to your disorders' (2.3.95–7), he tells Sir Toby, and one can well imagine that the Countess did say something of the sort; the party is very noisy, and surely the Countess deserves some observation of decorum in her own house. The witty and sensible Maria is astonished to discover what a 'caterwauling' the revellers are making, and warns them that Olivia has 'called up her steward Malvolio and bid him turn you out of doors' (72–4). At the same time, Malvolio's manner of issuing his ultimatums is so smug and officious that he quickly loses any sympathy he might otherwise have garnered. Most of all, his own secret ambition to be 'Count Malvolio' merits all the satirical vengeance that Maria and Toby and the rest can muster.

'Dost thou think, because thou art virtuous, there shall be no more cakes and ale?' Sir Toby accosts Malvolio (2.3.114–15). No anti-Puritan satirist could have said it better. The Puritans were disliked by many because of their disapproval of church-ales, May games, Maypoles, dancing, drinking, and other forms of social entertainment. The dislike was intensified by the common perception that such blue-nosed legislators of public morality might themselves be secretly lecherous and worldly. Here again Malvolio fits the mold. He is guilty of 'practicing behavior to his own shadow' and of fantasizing about the Countess Olivia as his sexual partner. He meditates in soliloquy about precedents for his becoming 'Count Malvolio': 'the lady of the Strachy' is reported to have 'married the yeoman of the wardrobe' (2.5.16–39). He prides himself on his 'familiar smile' (65), even while we know that he is famous for his scowl. He longs secretly for the power of being Count Malvolio not simply for the wealth it would bring him but more importantly for the authority it would give him to berate Toby and Andrew and drum them out of the Countess's household. Malvolio is even like the stereotypical Puritan in the way he reads and interprets. When he finds a letter dropped in his way by Maria with handwriting in imitation of that of the Countess, Malvolio goes into intellectual contortions to fit the enigmatic message to himself. 'If I could make that resemble something in me!' he exclaims, as he reads the riddling 'M.O.A.I' (106–19). Maria has indeed chosen cunningly: 'M' and 'O' begin and end Malvolio's name, while 'A' and 'I' are the second and next to last letters. Puritans were often accused of torturing a biblical text to make it say what they wanted it to say. Malvolio sees the opportunity to do just this in the letter. 'And yet, to crush this a little, it would bow to me', he says, 'for every one of these letters are in my name' (137–8).

Malvolio thus conforms in many important particulars to the stereotype of the killjoy Puritan. He richly deserves his satirical punishment of being tricked into dressing in outlandishly festive costume and into smiling like an idiot. Even if we must bear in mind Maria's caution against tarring all Puritans with this brush, and even if the punishment of Malvolio goes too far in its use of humiliating incarceration, we are plainly invited to rejoice in the comeuppance of this humourless spoil-sport. Seldom in Shakespeare are the sympathies so clearly tilted to one side. Presumably the reason for this uncharacteristic tilt of sympathies is that Malvolio is the enemy of all that theatre stands for. Many Puritan preachers hated theatre, as we have seen, and Malvolio is plainly an apostle of the same persuasion. When he storms off in the final act, vowing that 'I'll be revenged on the whole pack of you!' (5.1.378), his declaration of war has a chilling effect. Ultimately, in 1642, the Puritans did close down the London theatres as they had longed to do for well over a half century. The battle lines are drawn in *Twelfth Night*. 'What's to come is still unsure', sings Feste (2.3.49).

Elsewhere, too, Shakespeare appears ready to invite genial but satirical laughter at persons of a reforming persuasion. The name of Sir Oliver Mar-text in *As You Like It* offers a clue to his character: he is a 'hedge-priest' of the rustic sort who might be asked to marry Touchstone and Audrey 'under a bush like a beggar' (3.3.77). Marring texts through pointlessly literal exegesis was a practice held against Puritan-inclined writers, as in the case of Malvolio's torturing of 'M.O.A.I.' Mar-text is a 'vicar of the next village' (40); he officiates in a 'chapel' (62). Like many a Puritan-inclining parish priest of the Anglican church, he refuses to be deterred in his zeal by Jaques's scorn for the humble circumstances of his calling. "'Tis no matter', he mutters defiantly when left alone on stage. 'Ne'er a fantastical knave of them all shall flout me out of my calling' (98–9). Sir Hugh Evans, a Welsh parson in *The Merry Wives of Windsor* with a propensity for citing the metrical Psalms (3.1.23) and for threatening the schoolboys under his tutelage with whippings if they fail to recite their Latin paradigms correctly (4.1.15–78), is the target of some good-natured practical joking. The curate Nathaniel and the pedantic schoolmaster Holofernes in *Love's Labour's Lost* offer examples of the sorts of instructors of youth one might encounter in rural England as a consequence of Protestant educational reform. Hotspur, in *1 Henry IV*, professes to be amused by his wife's swearing of primly decorous oaths, such as 'Not you, in good sooth', and 'as true as I live', and 'as God shall mend me', and 'as sure as day', as if she were 'a comfit maker's wife' or a London citizen's spouse who has never ventured further than Finsbury (3.1.245–50). Such pious mannerisms were characteristic of the bourgeois citizenry of England's largest and most Puritan-leaning city.

Shakespeare's interest in Calvinist thought is difficult to appraise, partly because as a dramatist he does not discuss the matter directly and partly because the differences between Calvinist theology and that of other religious persuasions are not always clearly distinguished in Renaissance playwriting. Certainly Calvinism exerted a profound influence on the reformed English church of the sixteenth and early seventeenth centuries. During the years of the mid sixteenth century, when the Catholic Queen Mary reigned in England, many clergymen went into exile, especially to Geneva; they returned home fortified with Calvinist doctrine. Cambridge University became a centre for Calvinist-inspired teaching. The intellectual ferment created there by William Perkins and others is manifest, for example, in Christopher Marlowe's powerful depiction in *Doctor Faustus* (1588–9) of a learned man whose 'hellish fall' and 'fiendful fortune' stand as a warning to all those who 'practice more than heavenly power permits' (A-Text Epilogue); Faustus is a terrifying example of the Calvinist unregenerate human being whose damnation seems unavoidably predetermined despite his knowledge of Christian doctrine. Marlowe went to Cambridge; Shakespeare did not, and yet Calvinism was everywhere in the culture. What traces, if any, does it leave in his writings?

The edifying contrast between Hamlet's dead father and his living uncle Claudius is suggestive in Calvinist terms. 'Look here upon this picture, and on this', Hamlet urges his mother, as he shows her the likenesses of these two men, perhaps in lockets worn by Hamlet and Gertrude about their necks. The likeness of the dead Hamlet senior shows 'Hyperion's curls, the front of Jove himself, / An eye like Mars to threaten and command', while Claudius's image is that of 'a mildewed ear, / Blasting his wholesome brother' (3.4.54–66). Earlier, Hamlet has lauded his dead father as 'So excellent a king, that was to this [i.e., compared to Claudius] / Hyperion to a satyr' (1.2.139–40). These contrasts are Hamlet's, and are no doubt coloured by his own idealization of his father and intense hatred for Claudius, but other evidence in the play points as well to the idea that Claudius is an unregenerate man of the sort Calvin describes. The ghost of Hamlet's father certainly shares his son's perception of an impassable gulf between the virtuous and the damned: 'virtue, as it never will be moved, / Though lewdness court it in a shape of heaven, / So lust, though to a radiant angel linked, / Will sate itself in a celestial bed / And prey on garbage' (1.5.54–8). Claudius is one of the damned. When he attempts to pray and seek heaven's forgiveness for his sins, having been frightened into an intense recollection of the murder he committed by watching Hamlet's 'mousetrap' play of 'The Murder of Gonzago', Claudius discovers to his utter terror that he is a man who 'cannot repent'. He finds that he is unable to pray 'Though inclination be as sharp as will'. As one who has been born into a Christian culture and has been given all the presumed benefits of a Christian education, Claudius knows perfectly well what is required of him if he is to hope for salvation: he must be truly penitent. Christ's teaching welcomes the penitent sinner, and Claudius is a sinner. 'Is there not rain enough in the sweet heavens / To wash it [Claudius's blood-covered hand] as white as snow?' he ponders in soliloquy. 'Whereto serves mercy / But to confront the visage of offense?' (3.3.38–66). Yet at once comes the painful explanation that God's mercy is not for Claudius.

> But oh, what form of prayer
> Can serve my turn? 'Forgive me my foul murder'?
> That cannot be, since I am still possessed
> Of those effects for which I did the murder:
> My crown, mine own ambition, and my queen.
> May one be pardoned and retain th'offense?
>   (3.3.51–5)

The question answers itself. In this corrupted world one can hope to 'shove by justice'; tainted money 'Buys out the law. But 'tis not so above. / There is no shuffling, there the action lies / In his true nature' (57–62). Claudius understands all too well that what he has to do is to give up the Danish crown and the widow of the brother he has murdered, and promise in his heart and soul to lead a new life. That is all that God, in his infinite mercy, asks of him. Yet this is precisely what Claudius is unable to will himself to do.

Why are some humans unable to will themselves to lead godly lives? Calvin's answer lays stress on the infinite power and foreknowledge of God: since he knows all that will happen, he knows that some humans will fail spiritually and be eternally damned. God does not will each person's actions, but he does evidently grant that some will be saved and some will not. We must not blame God for this, or see him as the author of evil; that is the ultimate heresy. Rather, we must understand that mercy is God's gift to give or not to give as he sees fit in his mysterious and infinite wisdom. We as humans cannot hope to earn salvation; it is a gift of grace. We must conduct our lives as well as we can, hoping that virtuous conduct may be a sign that we are among the elect.

Hamlet shows repeatedly that he has pondered these ideas with great care. When he asks Polonius to see that the visiting players are 'well bestowed' in Elsinor Castle, Polonius assures Hamlet, 'My lord, I will use them according to their desert.' This answer does not satisfy Hamlet. 'God's bodikin, man', he retorts, 'much better. Use every man after his desert, and who shall scape whipping?' (2.2.522–30). That is to say, we all could hope for nothing but punishment if we were to be given our just deserts. The idea recurs when Hamlet confronts Ophelia with their failed love relationship:

> Get thee to a nunnery. Why wouldst thou be a breeder of sinners? I am myself indifferent honest, but yet I could accuse me of such things that it were better my mother had not borne me: I am very proud, revengeful, ambitious, with more offenses at my beck than I have thoughts to put them in, imagination to give them shape, or time to act them in. What should such fellows as I do crawling between earth and heaven? We are arrant knaves all; believe none of us. (3.1.122–30)

Although he sees himself as less corrupt than many people, Hamlet is obsessed with the fallen state of humanity. The sins he ascribes here to himself – pride, vengeful anger, worldly ambition – are the very 'crimes' that have sent old Hamlet to Purgatory for a time, because to be human is to commit such sins daily, to the peril of one's soul if one cannot obtain merciful forgiveness. The world in which Hamlet thus finds himself is 'an unweeded garden / That grows to seed. Things rank and gross in nature / Possess it merely' (1.2.135–7).

To be sure, these are the premises of medieval Christianity, going back to St Augustine and still earlier; the fallen state of humanity, and the consequent need for God's grace, were fundamental principles. Still, Calvinist thought had given these ideas a new urgency in the sixteenth century by underscoring the potential for spiritual failure. Shakespeare, in *Hamlet*, is continually aware of this danger. The unyielding malignity of Iago in *Othello* is no less unsettling. And how are we to explain, in *King Lear*, the appalling contrasts between Cordelia and her cruel sisters, or between Edgar and Edmund? Or, in *Richard III*, between Richmond and Richard? In *Macbeth*, between Banquo and Macbeth? Human and psychological explanations can go only so far. Ultimately, we are left with an awareness of a spiritual and cosmic battleground between good and evil that is at once medieval in its overview of humankind's fallen nature and Calvinist in its preoccupation with the intransigence of the reprobate.

How do the Weird Sisters in *Macbeth* know that they can prevail on Macbeth to commit a horrible murder, and yet cannot reach the heart of Banquo? Their baleful prophecies kindle in Macbeth a temptation that he is unable to resist, even though (like Claudius) he is fully aware of the spiritual and moral consequences of the act he is contemplating. He knows that 'Vaulting ambition' is the only motivation prompting him to go ahead with the murder of King Duncan, and is fully aware that ambition cannot hope to weigh in the scales of justice against the murder of a kinsman, a king, and an honoured guest (1.7.12–28); nonetheless, the murder proceeds. The Weird Sisters' uncanny foreknowledge that enables them to predict that Macbeth 'shalt be king hereafter' (1.3.50) must be based on a certainty that Macbeth is reprobate in Calvin's terms, like Marlowe's Doctor Faustus: he has free will as a human being, and yet he will do what is foreordained. This certain destiny is ineradicably part of who he is. It is fulfilled through his decisions, his acts; yet it also appears to have been fully predetermined. Banquo, contrastingly, knows how to contain his human frailty within the compass of moral conduct. 'Merciful powers', he exclaims, 'Restrain in me the cursèd thoughts that nature / Gives way to in repose!' (2.1.7–9). His prayer is answered because, though his human nature makes him inevitably prone to sinful ambitions, he is somehow possessed of a grace that enables him to pray efficaciously for the divine assistance without which he knows that he would fail. How are we to understand these crucial differences between Macbeth and Banquo? Presumably the answer lies somewhere in the paradoxes of determinism and free will that find their most incisive expressions in the Renaissance in the writing of Calvin and in works like *Macbeth*.

Was Shakespeare anti-Semitic? Certainly English culture in his day was intolerant of Jews. They had been expelled from England during the reign of Edward I in 1290, in response to hostile public opinion against the influential role that Jews had played in banking and finance. Some Jews lived in London and at court in the late 1590s and early 1600s, but they generally stayed out of view, and some adopted the tactic of conforming outwardly to the official Anglican religion. Public hysteria erupted in 1594 when a Portuguese Jewish physician, Dr Roderigo Lopez, was accused of having plotted against the life of Queen Elizabeth and that of Don Antonio, pretender to the Portuguese throne. Christopher Marlowe's *The Jew of Malta*, featuring a Jewish protagonist (Barabas) with an impressively long list of vengeful crimes, was successfully revived on this occasion. The late-fifteenth-century *The Play of the Sacrament* had dramatized the story of five Jews who bought a sacramental host from a corrupt clergyman and subjected it to tortures symbolic of Christ's crucifixion. The cycle plays of the late medieval period generally portrayed the Jews as guilty of the crucifixion and thus inveterately hostile to Christianity. As potential converts to the 'true' faith they were acceptable, but only on that condition.

Shakespeare's writings do at times reveal something of this mindset. 'If I do not love her, I am a Jew', says Benedick of Beatrice in *Much Ado About Nothing* (2.3.257–8). The metaphor is offhand; Benedick isn't saying anything about Jews. The very unreflective nature of this defamatory comparison betrays a prejudicial attitude in the culture as a whole. So too in *The Two Gentlemen of Verona* when the clownish Lance complains of his dog for not weeping at their farewell to their family: 'A Jew would have wept to have seen our parting' (2.3.11–12). One of Falstaff's colourful asseverations is to swear that he is telling the truth, 'or I am a Jew else, a Hebrew Jew' (*1 Henry IV*, 2.4.177).

The Weird Sisters in *Macbeth* include a 'Liver of blaspheming Jew' among the ingredients of their diabolical cauldron (4.1.26).

The Merchant of Venice is of course much more complicated, so much so that we can wonder if Shakespeare's audiences were not supposed to be distressed by Gratiano's abusive baiting of the defeated Shylock in the trial scene (4.1.311–98), or earlier by the account of Antonio spitting on Shylock's 'Jewish gaberdine' (1.3.110, 124). Great actors like Henry Irving and Laurence Olivier have shown how sympathetic Shylock can be in performance, especially in his 'Hath not a Jew eyes' speech (3.1.55–69). Shakespeare softens the brutal antagonisms of Christian–Jewish confrontation in a number of ways. Antonio seems disposed to welcome Shylock into Christian society if only he will stop lending money at interest. 'Hie thee, gentle Jew', Antonio says in farewell to Shylock, when Shylock agrees to lend money 'in a merry sport' without interest other than the forfeiture of a pound of flesh in the event of nonpayment. 'I'll seal to such a bond / And say there is much kindness in the Jew', Antonio declares. 'The Hebrew will turn Christian; he grows kind' (1.3.144–77). To be sure, this charitable disposition on Antonio's part is posited on the idea of conversion: if the Jew will 'turn Christian', then he will no longer be a Jew. The conversion of Shylock's daughter Jessica to Christianity as the wife of Lorenzo seems to reinforce the point; she is included in the play's festive gathering at Belmont at play's end (even if modern productions sometimes portray her as an uncomfortable outsider still). Jewishness is defined as a matter of faith, not of ethnicity.

Still, *The Merchant of Venice* does seem to privilege Christianity over Judaism. However much we are invited to sympathize with Shylock as a persecuted man, his gospel of prospering by his 'bargains' and his 'well-worn thrift' (1.3.47) is presented in the play as belonging to an older order of moral and ethical conduct. His defence of Jacob for having outwitted Laban over some sheep sounds like a defence of shystering: having agreed with Laban that parti-coloured lambs would be the wages of Jacob's labour, Jacob proceeded to stick rods with peeled streaks in front of the ewes in heat so that they would give birth to parti-coloured lambs. Shylock's interpretation of this Old-Testament story sounds like hair-splitting, self-interested calculation: 'thrift is blessing, if men steal it not' (74–88). The Christians, conversely, believe in risk, in adventure, in shooting an arrow after a lost arrow as a way of finding the first one (1.1.140–52). Antonio risks his life to enable his younger friend, Bassanio, to compete for the hand in marriage of Portia. Bassanio risks all in the choice of three caskets for the sake of romantic love and fortune. Lancelot Gobbo leaves the employment of Shylock to serve Bassanio because, as he says to Bassanio, 'The old proverb is well parted between my master Shylock and you, sir: you have the grace of God, sir, and he hath enough' (2.2.141–3). By 'enough' Lancelot means worldly prosperity but without spiritual grace. As Lancelot says, 'I am a Jew if I serve the Jew any longer' (107). Jessica decides to abandon her father because, as she tells Lancelot, 'Our house is hell' (2.3.2). However reckless and even thoughtless risk-taking can sometimes be, it is presented in the play as more gallant and more generous than the more wary posture adopted by Shylock. Risk-taking is part of a new dispensation, and it carries the day in the play's romantic ending. Modern productions often ironize this ending as a way of showing that the Christians in the play are heartlessly superficial, as they sometimes are, but a more balanced view may be that Shakespeare, for all his compassionate sensitivity to the evils of persecution (certainly far greater than anything manifested in Marlowe's *The Jew of Malta*), shared his culture's bias in favour of the purportedly new Christian ethic of grace.

Does Shakespeare 'believe' in fairies, ghosts, and other supernatural beings? They are certainly omnipresent in his plays. At the same time, they are there at least in part because they are so essential to his dramaturgy. To ask whether we are to 'believe' in the fairies in *A Midsummer Night's Dream* is a complicated question. On the one hand, they are certainly real in the sense of being dramatic characters on stage. They have their quarrels and their sense of fun; they provide for us an amusing perspective on human folly, especially in love. 'Lord, what fools these mortals be!' exclaims Puck as he and Oberon prepare to witness the 'fond pageant' (3.2.114–15) of the altercation caused by Puck himself in mistakenly anointing Lysander's eyes with the magical herb instead of Demetrius's, so that the two young men are now competing for the love of Helena. The fairies are essential to the play's handling of point of view. They make themselves 'invisible', presumably with a gesture or some quick change of garment. 'I am invisible', says Oberon (2.1.186), and we as audience assume that he is so, able thus to wander in among the mortals without being 'seen'. (Prospero in *The Tempest* can do the same thing.) The very self-awareness of this theatrical device puts us on notice that their 'invisibility' is a stage convention, and so too, perhaps, is any sense of their objective existence. In a sustained dramatic irony, the humans of this play are never aware of the extent to which their actions are being directed by unseen creatures of the dark. Our awareness of this irony is part of our pleasure in theatrical performance. At the same time, Shakespeare seems to be playing with popular belief in fairies, leprechauns, goblins, and the like. This belief was undoubtedly widespread among many people in the Renaissance. Perhaps the best sense in which Shakespeare's fairies are 'real' is that they are immortal in his art. They still parade before us in our imaginations, and will do so as long as his plays are read and performed. Such an immortality is something that we mere mortals cannot hope to enjoy.

Much the same can be said of Shakespeare's dramatic employment of ghosts. Whether ghosts and demons were real was a much-debated topic in the Renaissance. Protestant writers like Samuel Harsnett tended to decry ghosts and demons as the figments of a corrupted Catholic fantasy; his *A Declaration of Egregious Popish Impostures* (1603) is unremittingly sceptical in its denunciation of exorcism. King James I weighed in with a similar scepticism on the subject of witchcraft. Shakespeare's ghosts are everywhere, and they are capable of remarkable stage trickery. Hamlet's father's ghost can make himself visible to the guards on watch and to Hamlet and Horatio, but he can also make himself simultaneously visible to Hamlet and not to Gertrude (*Hamlet*, 3.4.136–45). Some readers take this as evidence that the ghost is a product of Hamlet's overactive imagination, but an equally plausible explanation is that this ghost simply has no wish to communicate with Gertrude. What would they have to talk about?

At all events, ghosts in Renaissance lore are fully capable of such tactics. The Weird Sisters manifest themselves to Banquo and Macbeth and then '*vanish*' in such a way that Ross and Angus do not see them: 'The earth hath bubbles', says Banquo, 'as the water has, / And these are of them' (*Macbeth*, 1.3.78–80). Banquo's ghost in *Macbeth* twice reveals himself to Macbeth while the guests at the banqueting table see nothing (3.4.38–108). Even Lady Macbeth is convinced that 'This is the very painting of your fear' (61). Yet the stage direction seems plain enough: '*Enter the Ghost of Banquo, and sits in Macbeth's place*' (37 SD). This ghost is real in the theatre. So is '*the Ghost of young Prince Edward, son [of] Harry the Sixth, to Richard*', and so are the ghosts of Henry VI, Clarence, Rivers, Grey, Vaughan, Hastings, the two young Princes, the Lady Anne, and Buckingham, all of whom in turn visit King Richard and then Richmond with alternating prophecies of defeat or victory in the next day's battle (*Richard III*, 5.3.118–76). Richard and Richmond are both asleep in their respective tents, and yet the ghosts seem 'real' in the sense that they are not confined to one dream. Their collective intent to 'sit heavy' on the soul of Richard in the battle of Bosworth Field raises the possibility that as spirits they can have a decisive influence on the doings of mortals. '*The Ghost of Caesar*' appears to Brutus on the eve of the battle of Philippi in *Julius Caesar* without being perceived by the soldiers who are guarding Brutus (4.3.276–304), and yet a candle or taper burns 'ill' as though signalling the presence of something otherworldly (278). 'Thou shalt see me at Philippi', announces this 'evil spirit' to Brutus, plainly implying that the defeat of Caesar's assassins at Philippi is foreordained (284–5). Shakespeare's ghosts, being dramatic creations, occupy an ambiguous world of art that invites us to speculate about their relation to the mundane world without having to propound any dogmatic answers.

Witches occupy a similarly ambivalent dramatic space. The Weird Sisters in *Macbeth* are introduced in the play's opening stage direction with '*Enter three Witches*', and are elsewhere identified by the same name. 'Aroint thee, witch!' says a sailor's wife to one of them (1.3.6). 'Witches' mummy' is one of the ghastly ingredients of their diabolical cauldron (4.1.23). Hecate, goddess of night and of witchcraft, meets with them in what appears to be a non-Shakespearean scene (3.5). Witchcraft 'celebrates / Pale Hecate's offerings' (2.1.52–3). The three apparitions that the Weird Sisters show to Macbeth emerge from and then disappear into the space below the Elizabethan stage associated with the realm of hell ('Why sinks that cauldron?', 4.1.106). When the Duchess of Gloucester, in *2 Henry VI*, engages a witch named Margery Jordan to conjure up spirits for her, Margery and her cohorts '*do the ceremonies belonging, and make the circle*', reciting 'Conjuro te' (I conjure you), etc., '*It thunders and lightens terribly; then the Spirit riseth*' (1.4.1–41). '*Riseth*' would seem to mean rising up out of a trapdoor in the main stage. Fiends enter to Joan la Pucelle (i.e., Joan of Arc) in *1 Henry VI*, hanging their heads in defiance and refusing her offer of allowing them to sup at her body by way of indicating that her charmed days of victory over the English are coming to an end (5.3.1–24). These fiends too presumably emerge onto the stage from a trapdoor.

Omens are also commonly reported in Shakespeare's plays, with portentous suggestion. In *Julius Caesar*, many ominous portents are said to occur on the night before Caesar's assassination: hands burning without consuming the flesh, lions wandering in the streets of Rome, owls hooting and shrieking at noon, and still more (1.3.15–32). The eagles that accompany Cassius and Brutus to Philippi, feeding from the soldiers' hands, desert them in place of ravens, crows, and kites as the time of battle approaches, persuading even the sceptical Cassius to 'partly credit things that do presage' (5.1.81–92). The occult is thus an integral part of Shakespeare's dramaturgy, but always presented in such a way as to raise questions about the 'reality' of what the audience sees and hears.

The spiritual world of Shakespeare's drama is thus an eventful scene, evoking a cosmos in which spirits, demons, and fairies exert a seemingly powerful and yet uncertain control over human destiny. What sorts of spiritual values inhabit this cosmos? Does religion provide any sort of answer or consolation for life's manifest disappointments? Different plays supply different insights, of course, and different genres set up different expectations. Still, we can perhaps ask whether Shakespeare gives special privilege to social bonds of friendship, understanding, love, and compassion that can help atone for life's tragic circumstances and provide fulfillment for life's happier ventures. These redeeming qualities are generated out of human kindness and the ability to forgive, doing battle with humankind's worser propensity for cruelty and indifference. They are not, broadly speaking, sacramental; that is, they are not brought about by the workings of church liturgy and practice. They are generally compatible with Christ's parables extolling virtue and forbearance, but they do not depend on the promise of an eternal heavenly existence after bodily death. They are, in this sense, secular and humanistic without being hostile to organized religion, and generally without denying an ultimate role of a benign providence in human affairs (though such a providence is not to be found in the Roman plays).

When Duke Senior in *As You Like It* reflects on what he and his forest companions miss most in the society that they have left behind in their involuntary exile, he notes three main things: being knolled to church 'with holy bell', sitting 'at good men's feasts', and wiping one's eyes 'Of drops that sacred pity hath engendered' (2.7.119–22). In saying this he is echoing the very qualities of civilized life to which Orlando has just appealed in his request for aid in his time of dire need.

Church-going has its proper place in this roster, perhaps more as a social custom than as a sacramental and ritual event, since it is immediately paired with the social custom of feasting in company and with acts of charity that are prompted by knowing what it is 'to pity and be pitied' (116). People need one another, and best fulfill themselves by charitable deeds.

Paradoxically, the force of Shakespeare's dramatization of charitable values can be seen with special clarity in a non-Christian setting, where the universality of those values rises above cultural particularity. A notable case in point is *King Lear*. Nominally set in mythic pre-Christian Britain, and filled with oaths to the gods and goddesses of a non-Christian cosmos ('Hear, Nature, hear! Dear goddess hear!' 1.4.274, 'You see me here, you gods, a poor old man', 2.4.274), *Lear* is suffused with idealisms that our culture tends to associate with Christianity because it is the religion closest at hand for many. No doubt this proximity and familiarity of Christian teaching would have invited Shakespeare's first audiences to recognize the connections. An instance occurs in the play's first scene. When the King of France learns that Cordelia has been banished by her father, he naturally supposes that her offence must have been 'of such unnatural degree / That monsters it'. Cordelia begs her father to assure France that she is guilty of 'no vicious blot, murder, or foulness, / No unchaste action or dishonored step', and that she has been banished simply for lacking 'A still-soliciting eye and such a tongue / That I am glad I have not' (1.1.222–35). France immediately understands the point: Cordelia has not practised the calculated flattery that is too often the way of the world. He puts the question squarely to his rival for the hand in marriage of Cordelia:

> My lord of Burgundy,
> What say you to the lady? Love's not love
> When it is mingled with regards that stands
> Aloof from th'entire point. Will you have her?
> She is herself a dowry.   (1.1.241–5)

This selfless idealism seems rather strange in the mouth of a powerful king who might be expected, like the Duke of Burgundy, to consider a dowry the *sine qua non* of any marriage agreement between two royal or noble families, but that very strangeness underscores the thematic opposition here between worldliness and a gospel of *agapē*, or love that is utterly unselfish. Love, in France's view, cannot properly be called love unless it is benevolent, generous, and pure. France further clarifies what he means when he addresses Cordelia herself, explaining why he has chosen her in the face of her having been banished by her father and rejected by the worldly Duke of Burgundy:

> Fairest Cordelia, that art most rich being poor,
> Most choice, forsaken, and most loved, despised,
> Thee and thy virtues here I seize upon,
> Be it lawful I take up what's cast away.
>
> (1.1.254–7)

These are the paradoxes of the Beatitudes in Christ's Sermon on the Mount: 'Blessed are the meek, for they shall inherit the earth', 'Blessed are they which do hunger and thirst after righteousness, for they shall be filled', 'Blessed are they which are persecuted for righteousness' sake, for theirs is the kingdom of heaven', etc. (Matthew 5: 3–12; see also Luke 6: 20–3). Christianity of course does not hold a monopoly on such idealisms, and accordingly these ideas seem perfectly appropriate to the pre-Christian world of *King Lear*, but they resonate strongly here as a guide to audience sympathy. Clearly we are intended to admire Cordelia's unblemished honesty, however imprudent it may seem, and we admire France for honouring her in these terms. Moreover, this value system operates throughout the play. Kent, heroic in his honest loyalty, pays the price of exile. Edgar is forced to flee in order to save his life. The worldlings, meanwhile, prosper insolently and nearly succeed in taking over the entire kingdom.

The painful truths of the play's inversions of wisdom and folly, seeing and blindness, are repeatedly pointed out by Lear's Fool, describing Lear as one who 'bor'st thine ass on thy back o'er the dirt' and who 'mad'st thy daughters thy mothers' 'when thou gav'st them the rod and putt'st down thine own breeches' (1.4.159–71). The Fool's ironic advice to any who wish to succeed is to 'Let go thy hold when a great wheel runs down a hill lest it break thy neck with following; but the great one that goes upward, let him draw thee after' (2.4.70–3). Plainly the Fool does not want any decent person to follow his advice; he himself clings loyally to Lear at the very nadir of Lear's fortunes. What the Fool is doing is to define 'wisdom' and 'folly' in two radically opposite senses. 'Wisdom' is for worldlings the creed of self-interest, whereas for the pure in heart wisdom is the knowledge and practice of goodness; conversely, 'folly' is guilelessness to worldlings, innocence to the virtuous. Erasmus had made the analogy to Christianity explicit in his *In Praise of Folly* (*Moriae Encomium*, 1509, translated into English in 1549): Erasmus sees Christ as wise fool because his teaching is at once so unworldly and so exalted in its vision of what is ultimately true and good. *King Lear* is a dramatic tribute to Erasmus's great idea.

A similar idealism manifests itself throughout the Shakespeare canon. Forgiveness is often for Shakespeare both a beautiful idea and a device of dramatic structure. In *Cymbeline*, for example, in a mythic pre-Christian setting like that of *King Lear*, much of the action turns on the deep penitence of Posthumus Leonatus for having ordered the execution of his wife Imogen on a fabricated charge of adultery. Thinking that he has succeeded in his benighted wish to end her life, Posthumus makes his way back from Italy to Britain with the intent of being captured and put to death. 'So I'll die / For thee, O Imogen', he declares in soliloquy, 'even for whom my life / Is every breath a death' (5.1.25–7). Death will be for him part expiatory act and part a gesture of the despair he feels at having committed an unforgivable crime. He is saved from his worst self by the tragicomic form of a story in which Imogen is not in fact dead, and by her willingness to forgive what he has done. In *The Winter's Tale*, as well, Leontes's despairing refusal to forgive himself for having caused the death of his virtuous queen Hermione by accusing her unjustly of adultery leads to a similar conclusion: after some sixteen years of penitent grief, Leontes is restored by a seeming miracle and is thereby reunited with the wife he thinks he has destroyed. Her forgiveness of him is so simple that it does not even require words: it is like Imogen's forgiveness of Posthumus Leonatus, or Cordelia's of King Lear, who, when her father begins to recover his sanity and observes to her that she has 'some cause' to hate him, replies simply, 'No cause, no cause' (*King Lear*, 4.7.75–8). Prospero, in *The Tempest*, grapples with the difficult task of forgiving his enemies.

This theme of forgiveness is especially insistent in *Lear* and the late romances, but it is everywhere in the earlier plays as well: in Julia's forgiveness of the inconstant Proteus in *The Two Gentlemen of Verona*, in Hero's forgiveness of Claudio in *Much Ado About Nothing*, in Oliver's conversion from a villain into a loving brother eager to make restitution to Orlando for all the wrong done him in *As You Like It*, in Duke

Frederick's resolve to bequeath his ill-gotten title to his banished brother in the same play, in Helena's willingness to renew her marriage with Bertram after his many attempts to repudiate her in *All's Well That Ends Well*, in Henry IV's belated but sincere reconciliation with his son in *2 Henry IV*, in Desdemona's forgiveness of her husband even as she lies dying at his hands in *Othello*, and still more. *Measure for Measure* is a veritable feast of forgiveness and reconciliation: Angelo and Lucio are pardoned by the Duke, Mariana takes Angelo as her husband despite the penchant for evil that he has so abundantly demonstrated, Isabella shows herself capable of forgiving Angelo for having (as she believes) executed her brother, she and her brother learn to forgive each other and themselves for their painful quarrel, Claudio is restored to his Juliet and to his sister Isabella, Pompey is taught a trade rather than being executed as a criminal, the Provost is excused for having disobeyed an order, Escalus is pardoned for having been misled into supporting Angelo's abuse of justice, and even the life of the dissolute prisoner Barnardine is spared. It is as though Shakespeare sees forgiveness as one important answer to human insensitivity and brutishness: people must learn to forgive the unforgivable. The analogies to Christian teaching are marked, though not in such a way as to exclude other religious ideas. We must bear in mind too that forgiveness is an essential structural device for Shakespeare, especially in the comedies and late romances, so that the emphasis has theatrical as well as ideological implications. Yet even if we cannot say with any certainty that Shakespeare personally 'believed' in the values of forgiveness, charity, compassion, generosity, and unselfish love, we can say that as a playwright he found these values essential in the stories he chose to dramatize in this way.

Perhaps we can also say that Shakespeare seems far more interested as a dramatist in the cleansing emotional and spiritual effects of contrition and forgiveness than he is in more theological instructions about avoiding sin in order to escape the torments of hell and ensure an eternal life in heaven. That idea of eternal life in God seldom manifests itself in Shakespeare's writings. To be sure, Hamlet does choose not to kill Claudius at prayer lest he send the man's soul to heaven (3.3.74–8). Queen Katharine in *Henry VIII* spends her last moments meditating on 'that celestial harmony I go to' and is rewarded with a vision of 'Spirits of peace' while she holds up her hands to heaven (4.2.80–3). Yet these are rare instances, and even here we can regard the speakers' pronouncements as more indicative of their states of mind (Katharine is portrayed as a deeply devout woman) than of any larger sense in any of Shakespeare's plays that heaven will reward the virtuous and that hell will punish the vicious. Othello cries out in anguish, when he realizes that he has killed an innocent wife, 'Whip me, ye devils, / From the possession of this heavenly sight! / Blow me about in winds! Roast me in sulfur! / Wash me in steep-down gulfs of liquid fire!' (*Othello*, 5.2.286–8). Emilia feelingly speaks of Desdemona as 'the more angel she, / And you [Othello] the blacker devil' (134–5). Once again, however, these speeches evoke the emotional states of the speakers. The play of *Othello* does not, for most critics at least, ask us to consider whether Othello is to be imagined as going to everlasting punishment in hell while Desdemona basks in eternal glory. Shakespeare's plays don't work that way. What this may suggest about Shakespeare's own religious views is a matter of debate.

The ideas about religious faith and belief presented in Shakespeare's plays are of a piece, as are his ideas about sexuality and about politics. Ideas about religion are explored with a special intensity as he turns in his writing career to the genres of the problem play and of tragedy. These plays especially, but also the canon as a whole, show a detailed and incisive familiarity both with Catholic dogma and with Calvinist emphasis on the inseparable gulf between the elect and the damned. In his approach to the heated religious controversies that were so characteristic of the age in which he lived, he tends to be generous and moderate, allowing charitably for redeeming qualities in the followers of various rival persuasions. His anticlericalism is mild compared with that of other dramatists and writers of the period. In his historical evaluation of both King John and Henry VIII, he is balanced. With Puritan reformers he is less sympathetic, if only because they are so often vociferous enemies of theatre. Although his treatment of Jews is coloured by the ingrained prejudices of his age against a religion that was seen as inimical to Christianity, he is more forbearing by far than other contemporary writers. He puzzles out the paradoxes of determinism and free will in such a way as to allow free play for both sides of the argument. He handles adroitly the fraught question of belief in ghosts and other spirits by treating their many appearances in his plays as a necessary part of theatrical experience. He says very little about salvation through Christ or about a promise of eternal life in heaven as a reward for virtuous behaviour. Instead, he holds up charitable generosity as its own reward and sincere penitence for human failings as one sure way to find happiness and reconciliation. Forgiveness is a double blessing, like heavenly grace itself: to quote Portia in *The Merchant of Venice* (4.1.185), 'It blesseth him that gives and him that takes.'

We have not yet examined more sceptical ways of thinking about religious difference and about the place of humanity in the cosmos. These issues come next, in what is perhaps a logical extension of what we have already seen. Religious doubt was heresy in Shakespeare's time. It was also, for some, an unavoidable challenge to more orthodox thinking. Whatever conclusions Shakespeare may have arrived at personally, his writings in the early seventeenth century suggest that he came to these questions gradually in the course of his career as a dramatist. The genre of tragedy that he embraces with a flourish around 1599 is for him the primary idiom in which such an exploration can take place.

6

Is Man No More Than This?
Shakespeare's Ideas on Scepticism, Doubt, Stoicism, Pessimism, Misanthropy

The values of generosity, unselfish love, and forgiveness we have examined in the last chapter do not go unchallenged. In the years around 1599–1601, when he wrote *Julius Caesar*, *Hamlet*, *Troilus and Cressida*, and probably some of the late sonnets, Shakespeare seems to have taken a new and sceptical look at humanity's often misguided quest for happiness and self-knowledge. In part this shift may have been occasioned by a desire to explore new dimensions in literary and dramatic genres, in the so-called problem plays and in tragedy. He had studied the potential for tragedy in early history plays like *Richard II* and *Richard III*, *King John*, and the *Henry VI* trilogy, and had written two tragedies in *Titus Andronicus* and *Romeo and Juliet*, but not until 1599 or thereabouts did he begin to grapple more fully with issues of doubt and moral relativism. At this same time, as we have seen in Chapter 2, Shakespeare also began to consider the consequences of real, as opposed to fantasized, sexual infidelity. Misanthropy and misogyny come together in an all-embracing indictment of humanity's capacity for proving to be its own worst enemy.

Whether this new shift toward pessimism was the result of some misfortune in Shakespeare's life has long been speculated, but without any convincing evidence. The death of his only son Hamnet in 1596 was undoubtedly a terrible blow to Shakespeare, but that event occurred some years before the writing of *Hamlet*, *Troilus*, and the rest; the years immediately following Hamnet's death witnessed a succession of buoyantly upbeat plays (even if tinged with melancholy) like *Much Ado About Nothing*, *The Merry Wives of Windsor*, *As You Like It*, *Twelfth Night*, the *Henry IV* plays, and *Henry V*. Again, we must be careful not to theorize too glibly about Shakespeare's own personal views. A sounder approach, perhaps, is to regard the plays around 1599–1601 as theatrical experiments in a more disillusioning and philosophically interrogating spirit than he had previously employed. New and more sceptical questions opened up for him new avenues of thought about the human condition.

Troilus and Cressida (1601) sees the Trojan War as one in which all values become suspect. The love affair of the title characters falls apart. The war itself, in Thersites's mordant view, is an argument about 'a whore and a cuckold' (2.3.71–2), that is, Helen and her estranged husband, Menelaus. The Prologue agrees: the Greeks have come to the coast of Asia Minor 'To ransack Troy, within whose strong immures / The ravished Helen, Menelaus' queen, / With wanton Paris sleeps; and that's the quarrel' (8–10). The abduction of Helen was in turn prompted by a similar earlier event, when the Greek Telamon, father of Ajax, took as his prize Hesione, the sister of King Priam of Troy (2.2.77–80). The conflict thus began as a power struggle over women. The rights and wrongs are now so hard to determine that the leaders of both sides disagree among themselves.

In the demoralized Greek camp, Achilles keeps to his tent, refusing to fight and encouraging those around him, especially Patroclus and Thersites, to lampoon the mannerisms of the generals, especially Agamemnon and Nestor (1.3.146–78). As Ulysses laments, 'The specialty of rule hath been neglected', resulting in the formation of 'many hollow factions' (78–80):

> Oh, when degree is shaked,
> Which is the ladder to all high designs,
> The enterprise is sick. . . .
> Then everything includes itself in power,
> Power into will, will into appetite;
> And appetite, an universal wolf,
> So doubly seconded with will and power,
> Must make perforce an universal prey
> And last eat up himself.
>
> (1.3.101–24)

Anarchy and lack of respect for authority are so universal in the Greek camp that the wise observer Ulysses is himself driven to devious means in an attempt to bring Achilles and the others to their senses.

Among the Trojans, disagreement is no less sharp. Should the Trojans continue to keep Helen? The oldest and wisest of Priam's sons, Hector, argues cogently in a council of war that they should 'Let Helen go' (2.2.17). Knowing as they do that Helen is Menelaus's wife, the Trojans, in Hector's view, have a sacred obligation to honour the 'moral laws / Of nature and of nations' that 'speak aloud / To have her back returned' (184–6). Helen is 'not worth what she doth cost / The holding' (51–2). Challenging this powerful argument, Hector's younger brother Troilus offers an appeal based on a more relative set of values. 'What's aught but as 'tis valued?' he asks (52). Does not Helen's value reside in Trojan wills and desires? Having taken Helen in the conduct of such wills, how can the Trojans give Helen back? Hector has a firm answer:

> But value dwells not in particular will;
> It holds his estimate and dignity
> As well wherein 'tis precious of itself
> As in the prizer. 'Tis mad idolatry
> To make the service greater than the god;
> And the will dotes that is inclinable
> To what infectiously itself affects
> Without some image of th'affected merit.
>   (2.2.53–60)

That is to say, will is mere wilfulness when it is derived from the will's own diseased affection without some visible sign of merit in the thing desired. Hector holds to the principle that some values are inherent, in nature and in the social contracts among men. His fear of unbridled will is essentially that of Ulysses as well: it spirals downward into an appetite for will and power that ends up consuming itself. Yet Hector yields to the pressures of family loyalty. The war goes on. Hector loses his life as victim of a savage appetite for revenge that has gone out of control. Troilus, the proponent of continuing the war, learns that he must give up Cressida as a condition of that mindless continuation. Paris sleeps with Helen still, though the relationship now seems pitifully enervated and tawdry (3.1). The audience is presumably aware that Troy will shortly be burned to the ground.

The scepticism of the play thus destabilizes human ideals by exposing them to pragmatic and brutal realities. Prevalent commercial metaphors anticipate those of Thomas Hobbes, in which fixed and divinely sanctioned concepts must yield to a new gospel of value declaring that 'the value or worth of a man is, as of all other things, his price' (*Leviathan*, Chapter 10). Conflicts in the name of honour inevitably dissolve into conflicts of power. As Achilles comes to realize, fame quickly deserts the person who does not burnish his reputation with continuous accomplishments:

> men, like butterflies,
> Show not their mealy wings but to the summer,
> And not a man, for being simply man,
> Hath any honor but honor for those honors
> That are without him – as place, riches, and favor,
> Prizes of accident as oft as merit;
> Which, when they fall, as being slippery standers,
> The love that leaned on them, as slippery too,
> Doth one pluck down another and together
> Die in the fall.   (3.3.78–87)

Honour is capricious and arbitrary. It is awarded usually for external and superficial qualities such as official position, wealth, and good looks. Shakespeare may have in mind here Seneca's moral essay 'On Values' (42.1–10) and Montaigne's *Essays* (translated by John Florio, 1603, pp. 139–40). The idea here of the slipperiness of friendship is also a philosophical commonplace, as in traditional medieval images of Fortune's wheel.

In its language and structure, *Troilus and Cressida* revels in divided consciousness. 'This is and is not Cressid', laments Troilus (5.2.150), as he seeks to understand how the Cressida he has idealized in his fantasy world is so unlike the Cressida that deserts him for the Greek Diomedes. Troilus himself is caught between the boundlessness of his desire and the limits of his own physicality. 'This is the monstrosity in love, lady', he tells Cressida as they are about to consummate their love relationship, 'that the will is infinite and the execution confined, that the desire is boundless and the act a slave to limit' (3.2.80–2). Cressida knows this only too well. 'They say all lovers swear more performance than they are able', she says, 'and yet reserve an ability that they never perform, vowing more than the perfection of ten and discharging less than the tenth part of one' (83–6). The event shows how right she is. The play ends anticlimactically, in utter disillusionment, with the senseless death of Hector, the drifting apart of Troilus and Cressida, and the continuation of the war in a spirit of blind fury. The very disjunctive and non-sequential character of the plot is itself a wry comment on the destructive interplay of lechery and war. The play is unusually rich in contrastive styles, with a striking number of newly coined words tending to reinforce the negative: 'disorbed', 'distaste', 'uncomprehensive', 'languageless', and still more. Images of cooking and the spoiling of food underscore the play's obsession with self-consuming appetite, as when Troilus bitterly laments of Cressida that 'The fractions of her faith, orts of her love, / The fragments, scraps, the bits and greasy relics / Of her o'ereaten faith, are bound to Diomed' (5.2.162–4). 'Fractions' are fragments; 'orts' are leftovers. Cressida's desertion signals for Troilus the falling apart of the universe itself: 'The bonds of heaven are slipped, dissolved, and loosed' (160).

Hamlet's preoccupations are of a similar kind. Images of decay, disorder, sterility, and sickness abound. Hamlet's disillusionment about his father's death and his mother's overhasty marriage expands into a generalized disappointment about the human condition:

> Oh, God, God,
> How weary, stale, flat, and unprofitable
> Seem to me all the uses of this world!
> Fie on't, ah, fie! 'Tis an unweeded garden
> That grows to seed. Things rank and gross in nature
> Possess it merely.   (1.2.132–7)

To Rosencrantz and Guildenstern he admits that he has lost all his mirth and that 'this goodly frame, the earth, seems to me a sterile promontory; this most excellent canopy, the air, look you, this brave o'erhanging firmament, this majestical roof fretted with golden fire, why, it appeareth nothing to me but a foul and pestilent congregation of vapors' (2.2.299–304). The problem then is not with the world itself but with those who have corrupted it and themselves. 'What a piece of work is a man! How noble in reason, how infinite in faculties, in form and moving how express and admirable, in action how like an angel, in apprehension how like a god! The beauty of the world, the paragon of animals! And yet, to me, what is this quintessence of dust?' (304–9). Again and again, Hamlet's inquiring mind and melancholy disposition lead him into a broad and desolate view of the vanity of human wishes. Ophelia's grave prompts him to reflect on the unavoidable condition of death and the consequent end of all human striving. 'Alexander died, Alexander was buried, Alexander returneth to dust, the dust is earth, of earth we make loam, and why of that loam whereto he was converted might they not stop a beer barrel?' (5.1.209–12). The thought is, to be sure, a commonplace, derived from the rite for the burial of the dead ('ashes to ashes, dust to dust'), Ecclesiastes ('Vanity of vanities, saith the Preacher, vanity of vanities; all is vanity', 1.2), and similar texts, and does at last offer Hamlet some comfort in his reflection that death is a great equalizer and a terminator of injustice; but until he reaches that point his view of life is darkly pessimistic.

Hamlet is especially distressed by the sexual behaviour of his mother and her new husband, Hamlet's uncle. The marriage is incestuous, both to Hamlet and to his father's ghost. Even before Hamlet learns the truth of what the Ghost has to tell him about the murder, Hamlet deplores the 'dexterity' with which his mother has posted 'to incestuous sheets' (1.2.156–7). The Ghost holds to the same view: Claudius is 'that incestuous, that adulterate beast' against whom he adjures Hamlet to proceed lest 'the royal bed of Denmark be / A couch for luxury [lechery] and damnèd incest' (1.5.43, 83–4). Hamlet longs to kill Claudius 'When he is drunk asleep, or in his rage, / Or in th'incestuous pleasure of his bed' (3.3.89–90). When he does at last stab Claudius fatally and force him to drink from the poisoned cup, Hamlet addresses the King as 'thou incestuous, murderous, damnèd Dane' (5.2.327). Most people nowadays do not regard marriage of a man with his deceased brother's wife as incestuous, but it is akin to the marriage of a man with his deceased wife's sister that so agitated British public opinion in the nineteenth century, and can come within the purview of forbidden unions if a society so determines. In Hamlet's case, incest clearly adds to the horror.

Hamlet hates to think of what his mother has done, and yet he dwells on it obsessively. 'Let me not think on't; frailty, thy name is woman!' (1.2.146). Gertrude's failure to honour her dead husband's memory is generalized into an indictment of all women. When he arraigns his mother in person, he explodes with fury at her polluted act. 'Have you eyes? / Could you on this fair mountain leave to feed / And batten on this moor?' (3.4.66–8). He is outraged that she still has sexual feeling at all. 'At your age / The heyday in the blood is tame, it's humble, / And waits upon the judgment' (69–71). Evidently Hamlet is of the view that sexual desire ceases, or at least should cease, at menopause in women, since they are past childbearing age and have no reason for practising sex other than out of absolute lust. 'Rebellious hell', he exclaims, 'If thou canst mutine in a matron's bones, / To flaming youth let virtue be as wax / And melt in her own fire' (83–6). Women of matronly years should set an example of restraint for younger women, not of unseemly desire. The image of Gertrude and Claudius as sexual partners is unbearable for Hamlet, and yet he cannot let it go. 'Nay, but to live / In the rank sweat of an enseamèd bed', he accuses her, 'Stewed in corruption, honeying and making love / Over the nasty sty!' (93–6). 'Enseamèd' here means saturated in the grease and filth of passionate lovemaking. Hamlet leaves his mother with a warning that again betrays his prurient curiosity about her sexual behaviour. He would not have her do what he ironically bids her to do, that is,

> Let the bloat king tempt you again to bed,
> Pinch wanton on your cheek, call you his mouse,
> And let him, for a pair of reechy kisses,
> Or paddling in your neck with his damned fingers,
> Make you to ravel all this matter out
> That I essentially am not in madness,
> But mad in craft.   (3.4.189–95)

Gertrude's carnality is thus for Hamlet an emblem of the fallen condition of the world he no longer wishes to inhabit.

Part of what Hamlet finds so depressing in human behaviour is its complacent mediocrity and its fatuous belief in its own powers of observation. Polonius is a special target of his ire. 'If circumstances lead me, I will find / Where truth is hid, though it were hid indeed / Within the center' (2.2.157–9), Polonius solemnly assures the King and Queen by way of asserting his ability to clear up the mystery of Hamlet's erratic goings-on. Sure enough, Polonius has no doubt that he has 'found / The very cause of Hamlet's lunacy' (48–9), namely, that Hamlet is mad for love of Ophelia. Who could doubt this wise conclusion? 'Hath there been such a time – I would fain know that –', he asks the King and Queen, 'That I have positively said " 'Tis so," /

When it proved otherwise?' (153–5). Polonius is confident of knowing the answer because he professes to understand all about falling in love. 'Truly in my youth I suffered much extremity for love, very near this', he reflects (189–91). Polonius's professional reputation is at stake: it is his business to know everything that goes on at court. Polonius is thus the perfect opposite of what Hamlet believes, that one must strive to know oneself and be aware that such knowledge is extraordinarily difficult to achieve, since human beings are infinitely complex. Hamlet sees himself as especially so. For that reason he resents and detests the intrusive efforts of others to figure him out.

Rosencrantz and Guildenstern are no less guilty, in Hamlet's view, of callow intellectual arrogance. They assume that Hamlet is frustrated in his political ambition to be king, as well we might expect them to do, since they themselves think in just such political terms. Hamlet leads them on in this supposition, and then launches into a tirade against such pitiful oversimplification. Inviting them to play on a recorder – a thing no one can do without diligent practice – and eliciting from them a confession that they have not the skill to play the recorder, Hamlet spells out for them the lesson of their foolishness in presuming that they can plumb the mystery of something vastly more complex than a musical instrument:

> Why, look you now, how unworthy a thing you make of me! You would play upon me, you would seem to know my stops, you would pluck out the heart of my mystery, you would sound me from my lowest note to the top of my compass, and there is much music, excellent voice, in this little organ, yet cannot you make it speak. 'Sblood, do you think I am easier to be played on than a pipe? Call me what instrument you will, though you can fret me, you cannot play upon me. (3.2.362–71)

Two ideas seem especially important to Hamlet in this passage: the uniqueness of the individual, and the difficulty of knowing. As one who attempts to know himself, he has nothing but impatience for those who think they have everything figured out.

The person Hamlet most loves and admires, Horatio, is one with whom he can share a disdain for such worldly folly. Horatio is a stoic. Shakespeare uses the word only once in all his writings, and then only in a lighthearted moment in *The Taming of the Shrew* when the servant Tranio urges his master, Lucentio, that they not apply themselves too diligently to their studies: 'Let's be no stoics nor no stocks, I pray, / Or so devote to Aristotle's checks / As Ovid be an outcast quite abjured' (1.1.31–3). Yet even without the explicit epithet of 'stoic', Horatio is an admirable practitioner of that Roman ethic. He is, as Hamlet praises him, 'one, in suffering all, that suffers nothing, / A man that Fortune's buffets and rewards / Hast ta'en with equal thanks' (3.2.65–7). Shakespeare is sufficiently conversant with stoic philosophy to understand that true stoicism cannot be defined simply as the ability to withstand adverse luck; one must also resist the temptation to hope for anything that Fortune can bestow. Hamlet has only admiration for such persons. 'Blest are those / Whose blood and judgment are so well commeddled / That they are not a pipe for Fortune's finger / To sound what stop she please', he says to Horatio. 'Give me that man / That is not passion's slave, and I will wear him / In my heart's core, ay, in my heart of heart, / As I do thee' (67–73). Hamlet longs to be like Horatio. Stoical philosophy offers rich consolations for one who is faced with agonizing decisions, as Hamlet is; such a philosophy invites one to consider whether forthright action is best, or whether one should adopt a more passive and reflective invulnerability to the assaults of injustice and misfortune. The passive view does not address the Ghost's command that Hamlet perform an act of revenge, but it has its attractions nonetheless.

Horatio is also a sceptic in the sense of not being easily taken in by myths and legends. He is sceptical about ghosts. 'Tush, tush, 'twill not appear', he assures the guard on watch as they await the reappearance of the ghostly spirit the guardsmen have twice seen (1.1.34). When the Ghost does in fact appear, Horatio is convinced: 'Before my God, I might not this believe / Without the sensible and true avouch / Of mine own eyes' (60–2). Horatio is an empiricist who insists on tangible and verifiable evidence. Now that he has such evidence, he credits the thing of which he was sceptical before. The testimony of such a scientifically minded gentleman does much to reify the ghost of this play: for the purposes of *Hamlet*, the Ghost is undeniably real.

For all their mutual fondness and admiration, Horatio and Hamlet disagree about scepticism. Hamlet is eager to convince Horatio that he is taking a wrong philosophical approach to things. When Horatio has marvelled at the strangeness of the Ghost's bidding him and Marcellus to swear to keep their vows of silence about what they have seen, Hamlet urges him to take the lesson to heart. 'There are more things in heaven and earth, Horatio, / Than are dreamt of in your philosophy' (1.5.175–6). By 'your philosophy' Hamlet means this subject called 'natural philosophy' or 'science' that one hears so much talk about. One can imagine these two dear friends arguing about this matter at length during their student days in Wittenberg; now, the crisis to which Hamlet finds himself subjected lends new urgency to what had been a philosophical debate. Why does Shakespeare make such a point of contrasting Hamlet and Horatio on the subject of scepticism?

Hamlet is a Christian. For all his profound disillusionment about people, he holds to a belief in the supreme deity. 'Angels and ministers of grace defend us!' he exclaims when he sees his father's Ghost for the first time (1.4.39). 'O all you host of heaven!' (1.5.93). He regretfully wishes that 'the Everlasting had not fixed / His canon 'gainst self-slaughter' (1.2.131–2); suicide might appeal to him as a solution to his world-weariness if it were not forbidden by divine command. Although death is 'a consummation / Devoutly to be wished', one comes up against a 'rub' when one considers how to die: 'in that sleep of death what dreams may come, / When we have shuffled off this mortal coil, / Must give us pause' (3.1.64–9). Even if the afterlife is an 'undiscovered country from whose bourn / No traveler returns' (80–1; an odd observation in view of the fact that Hamlet has just been talking with his father's Ghost returned from Purgatory), Hamlet does not doubt that some kind of existence will continue after the body's death. Hamlet knows that 'the devil hath power / T'assume a pleasing shape' and that the devil 'is very potent' with sufferers of melancholy like himself (2.2.600–3). Damnation is an ever-present danger: perhaps, Hamlet speculates, the devil 'Abuses me to damn me' (604). He sees himself as existing in a cosmic arena, with his own soul as the prize being fought over by the forces of good and evil. 'What should such fellows as I do crawling between earth and heaven?' (3.1.128–30). In Chapter 5 we saw his knowledgeable acquaintance with Catholic church liturgy regarding last rites. He hesitates to kill Claudius at prayer for fear that Claudius would then go to heaven (3.3.74–5). His Christian faith thus complicates his mission of revenge. Yet when the time approaches for the completion of that task, Hamlet's religious faith seems to come to his assistance. Assured that 'There's a divinity that shapes our ends, / Rough-hew them how we will' (5.2.10–11), Hamlet comes to the philosophical conclusion that 'There is special providence in the fall of a sparrow', and that 'If it be now, 'tis not to come . . . The readiness is all' (217–20). 'Let be' (222), he counsels Horatio. This sounds close in some ways to Horatio's stoicism, but it is a Christian stoicism that places all events in the hands of Providence. As such it is profoundly at odds with Horatio's Roman scepticism.

Hamlet and Horatio thus have markedly different interpretations of the tragic story now coming to its close. To Hamlet, the events of the play's last scene appear to confirm his belief in a 'special providence' that controls and makes use of every seeming accident for its own purposes. Hamlet's killing of Polonius in his mother's chambers, he sees, was an error on his part, and one of distressingly unhappy consequences for Laertes and Ophelia, but it has led ineluctably by a chain of events to Laertes's return to Denmark determined to avenge his father's death, his conspiring with Claudius to kill Hamlet by means of a poisoned sword or poisoned cup, and his entering into a duel with Hamlet that concludes not with what Laertes or anyone else has expected but with the deaths of himself, Hamlet, Gertrude, and Claudius. Hamlet obtains his revenge without committing premeditated murder, and dies honourably as he has long wished. This is the sense in which he has hoped to be heaven's 'scourge and minister' (3.4.182), providing human agency for heaven's purposes in punishing those who deserve to be punished and rewarding those who deserve reward.

Horatio's grief at the death of Hamlet does not prevent him from seeing Hamlet's story in very different terms. When he has his chance to 'speak to th' yet unknowing world' as to how so many deaths have come about, his account will stress accident and mistaken human agency devoid of any transcendental explanation:

> So shall you hear
> Of carnal, bloody, and unnatural acts,
> Of accidental judgments, casual slaughters,
> Of deaths put on by cunning and forced cause,
> And, in this upshot, purposes mistook
> Fall'n on the inventors' heads.   (5.2.382–7)

'Casual' means 'occurring by chance'. Horatio does see a pattern in this history, but it is a profoundly secular and ironic one; it tells of human beings who are their own worst enemies and who bring down upon themselves a catastrophe that is deserved even while it is unexpected. Shakespeare, with his characteristic delight in debate, offers us a dual explanation in which the alternatives are mutually incompatible. Perhaps we can see this as a way in which the play of *Hamlet* is itself so profoundly sceptical.

Julius Caesar, written about the same time as *Hamlet*, is sceptical about history in ways that resemble the scepticism of Horatio, who, after all, declares in Act 5 of *Hamlet*, as he attempts to take poison, 'I am more an antique Roman than a Dane' (5.2.343). The pagan world of ancient Rome provides Shakespeare a forum in which to explore philosophical ideas without the surrounding context of Christianity that we find in *Hamlet*. As a result, we can see in *Julius Caesar* that Shakespeare has a firm grasp on Roman ideas about scepticism and stoicism. He seems particularly attracted to the philosophical ideas of Cicero.

In the stormy night before the assassination of Julius Caesar on the ides of March (historically 44 BC), many wonders are reported to have occurred. Our interest here is in how various Romans respond to and interpret these alleged events. Casca, for one, has been characterized in scene 2 of the play as sardonically scornful of the adulation bestowed on Caesar by 'the common herd' and of Caesar's courting their favour by offering his throat to be cut. 'There's no heed to be taken of them', Casca concludes. 'There was more foolery yet, if I could remember it' (1.2.263–87). Casca is what we might call a cynic, though not in the historical philosophical sense of one who holds that virtue is the only good and that its essence lies in self-control and independence; he is instead a faultfinding, captious critic who is contemptuously distrustful of human nature and motives, believing as he does that human nature is motivated wholly by self-interest. All the more remarkable, for that reason, is his response to the stormy night. Breathless and staring wildly, he relates to Cicero what he has seen or heard. A common slave 'Held up his left hand, which did flame and burn / Like twenty torches joined, and yet his hand, / Not sensible of fire, remained unscorched'. Casca vouches that he personally 'met a lion, / Who glazed upon me and went surly by / Without annoying me'. He has talked with 'a hundred ghastly women, / Transformèd by their fear, who swore they saw / Men all in fire walk up and down the streets'. Reportedly, an owl 'did sit / Even at noonday in the marketplace, / Hooting and shrieking' (1.3.15–28). Some of this is second-hand report; some is direct testimony of what Casca himself has seen. In any event, the cynical Casca is in a panic of fear. He has become persuaded by sheer terror. He gives no credit to those who might say these events are reasonable and natural; 'I believe they are portentous things / Unto the climate that they point upon' (30–2).

Cicero, throughout this recitation, maintains his calm. His considered view is that strange events may indeed be taking place, but that thoughtful persons must be wary of interpretation:

> Indeed, it is a strange-disposèd time.
> But men may construe things after their fashion,
> Clean from the purpose of the things themselves.
>
> (1.3.33–5)

The reason for caution in interpreting what one hears or sees is that anyone is prone to evaluate events according to personal predisposition. The interpretation is apt to say more about the observer than about the thing supposedly observed or heard about.

Cicero is, for Shakespeare, the wise philosopher and statesman, choosing to side with the republican cause because of his hatred of tyranny but also acting as a moderating force and insisting above all on calm, deliberative reasoning. The conspirators consider drafting him as one of their members because of his 'judgment' and 'gravity', and because 'his silver hairs / Will purchase us a good opinion / And buy men's voices to commend our deeds', but they decide against asking him because 'he will never follow anything / That other men begin' (2.1.141–54). That is, Cicero is too independent for their purposes. Historically, indeed, he held aloof from conspiracy, choosing instead to guide policy as well as he could by his 'Philippics' in the Senate after the assassination of Caesar. Cicero was highly regarded in the Renaissance, as orator, statesman, and philosopher. Yet in *Julius Caesar* Cicero becomes a victim of the increasing polarization in Rome that he has attempted to prevent. At Philippi, Brutus receives a report of seventy senators that have died by the proscriptions of Antony and Octavius, 'Cicero being one'. Cassius can scarcely believe the news. 'Cicero one?' Messala confirms the stark truth: 'Cicero is dead, / And by that order of proscription' (4.3.177–9). Proscription is the branding of a man as an outlaw, the confiscation of his property, the offering of a reward for his murder, and the prohibition of his offspring from holding public office – a devastating penalty, especially for one who was such a great public figure. Cicero's death symbolizes more than any other single event the sad, ironic failure of a rebellion against tyranny that has had the effect only of impairing Rome's liberties.

Shakespeare thus gives Cicero a central role in defining how one should attempt to determine truth in difficult times. Cassius's response to the stormy night before the assassination is markedly and characteristically different. He boasts to Casca that he has

> walked about the streets,
> Submitting me unto the perilous night,
> And thus unbracèd, Casca, as you see,
> Have bared my bosom to the thunder-stone;
> And when the cross blue lightning seemed to open
> The breast of heaven, I did present myself
> Even in the aim and very flash of it.   (1.3.46–52)

Even to the sardonic Casca, this tempting the heavens is reckless and impious. 'It is the part of men to fear and tremble / When the most mighty gods by tokens send / Such dreadful heralds to astonish us', he protests (53–6). But Cassius will have none of this. He insists that he knows 'the true cause' of all these fires and 'gliding ghosts', namely, that 'heaven hath infused them with these spirits / To make them instruments of fear and warning / Unto some monstrous state' (62–71). If the heavens are angry, it is because of Caesar's hubris. Cassius thus dares to unfasten his doublet to the thunderbolt and lightning. The gesture is at once psychological and philosophical: Cassius is choleric and intemperate, but he is also an epicurean. 'You know that I held Epicurus strong / And his opinion' (5.1.80–1), he says to Messala at Philippi as they brace themselves for battle with the forces of Antony and Octavius.

Again, Shakespeare seems to have a solid grasp of ancient philosophy. By 'epicurean' Cassius does not mean, in the familiar modern sense, that he is a bon vivant, taking pleasure in eating and drinking and preening himself as a connoisseur with a fastidious taste for the voluptuous. Shakespeare does, to be sure, employ the term in this sense elsewhere: 'Epicurean cooks, / Sharpen with cloyless sauce his appetite', says Pompey of Antony in *Antony and Cleopatra* (2.1.24–5), and 'What a damned Epicurean rascal is this!' says Master Ford of the lecherous

Falstaff in *The Merry Wives of Windsor* (2.2.275). 'Epicurism' is equated with lust in *King Lear* (1.4.241). Cassius means to the contrary that, like Epicurus, he has believed the gods to be indifferent to human affairs, for which reason he has spurned superstitious belief in omens. As a hedonist of the true epicurean stripe committed to the doctrine that happiness or pleasure is the sole or chief good in life, Cassius has striven (not always successfully) toward the highest good, namely an imperturbable emotional calm; and because intellectual pleasure is to be preferred before all other pleasures, Cassius has attempted to renounce the momentary in favour of more permanent pleasures. Now, at Philippi, without turning his back on the idea of philosophical calm, Cassius is partly ready to 'credit things that do presage' (5.1.82). Two eagles that have accompanied the republican forces to Philippi have deserted them, leaving nothing but 'ravens, crows, and kites' to look downward on the beleaguered soldiers 'As we were sickly prey' (83–90). Cassius believes in the ominousness of this sign only partly (93), but he has abandoned the intellectual and philosophical arrogance with which he arraigned Casca in 1.3. Like Cicero, he has learned to doubt wisely. This wisdom is too late to save the republican venture from defeat, but it does tend to confirm that Cicero was right. The idea is Platonic as well: our best wisdom as frail mortals is to know that we understand practically nothing of importance. Shakespeare seems very drawn to this idea in a play where the consequences of such a view are borne out by the action of the plot. The protagonists in Rome's struggle for power have no way of guessing what will be the result of all their efforts. The sustained and at times almost comic ironies of *Coriolanus* lead to a similarly dispiriting conclusion.

Brutus is presented in *Julius Caesar* as a stoic, even though that term is not used. His response to the stormy night is, like Casca's or Cassius's or Cicero's, in character. He is oblivious to the portents that so amaze most Romans. 'The exhalations whizzing in the air / Give so much light that I may read by them' (2.1.44–5), he observes to himself as he opens a letter thrown in his window urging him to come to the rescue of Rome's liberties. The remarkable phenomena in the night sky are nothing more to him than a means of illuminating the letter he is reading. His calm is both temperamental and philosophical. He believes that a wise man should free himself from passions of joy or grief, and should make every effort possible to be indifferent to pleasure or pain.

The test case for Brutus, as it is for any stoic believer, is the loss of any family member or spouse. Should the true stoic be indifferent to the death of one who is so close and dear? Brutus's attachment to Portia is very strong. She is the daughter of the Cato the Younger of Ithaca famous for having sided with Pompey the Great against Julius Caesar in 48 BC and for having committing suicide rather than submit to Caesar's tyranny. Portia is like her father in personal integrity. She has shown her strength of resolution by giving herself 'a voluntary wound' in her thigh simply to demonstrate her constancy (2.1.300–2). Brutus admires his wife with sincere and mature devotion. 'O ye gods, / Render me worthy of this noble wife!' he exclaims (303–4), when she justly reproaches him for not sharing with her his anxieties about his dealings with the conspirators. Accordingly, when Brutus receives at Philippi the report of Portia's having 'swallowed fire' (4.3.155) in a dauntingly painful and courageous suicide rather than outlive the infamy of Brutus's imminent defeat (Plutarch, in Thomas North's translation, writes that she 'took hot burning coals and cast them in her mouth, and kept her mouth so close that she choked herself'), we as audience are naturally curious to know how Brutus will take the news.

Interestingly, the text of *Julius Caesar* gives us two different accounts. The seeming redundancy used to be regarded as a textual confusion resulting from the Folio compositor's having failed to delete one that had been marked for cancellation. Instead, the double report is now generally viewed as Shakespeare's intentional way of indicating Brutus's divided state of mind. In the first version, Brutus and Cassius are alone; they have quarrelled terribly, so much so that Brutus now offers as his excuse that he is 'sick of many griefs'. Cassius, understandably, takes Brutus up short on this point: 'Of your philosophy you make no use / If you give place to accidental evils' (143–5). Brutus is known for being a noble stoic: how can he give in to grief? Brutus's answer is eloquent in its stark simplicity: 'No man bears sorrow better. Portia is dead' (146). Cassius realizes that the classic challenge to stoical philosophy has just presented itself. 'How scaped I killing when I crossed you so?' he offers by way of apology. The two say little more than this. 'O ye immortal gods!' is Cassius's final comment. What can one possibly say on such an occasion? The silence is eloquent: they both feel the loss, and share its terrible burden in wordless communion. 'Speak no more of her', says Brutus (149–57).

But then other officers arrive, one of them bringing the news of Portia's death that Brutus and Cassius have already shared in private.

Messala is reluctant to be the bearer of sad tidings, but Brutus will have none of this reluctance; knowing that something is amiss, he insists, in the best tradition of the Roman stiff upper lip, 'Now, as you are a Roman, tell me true' (186). When Messala then reports that Portia 'is dead, and by strange manner', Brutus asks for no further details. 'Why, farewell, Portia. We must die, Messala. / With meditating that she must die once, / I have the patience to endure it now' (188–91). Messala is amazed, even though he knows Brutus's reputation for stoic resolve: 'Even so great men great losses should endure.' Cassius joins in, though having heard the news earlier in the scene: 'I have as much of this in art as you, / But yet my nature could not bear it so.' By 'art' he must mean the acquired philosophical wisdom of stoicism as contrasted with what human 'nature' can muster on its own. Brutus cuts off the discussion: 'Well, to our work alive' (192–5). In company, then, Brutus plays out his role as stoic, having had time beforehand to arm himself with the appearance of calm. We see both the deep, unspoken personal grief and the public stance that goes with Brutus's public persona. Presumably he means this as an inspirational model for his soldiers; certainly Messala takes it that way. Shakespeare shows us the inner as well as the outer man, dramatizing the philosophical problem for which stoicism was so celebrated.

Julius Caesar offers still another study in contradiction. He is not identifiably a stoic or epicurean or disciple of any other philosophical school; he is a man on horseback. He does not even bother to theorize his claims to absolute authority. Like Bolingbroke in *1 Henry IV* (see Chapter 3), he acts in a simple belief that he is the best answer to a politically divided state. Caesar's self-confidence is at once his besetting weakness and the key to his amazing success. He cannot admit fear in himself, even though he knows that he has dangerous enemies. 'If my name were liable to fear', he tells Antony, 'I do not know the man I should avoid / So soon as that spare Cassius.' 'I rather tell thee what is to be feared / Than what I fear, for always I am Caesar' (1.2.199–212). He dares to confront danger itself as though it were a personal enemy: 'Danger knows full well / That Caesar is more dangerous than he. / We are two lions littered in one day, / And I the elder and more terrible' (2.2.44–7). Well might his wife Calpurnia say to him by way of admonition, 'Your wisdom is consumed in confidence' (49). Caesar freely acknowledges that what is 'purposed by the mighty gods' cannot be avoided, and that 'death, a necessary end, / Will come when it will come' (26–37), and yet his last statement before he is killed is to boast that he is 'constant as the northern star', being the only mortal on earth 'That unassailable holds on his rank, / Unshaked of motion' (3.1.61–71). His greatest weakness is to be utterly confident that he is not superstitious or vulnerable to flattery, when in practice he bids the priests do 'present sacrifice' (2.2.5) on the night before the Ides of March and then ignores their advice and that of his wife to stay at home. Decius Brutus need only appeal to his sense of vanity by warning that the senators will laugh at him if he heeds the council of his soothsayers and his wife. To Calpurnia's warning that she has dreamed of Caesar's statue running with pure blood while smiling Romans bathe their hands in it, Decius has the perfect flattering answer: the dream signifies that from such a bleeding statue 'great Rome shall suck / Reviving blood' (2.2.87–8). Caesar's response to the stormy night is in character, like that of Casca, Cassius, Cicero, and Brutus. He is his own worst enemy, the mightiest man of Rome and yet unwittingly complicit in his own undoing.

Julius Caesar is thus, among its other achievements, the story of great philosophical ideas in conflict. Those ideas seem to do their adherents little practical good. Cicero is slaughtered for his moderation. Caesar's wisdom cannot instruct him to know himself. Cassius comes too late to understand that what men believe, no matter how fiercely, must surrender to a deep uncertainty about the nature of gods and men. Brutus's stoicism leads him into a seemingly unresolvable ambiguity about the ethics of suicide. When asked by Cassius what he intends to do if they lose in battle to Antony and Octavius, Brutus is ready with a refutation of the very notion of taking one's own life:

> Even by the rule of that philosophy
> By which I did blame Cato for the death
> Which he did give himself – I know not how,
> But I find it cowardly and vile,
> For fear of what might fall, so to prevent
> The time of life – arming myself with patience
> To stay the providence of some high powers
> That govern us below.   (5.1.104–11)

Brutus would prefer not to follow the example of his father-in-law, Marcus Porcius Cato, Portia's father, who killed himself to avoid submission to Caesar in 46 BC. A true stoic must obey the will of higher powers and suffer misfortune with patience. Yet moments later, when asked by Cassius if he would be content to be led in triumph through the streets of Rome, Brutus is adamant:

> No, Cassius, no. Think not, thou noble Roman,
> That ever Brutus will go bound to Rome;
> He bears too great a mind. (114–16)

And so it is that when Brutus faces certain defeat, after the suicides of Cassius and Titinius, Brutus too runs on his own sword. He is 'Free from the bondage' that Messala and others are in. 'Brutus only overcame himself.' He is accorded in death a splendid tribute by Mark Antony, as one whose 'life was gentle', with 'the elements / So mixed in him that Nature might stand up / And say to all the world, "This was a man!"' (5.5.54–75). As an embodiment of stoicism, Shakespeare's Brutus shows to us what is at once noble and self-contradictory about that philosophy. Other characters reveal their inner weaknesses in similar ways. Cicero fares best in this competition of ideas, perhaps, because his quiet insistence that men 'may construe things after their fashion, / Clean from the purpose of the things themselves' is so tellingly confirmed in Shakespeare's dramatization of a great moment of history. This is one sense in which *Julius Caesar* is such a sceptical play.

Whether Shakespeare was also acquainted with the philosophical ideas of Epictetus, Cicero, and Seneca that go under the name of libertinism is a question that deserves some consideration. Adherents or admirers of this philosophical school, including John Donne, Michel de Montaigne, Sir Francis Bacon, and Thomas Harriot among others in the Renaissance period, maintained that reason and nature should take precedence over ideas of divine revelation. 'Natural' philosophy encouraged the study of the physical universe as a way of attempting to recover the ideals of the Golden Age. Shakespeare, as usual, avoids philosophical labels; although Jaques in *As You Like It* is characterized by Duke Senior as a 'libertine' (2.7.65), and Corin is addressed by Touchstone as a 'natural philosopher' (3.2.30), these phrases simply suggest licentiousness in the first instance and folk wisdom in the second without recourse to the history of ancient philosophy. At the same time, the ideas of natural reason and of a sceptical approach to divine revelation clearly did fascinate Shakespeare. No doubt he could have encountered these ideas in the intellectual culture of London, whether or not he read directly in philosophical treatises. The ideas percolate especially in *Othello* and *King Lear*.

The clash of ideologies in *Othello* and *King Lear* centres to a considerable extent on the existential challenges posed by Iago and Edmund to conventional ideas of moral order. Both men are disturbingly 'modern' in their scorn for traditional notions of morality; both are highly rational, intelligent, inventive, self-reliant, and confident that their gospels of self-promotion offer a sure key to success. The older order is vulnerable to their attack because of its trust in a concept of world order that, from a modern point of view, can be seen as superstitious and naïve. We as modern audiences and readers are made uneasy by the way in which the villains of these two plays are so intelligently iconoclastic.

Iago is a consummate deceiver. At the same time, he is arguably in the grip of a psychotic fantasy of jealousy and hatred. He is also the most audacious and compelling thinker in the play. His creed is one of self-reliance. 'Virtue? A fig!' he exclaims to Roderigo, when that hapless Venetian has complained that he lacks the 'virtue' to do anything about his infatuated desire for a woman (Desdemona) who ignores his advances. 'Virtue' here means strength, nature. Iago is contemptuous of the notion that anyone could be so lacking in will power. ''Tis in ourselves that we are thus or thus', he lectures. 'Our bodies are our gardens, to the which our wills are gardeners.' We have the ability to make choices, to foster the qualities in ourselves that best serve our purposes. The key for Iago, indeed, is reason. 'If the beam of our lives had not one scale of reason to poise another of sensuality, the blood and baseness of our natures would conduct us to most preposterous conclusions.' Iago is a realist about human nature, seeing in it an inevitable gravitating toward fleshly indulgence and laziness. Only by our minds can we right the balance and reassert control. 'We have reason to cool our raging motions, our carnal stings, our unbitted lusts.' Love is to him nothing better than a 'sect or scion', a cutting or offshoot, of this innate human carnality (1.3.320–35).

Iago's ability at times to control his own emotions, which he knows to be potentially unruly, gives him the advantage he needs to outmanoeuvre his victims. The weak-willed Roderigo is putty in his hands. Michael Cassio is similarly at a disadvantage. Knowing Cassio's infirmity as a drinker with a penchant for quarrelsomeness when under the influence of alcohol, Iago tempts Cassio into drinking as he is about to go on watch and then foments a quarrel between Roderigo and Cassio that ends in Cassio's dismissal from Othello's service. Iago is quick to sermonize on this sadly edifying spectacle. 'You see this fellow that is gone before', he says of Cassio to Montano. 'He's a soldier fit to stand by Caesar / And give direction; and do but see his vice. / 'Tis to his virtue a just equinox, / The one as long as th'other. 'Tis pity of him' (2.3.115–19). Virtue and vice, reason and sensual appetite, again stand opposite to one another in Iago's cosmology. He himself knows how to drink moderately without losing control. Iago similarly exploits Cassio's weakness for women by inveigling Cassio into a mirthful conversation about Bianca, Cassio's mistress, when Othello thinks he is overhearing a conversation about Cassio's love for Desdemona (4.1.109–45). Subsequently, Iago accuses Bianca of being complicit in the fighting that results in the wounding of Roderigo and Cassio – a quarrel for which Iago is himself to blame (5.1.85–112). 'This is the fruits of whoring', he piously intones (118). The fact that Bianca keeps company with Cassio, and is known to be a courtesan, is 'evidence' enough for Iago to be able to convince his hearers that Bianca is part of a plot. Iago can don the guise of the Puritan to good use when it serves his purposes of extolling the virtues of controlling carnal desires.

Iago not only praises the ascendancy of reason over emotion; he demonstrates that ascendancy by his own brilliance as a tactician in logical argument. His chief weapon is the syllogism. How is he to convince Roderigo that Desdemona is in love with Cassio? He begins with the axiomatic proposition that what people call 'love' is 'merely a lust of the blood and a permission of the will'. It follows that Desdemona's and Othello's love for each other is of this kind, since they are both human and thus subject to the generalization about love as wilful lust. 'It cannot be long that Desdemona should continue her love to the Moor . . . nor he his to her.' Moreover, their temperaments are such that they are sure to be incompatible: Moors 'are change- able in their wills', whereas Desdemona is a young woman subject like all such women to the desire for mates of their own age and inclina- tion. 'She must change for youth; when she is sated with his body, she must find the error of her choice. She must have change, she must' (1.3.337–54). The word 'must' underscores the syllogistic force of the argument: Desdemona is a young woman; young women desire mates of their own kind; Othello is an older man and a 'Moor'; ergo, therefore, she 'must' change.

'Nature' is also operative in such an irresistible chain of presumed causality. Desdemona's eye 'must be fed', Iago instructs Roderigo, 'and what delight shall she have to look on the devil? When the blood is made dull with the act of sport, there should be, again to inflame it and to give satiety a fresh appetite, loveliness in favor, sympathy in years, manners, and beauties – all which the Moor is defective in.' Again, Iago's axiomatic proposition is that love is lust and appetite; if one grants that, the rest follows logically enough. According to this train of thought, the love of a young white woman for an older black general is not 'natural'. 'Very nature will instruct her in . . . some second choice.' The next question is a simple and inevitable one: who will be Desdemona's second choice? 'Now, sir, this granted – as it is a most pregnant and unforced position – who stands so eminent in the degree of this fortune as Cassio does?' (2.1.228–40). Iago insists on the logical irresistibility of his syllogism. If one grants that 'nature' will turn Desdemona's appetite toward new interests – how could it be otherwise? – and if one specifies that the characteristics she will desire in a new mate are necessarily those of youth, handsomeness, and good manners, then how could one conclude other than that Cassio is the man? Roderigo is reluctant to accept this conclusion, because he believes Desdemona to be 'of most blessed condition', meaning that he questions Iago's premise about her necessarily sharing the appetites of other young women, but Iago has an answer for that too: 'Blessed fig's end! The wine she drinks is made of grapes' (252–5). The implied logic here again is unassailable in syllogistic terms: young women (like all young people) have sensual appetites; Desdemona is a young woman; ergo, Desdemona has sensual appetites. Roderigo quickly surrenders to this argument and proceeds to do as Iago instructs him.

Othello is of course Iago's chief target. Once again, Iago's weapon is 'logical' argument proceeding from axiomatic premises to nominally unassailable conclusions. His argument is essentially the one that he has used with Roderigo: 'natural' inclination will inevitably teach Desdemona the error of her choice. Having prodded Othello into wondering 'how nature erring from itself' might generate in Desdemona a restlessness about her marriage, Iago pounces:

> Ay, there's the point! As – to be bold with you –
> Not to affect many proposèd matches
> Of her own clime, complexion, and degree,

Whereto we see in all things nature tends –
Foh! One may smell in such a will most rank,
Foul disproportion, thoughts unnatural.

(3.3.244–9)

Iago has of course no physical evidence – how could he? Desdemona
has done nothing of the sort. Iago must instead rely on the syllogistic
argument, proceeding from a premise of what constitutes 'natural'
behaviour to the conclusion that Desdemona, being human and a
woman, must behave as women purportedly do.

Iago must also get Othello to agree to this chain of reasoning, not
merely nodding in approval but internalizing the argument as a part
of himself. Iago's uncanny ability to accomplish this feat bespeaks a
weakness in Othello himself. Part of him must be ready to believe
that it is not 'natural' for a young white woman to continue to love
an older black man. Sensual appetite may prompt her to be fascinated
at first with the exotic strangeness of it all, but that will soon wear
off. Iago has not long to wait for his poison to destroy Othello's
confidence in himself:

Haply, for I am black
And have not those soft parts of conversation
That chamberers have, or for I am declined
Into the vale of years – yet that's not much –
She's gone. I am abused, and my relief
Must be to loathe her. Oh, curse of marriage,
That we can call these delicate creatures ours
And not their appetites!   (3.3.279–86)

Othello's believing that men have a right to 'own' women makes him
fearful of loss of control. If he cannot control his wife's appetite, he
delivers into her hands the power to ruin his happiness. Iago can push
Othello over the edge into irrational jealousy because the syllogistic
logic he employs can resonate so fiercely with the workings of Othello's
own psyche.

We as audience are presumably able to see what is deeply fallacious
about Iago's argument. The problem is not in its logical structure,
but with the low premise about human nature and especially woman's
nature that then is generalized into an absolute basis upon which
to construct the conclusions that seem necessarily to follow. But

Desdemona is not 'all women'. Critics like W. H. Auden who assume that, given enough time, Desdemona will confirm Iago's and Othello's misogynist fears are giving in to Iago's insinuations about the inescapable carnality of women. The play seems to take some pains to refute this premise. To be sure, Desdemona does take pleasure in good company, music, dancing, and the like. She enjoys a loving relationship with Cassio. When she and Cassio kiss and whisper together on the occasion of Desdemona's arriving safely on Cyprus (2.1.167–77), Iago sees material upon which to construct his hypothetical case of her being interested in men besides her husband. She is of 'so free, so kind, so apt, so blessed a disposition' (by Iago's own admission, 2.3.313–14) that she is ready to plead for Cassio's reinstatement as Othello's second-in-command even when she perceives that for some reason she angers Othello by doing so. But her reasons are seemingly pure: she knows that Cassio means a lot to Othello, and she wants to see a reconciliation between these two men. Later, in her conversations with Emilia about marital infidelity, she is astonished to hear Emilia's playful argument that adultery is 'a small vice' and that Emilia would 'venture Purgatory' for it if the price were high enough (4.3.70–80). Desdemona has to ask Emilia if it is really true that 'there be women do abuse their husbands / In such gross kind' (64–5). She cannot bring herself to speak the word 'whore', scarcely grasping what it means (4.2.121–7). Her readiness to take the blame on herself for somehow having driven Othello to impatience ("'Tis meet I should be used so, very meet', 112) and her attempt to claim responsibility for her own death ('EMILIA Oh, who hath done this deed? / DESDEMONA Nobody; I myself', 5.2.127–8) testify to her astonishing and unassailable goodness. Desdemona is not like most other women. Emilia is fundamentally a good person, but even she falls short of Desdemona's innocence and generosity of heart. The sacrificial heroine of this play is, above all else, a refutation of Iago's premise about universal human carnality.

Iago's existential challenge to moral order is thus ultimately defeated and exposed for what it is by Desdemona's goodness, but up until the last moment in the play that challenge comes frighteningly close to success. Iago persuades Othello to kill the person he has held most dear, joining in a diabolical conspiracy based mutually on hatred and fear of women. 'Arise, black vengeance, from the hollow hell!' exclaims Othello. 'Yield up, O love, thy crown and hearted throne / To tyrannous hate!' (3.3.462–4). Why, when complete victory seems so near for Iago, is his work of evil undone to the crucial extent that Othello learns, albeit too late to save her life and his own happiness, that Desdemona was true? In good part, of course, this is because of Desdemona's unshakable virtue. Perhaps another reason is that Iago's championship of reason turns out to be so flawed. Paradoxically, this apostle of reason is himself profoundly out of control. He is able to manipulate others, and to curb his own appetites for sensual pleasures, but he can do nothing about his irrational jealousy and his hatred of Othello, Desdemona, Cassio, and all the rest. His hatred is all-embracing: his professed aim is to 'enmesh them all' (2.3.356). He acknowledges to himself that his fear of being cuckolded in his own marriage by Othello is baseless: 'I know not if't be true', he says to himself, 'But I, for mere suspicion in that kind, / Will do as if for surety' (1.3.389–91). The utter improbability of such unfaithfulness must be as apparent to him as to us; Othello is devotedly in love with Desdemona, and Emilia is stubbornly loyal in her unhappy marriage. Yet the thought will not leave Iago. He seeks revenge 'For that I do suspect the lusty Moor / Hath leaped into my seat, the thought whereof / Doth, like a poisonous mineral, gnaw my innards' (2.1.297–9).

Emilia, for all her talk of women's need to assert themselves and redress the unequal balance of power and pleasure dividing men from women, is not about to cheat on Iago; indeed, she commits what she comes to consider the unforgivable act of giving Desdemona's handkerchief to her husband in an attempt to 'please his fantasy' (3.3.315). Emilia knows why Iago is jealous: some men are just like that. 'They are not ever jealous for the cause, / But jealous for they're jealous', she tells Desdemona. 'It is a monster / Begot upon itself, born on itself' (3.4.161–3). Emilia has every reason to know. She has suffered the indignities of Iago's jealousy without giving him cause. Her reward is to die at his hands for attempting to tell everyone what she has long feared and suspected, that Iago's wanting the handkerchief was somehow a part of his plotting against Desdemona (5.2.199). In her astute analysis of the nature of jealousy, Emilia clarifies for us what is so troubling and false about the seeming appeal and incisiveness of Iago's scepticism.

Edmund in *King Lear* is, like Iago, a plausible villain who challenges traditional ideas with intellectual brilliance. The first targets of his scornful manipulation are his father, the Earl of Gloucester, and his brother, Edgar. Gloucester is especially vulnerable because he thinks in such conventional ways about the gods, the stars, and human destiny. 'These late eclipses in the sun and moon portend no good to us', Gloucester assures his bastard son. 'Though the wisdom of nature can reason it thus and thus, yet nature finds itself scourged by the sequent events. Love cools, friendship falls off, brothers divide; in cities, mutinies; in countries, discord; in palaces, treason; and the bond cracked twixt son and father' (1.2.106–12). Gloucester posits a meaningful connection between the movements of celestial bodies and every aspect of life on earth. To him, eclipses and earthquakes are not simply meta-phors of discord; they are signs of divine intention, warnings, predictors or confirmers of catastrophe. All is interconnected. Life as we know it responds to heavenly influence at all levels, from the family on up the chain of being to the heavens themselves. Disharmony in one realm of creation reflects disharmony in other realms. Disturbances in nature are a sign of divine displeasure, instructing us to reaffirm our obedi-ence to a divinely sanctioned order in the cosmos.

These ideas are graceful and even beautiful in their symmetries, but to Edmund they are 'the excellent foppery of the world'. They are superstition. They represent a lamentable disinclination among us human beings to accept responsibility for our own acts. We excuse our own failings by ascribing fate to some nebulous idea of superhuman agency. 'When we are sick in fortune – often the surfeits of our own behavior – we make guilty of our disasters the sun, the moon, and stars, as if we were villains on necessity, fools by heavenly compulsion, knaves, thieves, and treachers by spherical predominance, drunkards, liars, and adulterers by an enforced obedience of planetary influence, and all that we are evil in, by a divine thrusting on' (1.2.121–9). Edmund's contempt for astrology is likely to strike us as appealingly modern. He scorns the platitudes of his elders as without foundation. He is a true sceptic in the sense of interrogating received opinion, refusing to accept its timeworn notions without objective verification. In his view, such a verification would be impossible because the older ideas are worthless. They are the myths, in his view, that human society invents to perpetuate privilege and hierarchy. Edmund, as an illegitimate younger son unable to inherit property, is an outsider. His father's complacency about having sired a bastard makes Edmund's impatient fury all the more understandable. His iconoclastic stance has its appeal for viewers and readers today. Edmund is, arguably, a rebel with a cause.

Edmund's response to his outsider status is to declare himself to be self-reliant, like Iago in *Othello*. Any astrologically inclined person who might wonder if Edmund is 'rough and lecherous' because 'My father compounded with my mother under the Dragon's tail and my nativity was under Ursa Major' will totally misjudge the situation. 'Fut', he says in soliloquy, 'I should have been that I am, had the maidenliest star in the firmament twinkled on my bastardizing' (1.2.131–6). Edmund reckons himself bound to the services of Nature, who is his goddess (1–2). By 'Nature' Edmund means the sanction that governs the material world through mechanistic, amoral forces. He emphatically does not mean what 'Nature' means to King Lear when, outraged by Goneril's hardheartedness toward him, Lear implores, 'Hear, Nature, hear! Dear goddess, hear!' (1.4.274). Lear prays to Nature as one of the gods who should 'love old men' because the gods themselves are presumably old, and because their 'sweet sway' should foster obedience (2.4.191–3). Nature is to Lear a divinely ordained cosmos, and, since kings are the surrogates on earth of the gods, kings are or should be under the gods' special protection. 'Nature' is an extraordinarily important word in *King Lear*; it is used more often in this play than in any other in the Shakespeare canon (with *Macbeth*, *Othello*, and *Hamlet* following). The play is indeed a battleground over which rival concepts of nature are being fought. Gloucester uses the term in Lear's sense when he talks about 'the wisdom of nature' (1.2.107). Regan's definition is closer to that of Edmund when she says unfeelingly to her father, 'Oh, sir, you are old; / Nature in you stands on the very verge / Of his confine' (2.4.146–8). An anonymous gentleman evokes the concept of a battleground when he describes Cordelia as 'one daughter / Who redeems nature from the general curse / Which twain have brought her to' (4.6.205–7).

What is truly frightening about *King Lear* is that the battle over 'nature' seems to run in Edmund's favour to such an extraordinary degree and for so long a time. His creed of self-reliance gives him, as he readily perceives, a tactical advantage over others who credulously submit to the moral restrictions of the social order. Holding the view that moral codes are simply a part of the mythology by which the power structure enforces its grip on society, Edmund sees no reason not to lie, cheat, or otherwise overwhelm those who stand between him and the goals of his limitless ambitions. Confident that there are no gods to reward or punish, and no afterlife in which to suffer eternal pain,

Edmund proceeds with relentless energy and tactical brilliance. He turns his father against his brother Edgar by misrepresenting Edgar as a disloyal son. Finding a more compatible father figure in the Duke of Cornwall, Edmund betrays his own father as one who, by offering aid and comfort to old Lear, is an enemy to the state; since a French army under Cordelia has invaded Britain to succour Lear, any assistance offered him is technically treason. Cornwall rewards Edmund for his 'loyal' service by naming him Earl of Gloucester, in place of his condemned father. When Cornwall dies in a scuffle with a servant, Edmund parleys his sexual relationship with Regan into a bid to become Duke of Cornwall in her name. His adulterous affair with Regan's sister Goneril offers him an opportunity to aim at the life of Goneril's husband, the Duke of Albany. Named co-commander with Albany of the armed forces resisting Cordelia's invasion, Edmund is within an ace of becoming king of England. Edmund's proud declaration that 'the base / Shall top th' legitimate', and that the gods 'stand up for bastards' (1.2.20–2), seems for a very long time to be vindicated in practice.

Goneril and Regan achieve the same cruel success throughout most of *King Lear*. Their father plays right into their cynical stratagem: they tell him what he wants to hear until they have complete authority in their own hands. They are contemptuous of their virtuous sister, Cordelia, for having 'obedience scanted' (1.1.282), that is, for not having made effusive protestations of undying love for King Lear as they have done; in their view, Cordelia deserves what she gets. Their intent to repudiate their own offers of love to their father is evident before the close of the first scene. 'Pray you, let us hit together', says Goneril to Regan. 'If our father carry authority with such disposition as he bears, this last surrender of his will but offend us' (306–8). The Fool warns us and Lear as to what Lear can expect from such hard-hearted daughters, since Lear has committed the folly of making his daughters his mothers, i.e., has put them in authority over him (1.4.169–71), but the warnings are unheeded and come too late. Goneril and Regan do not theorize a secular philosophy in the way that Edmund does, but clearly they are all of a similar persuasion that nothing human or divine can touch them once they have achieved ascendancy. Goneril is openly contemptuous of her mild-mannered husband, Albany. 'Marry, your manhood! Mew!' she jeers, when Albany accuses her of being a fiend who is shielded from his wrath only by having 'A woman's shape' (4.2.68–9). When Albany attempts to call her to account by showing her an incriminating letter she has written to Edmund, and asks if she knows the writing to be hers, Goneril has her defiant answer: 'Say if I do, the laws are mine, not thine. / Who can arraign me for't?' 'Ask me not what I know', she declares, as she leaves the stage for the last time (5.3.161–3). Down to this moment in the play, the race goes to the swiftest.

Since deliberate evil prevails for such a long while, the existential challenge in *King Lear* is especially acute, more so than in any other Shakespeare play. Do the gods exist at all? Lear implores their help to no avail; instead of being succoured he is shut out in the storm, loses his reason, and eventually dies brokenhearted when Cordelia, his one remaining hope, is taken from him. Gloucester repeatedly invokes 'the kind gods' in his hour of greatest need (3.7.36, 73, 95), and clings to the hope that 'I shall see / The wingèd Vengeance overtake such children' (i.e., Goneril and Regan, 68–9), but these pleas for divine justice do not halt the inexorable brutality of his being blinded by Cornwall. The anonymous servants who witness this desecration pose disturbing questions about the threat of universal disorder that must surely result if crimes are unpunished by the gods: 'I'll never care what wickedness I do, / If this man [Cornwall] come to good', says one, to which his fellow servant replies, 'If she [Regan] live long, / And in the end meet the old course of death, / Women will all turn monsters' (3.7.102–5, in a passage occurring only in the quarto text, not the Folio). The Duke of Albany similarly worries that if human crimes are not punished by divine retribution, the consequence will be utter barbarism and chaos. 'If that the heavens do not their visible spirits / Send quickly down to tame these vile offenses', he says when he learns how cruelly King Lear has been treated by his daughters, 'It will come, / Humanity must perforce prey on itself, / Like monsters of the deep' (4.2.47–51). But what if the heavens do not attend to such injustices? When he hears of the death of Cornwall in the aftermath of the blinding of Gloucester, Albany exclaims, 'This shows you are above, / You justicers, that these our nether crimes / So speedily can venge!' (4.2.79–81). Yet Albany is at a loss to explain why Gloucester had to lose his eyes. Every attempt on the part of thoughtful persons in the play to see divine purpose in human action is immediately undercut by the dismaying reality that ruthless villains not only act with impunity but seem also to have the upper hand over those persons whose deeds are constrained by moral considerations.

The role of Edgar is crucial in sorting out these dilemmas of existential challenge in *King Lear*. Edgar is a realist and sceptic. He learns the hard way that things do not always turn out well. To hope for the best is to set oneself up for disillusionment. At the beginning of Act 4, for example, he considers his miserable plight as a hunted man in disguise as a wretched beggar and seeks consolation in the notion that at least his fortunes cannot deteriorate further: 'To be worst, / The lowest and most dejected thing of fortune, / Stands still in esperance, lives not in fear. / The lamentable change is from the best; / The worst returns to laughter' (4.1.2–6). Immediately, as though in deliberate confutation of his taking comfort in such a shopworn cliché, he meets his wretched old father, blinded, despairing, and intent on ending his life. 'O gods!' exclaims Edgar to himself. 'Who is't can say, "I am at the worst"? / I am worse than e'er I was.' Edgar realizes that he has selfishly considered only his own happiness; he now sees that another human being, one who is dear to him, is in more wretched condition than he. 'And worse I may be yet', he continues in an aside. 'The worst is not / So long as we can say, "This is the worst"' (25–8). So long as we can draw breath, the one thing we can be sure of is that things may get worse.

Edgar is learning, then, the counsel of stoicism. If one expects nothing from life, one cannot be disappointed. He is like his brother Edmund in his matter-of-fact understanding of nature. He recognizes that competition for survival is a fact of existence. He sees no reason to expect that good behaviour will be rewarded and bad behaviour punished by the gods; indeed, all the evidence induces him to conclude that the gods, if they do exist, simply do not play an active role in human affairs. Though he does not deny their existence, he does view most religious practices as delusional. At the same time, he perceives this compassionately, whereas his brother sees an opportunity for ruthless self-advancement. Edgar shares with Edmund the perception that their father's theology is a myth, but Edgar has no desire to take advantage of his father's intellectual weakness; to the contrary, Edgar props up his father's wavering faith in the gods by inventing for him a bogus suicide and a 'miraculous' survival (4.6.55), complete with a horned and thousand-nosed 'fiend' who has purportedly goaded Gloucester into trying to end his life (68–72). The deception works: Gloucester resolves to 'bear / Affliction till it do cry out itself / "Enough, enough," and die' (75–7). He accedes to Edgar's counsel of philosophical stoicism. Like Hamlet, he will let the gods decide when it is time for him to die. For his own part, Edgar sees through his father's self-delusions; the very fact that he invents a religion for old Gloucester suggests that Edgar understands formal religion as a kind of quaint and even beautiful poetry that is ultimately illusory from a sceptical point of view. This does not mean that Edgar is an atheist; that intellectual position is too arrogantly self-assured to satisfy his doubts. It does mean that, as sceptic, he sees that his only hope for philosophical calm is to banish all deceiving hopes that the powers above will assist him in his daily needs.

Edgar is like his brother in questioning any direct role of the gods in material human affairs, but differs from Edmund in one crucial respect. Edmund sees the absence of the gods in human life as providing an opportunity for cynical self-advancement. Edgar instead sees compelling reason to be generous, compassionate, and forgiving toward one's enemies. The lack of any hope of eternal or supernatural reward gives to his deep humanism a strength that Shakespeare seems to find compelling and attractive, for he makes Edgar a kind of viewpoint character through whose eyes we are invited to interpret the disasters of the play's story. Why should one be kind and generous to others if the gods are not watching? Edgar's answer would appear to be that it is simply better to be that way. One must answer to oneself and to a sense of human decency. Cordelia follows a similar path and without hope of supernatural reward, so far as we can tell, though she does not verbalize her philosophical views as Edgar does. She evidently believes that it is better even to die if necessary rather than be untrue to one's inner sense of what matters. She is a sacrificial victim of the play's omnipresent inhumanity. Her persevering in goodness, like that of Desdemona in *Othello*, atones for much that is otherwise unbearable in *King Lear*.

What is more, evil does ultimately prove to be its own undoing. Edmund dies at the hands of the brother he has wronged, striving at last (and too late) to do some good in recompense for all of his evil-doing. Goneril poisons her sister Regan and then takes her own life in a despairing suicide. The lives of these three would seem to offer vivid evidence of what the rewards of viciousness are sure to be. No gods are needed to punish them in any judicial sense; the villains punish themselves. Their story is one of lust and illicit ambition that turns them into the selfish monsters that Albany describes (4.2.31–51). Edgar says it well:

'The gods are just, and of our pleasant vices / Make instruments to plague us' (5.3.173–4). The gods do then have a role after all, in Edgar's view, but it is not fulfilled in the way that is described by most religions or in the way that Lear and Gloucester have prayed for. A cosmic justice distantly oversees human affairs only through human agency: if we give way to our 'pleasant vices', that is, our pleasure-seeking desires, we will create the means of our own well-deserved punishment.

Even old Gloucester, in Edgar's view, falls under this rubric. As Edgar says to the dying Edmund about their father, 'The dark and vicious place where he thee got / Cost him his eyes' (5.3.175–6). The pleasurable act of begetting Edmund out of wedlock, an act that Gloucester has regarded with the kind of complacency that goes with his wealth and rank ('there was good sport at his making, and the whoreson must be acknowledged', 1.1.23–4), has led to his being blinded. Edgar's cause-and-effect formulation is of course true in a literal sense: if Gloucester had never sired Edmund, the treacherous son would not have been on hand to conspire in the arrest of Gloucester for treason. Yet the causal link is also true in the larger sense that acts have their consequences. The sexual act, in particular, creates a life in such a way as to incur awesome responsibilities. Edmund agrees finally about moral cause and effect: 'The wheel is come full circle' (5.3.177). This is a crucial concession on Edmund's part: no longer the sardonic atheist, he allows that the complex circumstances of life must somehow be meaningfully interconnected. The concession cannot begin to atone for the injustice of Cordelia's death, which even Edmund has belatedly tried to prevent; that terrible event, and the death of Lear, remind the survivors at last that things can always go disastrously wrong in an existential world. Perhaps Edgar's declaration that 'The gods are just', however circumscribed in its meaning, is still too hopeful. Yet the play does leave us with the perception that evil has punished itself, and that Cordelia and Edgar, like Desdemona, have persevered in being true to themselves.

We looked at *Macbeth* in the previous chapter in terms of its Calvinist paradoxes of determinism versus free will, but something needs to be said here as well. Macbeth would seem at first glance to offer the reassurance that murder cannot be hid and that crime will be met by well-deserved punishment. Macbeth is not a villain in the way that Iago and Edmund are villains. He knows that his killing of Duncan is morally wrong and that he will eventually have to pay the price of his mad ambition to be king. The ending of the play brings a restoration of political and moral order, even if some modern productions (including Roman Polanski's film of 1971) flirt with the notion that a struggle for power is about to begin all over again. Yet even in this tragedy the powers of evil embodied in the Weird Sisters are so insidious and so able, with Lady Macbeth's assistance, to overwhelm Macbeth's spirit that we are left with a shattering sense that evil in the hearts of some human beings will achieve its own baleful triumph. Banquo offers an important counterpart in his readiness to resist the insidious temptations of evil, but even he knows what it is to experience 'the cursèd thoughts that nature / Gives way to in repose' (2.1.8–9). The heart of darkness within the human condition, and the diabolical forces to which that darkness owes allegiance, are incessantly ready to pounce on the susceptible sinner.

Shakespeare's pursuit of sceptical thought in these great tragedies and problem plays is unsparingly honest. It leads him to profound reflections on misogyny and misanthropy in *Hamlet*, on relativism of all human values in *Troilus and Cressida*, and on secular interpretations of history in *Julius Caesar*. As is his practice, he sets ideas in debate. Troilus's belief in the relativity of values is set in opposition to Hector's insistence that 'value dwells not in particular will'. Hamlet and Horatio argue lovingly about Christian providentialism versus a classical and Roman view of history in which 'accidental judgments' and 'purposes mistook / Fall'n on the inventors' heads' are common occurrences. Hamlet's admiration for Horatio's stoic philosophy of despising the rewards and disappointments of Lady Fortune must do battle with Hamlet's obligation to act as the avenger of his father's murder. In *Julius Caesar*, the philosophical responses to the ominous occurrences on the night before the assassination of Caesar are as varied as the characters themselves, from superstitious terror to atheistic bravura to Pyrrhonistic doubt to simple obliviousness. Brutus's own stoicism is severely put to the test. The defeat that he and Cassius suffer at Philippi would seem to demonstrate an ironic view of history similar to that of Horatio, namely, that noble intentions are seldom fulfilled in the way that the participants had hoped. Human beings experience terrible difficulties in knowing themselves and understanding their relationship to destiny. They are often their own worst enemy.

In *Othello* and *King Lear* the existential challenges posed by the operation of evil are especially devastating. Iago and Edmund are terrifyingly alike in that their scepticism seems so modern to us. Their assaults on conventional ideas of reason and order are logically astute. Iago's syllogistic manipulations raise serious doubts in Othello's mind as to the meaning of 'natural'. Iago and Edmund achieve nearly complete success in their drives for self-advancement and revenge because their victims are so vulnerably credulous. The older order that Edmund attacks represents hierarchy and degree and everything that is entailed in the myth of the Great Chain of Being. Order is restored at the end of *Othello*, to be sure, as in *Macbeth*. In the apocalyptic end of *King Lear*, on the other hand, the seeming indifference of the gods to human suffering, if indeed the gods exist at all, leaves the pitiably few survivors with little sense of where to turn next. Only the charitableness of Cordelia and Edgar and Kent offers any atonement for a seemingly universal barbarism. Edgar understands as a sceptic that the cosmos cannot be counted on to reward virtuous behaviour and punish vice, but he refuses to give in to his brother's logic that one might as well turn villain in that case. Shakespeare's admiration for those who persevere in goodness, and his dismay at the near-triumph of villainy, suggest how his dramatic art can offer great consolation for the fallen world in which his tragic protagonists must strive.

7

Here Our Play Has Ending
Ideas of Closure in the Late Plays

Either Shakespeare was conscious of fashioning an overall design to his career as dramatist and poet, or the intense critical scrutiny of centuries has found that pattern for him. It doesn't really matter which. In either case, his late plays seem especially interested in how things end: how human beings cope with ageing and loss of physical strength, how they come to terms with depression, despair, and misanthropy, how they seek new identities and occupations in retirement, how they reconcile themselves with the persons dearest to them in their personal lives, and how they prepare for death. These topics seem well designed to offer a reply to the intense philosophical challenges we have explored in the previous chapter. It is as though Shakespeare works his way through a dialectic of thesis and antithesis toward synthesis. In an artistically self-aware gesture, he seems interested in how a play ends and how a writer's career should end. Shakespeare seems to be summing up what it means to be a person, a man, a husband and father, a writer, a dramatist.

The prospect of death, and the necessity of preparing for that great event, is a commonplace of classical and medieval/early modern thought. John Donne reportedly slept in his coffin as a reminder of what was to come. An awareness of death is omnipresent in Shakespeare; the word is hugely important in the Shakespeare lexicon. The skull of a lawyer puts Hamlet in mind of human mortality: 'Where be his quiddities now, his quillities, his cases, his tenures, and his tricks?' (*Hamlet*, 5.1.99–100). Such *ubi sunt* ruminations were a conventional element in reflections on death. 'Skull' occurs more often in *Hamlet* than in any other play in the canon. The certainty of death is another omnipresent truth. 'Death's the end of all', opines the Nurse in *Romeo and Juliet* by way of comforting Romeo over his banishment (3.3.92). 'Death, as the Psalmist saith, is certain to all', ventures Shallow in *2 Henry IV* (3.2.38), perhaps citing Psalm 89, verse 48: 'What man is he that liveth, and shall not see death?' 'Thou owest God a death', says Prince Hal to Falstaff as they await the commencement of the battle of Shrewsbury (*1 Henry IV*, 5.1.126), to which Falstaff replies, ''Tis not due yet; I would be loath to pay him before his day.'

Death is at times perceived as a release from the burdens of human existence, as when the Duke in *Measure for Measure*, disguised as a friar, counsels the condemned Claudio with the reflection that to lose one's life is to 'lose a thing / That none but fools do keep' (3.1.7–8). 'Death' occurs in this play far more often than in any other Shakespearean comedy. Elsewhere, death is likened to sleep, 'that knits up the raveled sleave of care, / The death of each day's life, sore labor's bath, / Balm of hurt minds, great nature's second course, / Chief nourisher in life's feast' (*Macbeth*, 2.2.40–4). Sleep is the 'ape of death' (*Cymbeline*, 2.2.31). Death is often personified as a grim monarch, as when the Bastard in *King John* speaks of 'the rotten carcass of old Death' (2.2.457) or when King Richard II laments the collapse of his royal fortunes:

> Within the hollow crown
> That rounds the mortal temples of a king
> Keeps Death his court, and there the antic sits,
> Scoffing his state and grinning at his pomp,
> Allowing him a breath, a little scene,
> To monarchize, be feared, and kill with looks,
> Infusing him with self and vain conceit,
> As if this flesh which walls about our life
> Were brass impregnable; and humored thus,
> Comes in at last and with a little pin
> Bores through his castle wall, and – farewell, king!
> (*Richard II*, 3.2.160–70)

Death is thus both a great compensation for life's tribulations and an emblem of fruitless striving.

At times, the approach of death is an occasion of sheer horror and sterility. Macbeth, having fallen into 'the sere, the yellow leaf', knows only too well that the 'honor, love, obedience, troops of friends' that virtuous men can hope to enjoy will not be his: in their stead he will reap 'Curses, not loud but deep, mouth-honor' (*Macbeth*, 5.3.22–8). News of his Queen's death leaves him with the realization that 'all our yesterdays have lighted fools / The way to dusty death', suggesting that life is but a 'brief candle' lighting our way through a meaningless existence toward the oblivion of the grave:

> Life's but a walking shadow, a poor player
> That struts and frets his hour upon the stage
> And then is heard no more. It is a tale
> Told by an idiot, full of sound and fury
> Signifying nothing.   (*Macbeth*, 5.5.22–8)

Yet other characters know that death should be approached with resolution and calm, even if they do not always find that strength in themselves when the moment arrives. Julius Caesar finds it 'strange that men should fear, / Seeing that death, a necessary end, / Will come when it will come' (*Julius Caesar*, 2.2.35–7). Brutus, defeated at Philippi, runs on his own sword, addressing the spirit of Caesar with his last words: 'Caesar, be still. / I killed not thee with half so good a will' (5.5.50–1). Claudio, in *Measure for Measure*, stoutly insists that 'If I must die, / I will encounter darkness like a bride / And hug it in mine arms' (3.1.83–5), though when offered a desperate hope of evading his sentence of death he loses his nerve. Antony, refusing to 'basely die' in cowardly surrender to Octavius Caesar, chooses to be 'a Roman by a Roman / Valiantly vanquished' – that is, by his own hand; Cleopatra, having studied various means of killing herself, resolves to die 'after the high Roman fashion / And make death proud to take us' (*Antony and Cleopatra*, 4.15.57–60, 92–3).

These varying responses to death are commonplaces of the age, original with Shakespeare only in the remarkable elegance with which they are worded. Cumulatively, they do highlight the importance of the moment of death in summing up a person's life. To die well is to complete and justify one's existence and one's hope of being remembered as a worthy person; to die badly is to put the seal on a bad bargain and to concede failure. The art of holy dying, much practised in the Middle Ages and Renaissance, laid its emphasis on spiritual victory and hope of eternal life in heaven. Shakespeare does not exclude that vision, as when Horatio mourns the death of Hamlet with 'Good night, sweet prince, / And flights of angels sing thee to thy rest!' (*Hamlet*, 5.2.361–2), or when the death of Queen Katharine in *Henry VIII* is preceded by a vision of six 'Spirits of peace', '*clad in white robes, wearing on their heads garlands of bays, and golden vizards on their faces, branches of bays or palm in their hands*' (4.2.82–3). More often, though, the art of dying well in Shakespeare celebrates human achievement. The eternity desired by his heroes and heroines is generally one of wishing to be remembered as notable and heroic. 'No grave upon the earth shall clip in it / A pair so famous', declares Octavius Caesar of the deaths of Antony and Cleopatra (5.2.358–9). Antony's summation of Brutus in *Julius Caesar* is that 'His life was gentle, and the elements / So mixed in him that Nature might stand up / And say to all the world, "This was a man!"' (5.5.73–5).

Even those who die in spiritual agony are concerned with how they will be remembered. 'Speak of me as I am', Othello bids his hearers:

> nothing extenuate,
> Nor set down aught in malice. Then must you speak
> Of one that loved not wisely but too well;
> Of one not easily jealous but, being wrought,
> Perplexed in the extreme; of one whose hand,
> Like the base Indian, threw a pearl away
> Richer than all his tribe.   (*Othello*, 5.2.352–8)

As the Ghost of old Hamlet says, 'Remember me!' (*Hamlet*, 1.5.92). Such a hope of remembrance is considerably more dominant in Shakespeare than the hope of heavenly reward.

Old age is a matter of anxious concern in Shakespeare, and, not surprisingly, most of all in the late plays. The phrases 'old man' and 'old' occur with especial frequency in *King Lear*. 'Oh, sir, you are old', Regan chides her father. 'Nature in you stands on the very verge / Of his confine' (2.4.146–8). Regan and Goneril have already agreed between themselves that their father's irritability and 'poor judgment' can only increase with the years. 'You see how full of changes his age is', Goneril says to her sister (1.1.292–5). Lear, for his part, is furious that in his old age he is not receiving the adulation to which his seniority should entitle him. He savagely mocks the notion that as an old man he should have to beg his daughters' understanding and aid: 'Dear daughter, I confess that I am old; / Age is unnecessary. On my knees I beg / That you'll vouchsafe me raiment, bed, and food' (2.4.154–6). Regan and Goneril refuse to acknowledge the force of Lear's sarcasm. 'Good sir, no more', says Regan. 'These are unsightly tricks' (157). Lear's pleas to the gods on behalf of his advancing years are no less unavailing. 'O heavens', he cries, 'If you do love old men, if your sweet sway / Allow obedience, if you yourselves are old, / Make it your cause; send down, and take my part!' (190–3). Old age seems to have bestowed no benefits on him at all. Hamlet taunts Polonius by citing a 'satirical rogue' who says 'that old men have gray beards, that their faces are wrinkled, their eyes purging thick amber and plum-tree gum, and that they have a plentiful lack of wit, together with most weak hams' (*Hamlet*, 2.2.197–201). Lear's Fool has his gnomic advice for the King, too late of course to do any good: 'Thou shouldst not have been old till thou hadst been wise' (*King Lear*, 1.5.43–4). As Bette Davis put the matter some centuries after Shakespeare, 'Old age ain't no place for sissies.' Or Lillian Hellman: 'The only thing good about it is you're not dead.'

One particular anxiety of men in their advancing years can be the fear of decreasing sexual potency. Women are more apt to worry about the fading of their attractiveness to men. The protagonists in *Antony and Cleopatra* exhibit these fears. Historically, Antony was fourteen years older than Cleopatra, and nineteen or so years older than his great political rival, Octavius Caesar. Without mentioning numbers, Shakespeare makes a point of these age differences. Antony is painfully aware that he is being challenged by a younger man. 'Who knows / If the scarce-bearded Caesar have not sent / His powerful mandate to you', Cleopatra taunts Antony (1.1.21–3), not letting him forget that the young man who aided him in the defeat of Brutus and Cassius at Philippi is now sending out orders for Antony to 'Do this, or this; / Take in that kingdom, or enfranchise that' (23–4) as though the two were equals, with Octavius the stronger of the pair. Antony needs no reminding. 'Now I must / To the young man send humble treaties, dodge / And palter in the shifts of lowness', he laments after his disastrous defeat at Actium, 'who / With half the bulk o'the world played as I pleased, / Making and marring fortunes' (3.11.60–4). His jealous rage at Cleopatra's equivocal reception of the presumably young and handsome Thidias as Caesar's ambassador to her is fed by Antony's concern that Cleopatra, who has slept with Gnaeus Pompey and Julius

Caesar in her earlier years, 'besides what hotter hours, / Unregistered in vulgar fame, you have / Luxuriously picked out' (3.13.120–2), will now seek the companionship of the young man who is in the ascendant, Octavius Caesar. Antony cannot forget that gray hairs 'Do something mingle with our younger brown' (4.8.20).

Antony is just of an age to be undergoing what today we call midlife crisis. For some years, intermittently, he pursues an extramarital affair, having guiltily left his pillow 'unpressed in Rome' and having 'Forborne the getting of a lawful race, / And by a gem of women' (3.13.107–9). (Actually, Antony lived with Octavia in Athens for some years, and had children with her, but that only makes his desertion of her seem all the more reprehensible.) In his fitful worry that his male charisma is fading, he dreads the prospect of a younger rival. His career is in shambles. Dereliction of duty obliges him to return to Rome and apologize, as well as he can, to Caesar for the 'poisoned hours' that, as he says, have 'bound me up / From mine own knowledge'. 'As nearly as I may / I'll play the penitent to you' (2.2.96–8). Such an apology does not come easily from so proud a man. Worse is to come. His second-in-command in Asia, Ventidius, confides to a fellow officer that he dare not boast openly of his own victories, lest he offend Antony by taking credit for the achievements that Antony jealously hoards to himself (3.1). At Actium, Antony disgraces himself as a military leader by flying after Cleopatra at the height of the battle. 'Indeed, I have lost command', he confesses (3.11.23). 'I / Have lost my way forever' (3–4). 'Authority melts from me' (3.13.91). Like many men his age, Antony fears that he is running out of options.

In his despairing mood, Antony sees his infatuation with Cleopatra as a kind of madness, a manifestation of what the ancient Greeks called *atē* or blind folly. In Antony's description of this madness, indeed, we can see how clearly Shakespeare understands how *atē* works, even though the term itself was presumably foreign to him:

> when we in our viciousness grow hard –
> Oh, misery on't! – the wise gods seel our eyes,
> In our own filth drop our clear judgments, make us
> Adore our errors, laugh at 's while we strut
> To our confusion.   (3.13.113–17)

This blind folly begins with a loss of will power and a deplorable hardening of the appetite into enslavement with corrupt pleasure. It heightens into a blind unawareness of what is happening. The individual is out of control; the 'wise gods' are determining his fate, inducing in him a *hubris* or arrogant pride (another term not employed by Shakespeare) that is the prelude to his catastrophic fall. The process is a fulfillment of divine intent; the madness sets up the individual for a fall into 'confusion' or destruction through total loss of self-awareness, as though to bring about a deserved retribution. Antony sees all this about himself and yet can seemingly do nothing to stop the deterioration. Shakespeare presents this loss of agency as a painful symptom of ageing and self-indulgence.

Cleopatra confronts ageing in a way that Shakespeare presents as seductively feminine. She acknowledges that she is 'with Phoebus' amorous pinches black / And wrinkled deep in time' (1.5.29–30). Gone are her 'salad days', when she was 'green in judgment' (76–7). That was when, at the age of twenty-one (historically in 47 BC), she was 'A morsel for a monarch' (32), i.e., Julius Caesar; and she was young still when, as she boasts, she could cause Gnaeus Pompey to 'stand and make his eyes grow in my brow', that is, rivet his eyes on her face (32–3). At the time of her death (historically in 30 BC), she was thirty-eight, fourteen years younger than her middle-aged lover. Again, Shakespeare does not bother with dates, and he collapses and foreshortens time, but the impressions of age difference are as in Plutarch. Cleopatra fights a defensive war against the advancing years by a dazzling array of stratagems. At her famous meeting with Mark Antony on the river of Cydnus in southeast Asia Minor (historically in 41 BC), according to Enobarbus's account, she furnishes herself with a magnificent barge, handsomely attired attendants, a pavilion, and garments of 'cloth-of-gold of tissue', all designed to show her as 'O'erpicturing that Venus where we see / The fancy outwork nature' (2.2.201–28). She staged herself on that occasion as a work of art in which the artifice caught the eye and lent its splendour to her own person, of which Enobarbus can say only that it 'beggared all description'. She knows still how to feed the male appetite by addressing every mood, every desire. 'Age cannot wither her, nor custom stale / Her infinite variety', says Enobarbus. 'Other women cloy / The appetites they feed, but she makes hungry / Where most she satisfies.' Indeed, her essence is paradox: 'vilest things / Become themselves in her, that the holy priests / Bless her when she is riggish' (245–50). She is that marvel of the mythic imagination, the Lucretian Venus, both innocent and sensuous. She is, in other words, the embodiment of the male fantasy in its quest for romantic adventure, especially middle-aged extramarital adventure.

Cleopatra demonstrates these paradoxical qualities in everything she does. She teases Antony about his mannish wife Fulvia. She instructs her attendants that if they find Antony 'sad' (i.e., thoughtful), 'Say I am dancing; if in mirth, report / That I am sudden sick' (1.3.3–5). When Charmian ventures to suggest that she instead try soothing Antony by acceding to his moods and wishes, Cleopatra expresses her lofty contempt for such naïve advice: 'Thou teachest like a fool: the way to lose him' (10). She is the pro, instructing her servants how to keep a man off balance. She recalls with delight the practical joke she played on Antony by having her attendants tie a dead salted fish on his hook when he was trying to impress her with his prowess as a fisherman (2.5.15–18). She knows how to laugh him out of patience and then laugh him into patience (19–20). She remembers how 'next morn, / Ere the ninth hour, I drunk him to his bed, / Then put my tires and mantles on him, whilst / I wore his sword Philippan' (20–3). To Roman observers like Octavius, these gender-crossing episodes are signs of debauchery, but to the ageing Antony (and to Enobarbus) they are fascinating. Cleopatra is Antony's 'serpent of old Nile' (1.5.26). She is indeed like the Nile, an abundant source of life that also brings with it an overabundance of mud and slime.

For the ageing Antony, then, Cleopatra is both a destructive and a regenerative force. His career ends in ruins and suicide. He even bungles his death, acting on a false report from Cleopatra that she has committed suicide, and wounding himself so ineffectually that he lingers for quite some time in pain (4.14.27–34). To be sure, he has given her good reason to send him that false report of suicide by the extremity of his rage against her. Yet despite their manifest failures and self-betrayals, Antony and Cleopatra become in death emblematic of a great love that has dared to defy convention with a spiritual if not a worldly success. They have defied Octavius Caesar, whose ruthless pursuit of power and visceral distaste for sensual pleasure define the Roman values in this play as ultimately too arid and life-denying. Octavius's highest priority in defeating Antony and Cleopatra, it seems, is to take Cleopatra back to Rome as the *pièce de résistance* of his triumphal entry into the city. He feels a compelling need to capture this transgressive woman and force her to submit to male control. Once she has learned for certain that his plan is to have her hoisted up and shown 'to the shouting varletry / Of censuring Rome' (5.2.54–6), she knows what she must do. She will attire herself in her robe and crown and defeat Octavius's intent through suicide. To the asp she cradles at her breast, she expresses her 'Immortal longings': 'Oh, couldst thou speak, / That I might hear thee call great Caesar ass / Unpolicied!' (280–308). 'Unpolicied' means outwitted; she beats Caesar at his own game.

Conversely, Cleopatra's poetic imagination fashions in Act 5 an Antony who symbolizes mythic greatness. At his best, he has always been a valiant soldier, one whose heart seems so great that it might 'burst / The buckles on his breast' (1.1.7–8). He has been generous, brave, charismatic, loved by those who follow him. Even his flaws have been those of a large spirit: overindulgent in pleasure, reckless in war, imprudent in his generosity. Now, in death, he becomes a god in Cleopatra's conjuring up of his image:

> His legs bestrid the ocean; his reared arm
> Crested the world; his voice was propertied
> As all the tunèd spheres, and that to friends;
> But when he meant to quail and shake the orb,
> He was as rattling thunder. For his bounty,
> There was no winter in't; an autumn 'twas
> That grew the more by reaping. His delights
> Were dolphinlike; they showed his back above
> The elements they lived in. In his livery
> Walked crowns and crownets; realms and islands were
> As plates dropped from his pocket.   (5.2.81–91)

As Cleopatra insists, her Antony is 'past the size of dreaming' (96). His greatness is elemental and cosmic: he towers over land and sea, he rises up out of the ocean, he shakes the world with Jove-like thunder, he embodies the movement of the seasons of the year, he sings the music of the spheres. He is a life force, and so is she. They are Isis and Osiris (3.6.17), Venus and Mars (1.5.19), moon and sun (5.2.79, 240–1). He is a 'demi-Atlas of this earth' (1.5.24), a devotee of Hercules (4.3.21); she is 'fire and air', having given her other elements 'to baser life' (5.2.289–90). Antony imagines them both, after death, in the Elysian Fields, 'Where souls do couch on flowers'. There they will go 'hand in hand, / And with our sprightly port make the ghosts gaze. / Dido and her Aeneas shall want troops, / And all the haunt be ours' (4.14.50–4). Even Octavius Caesar concedes that 'No grave upon the earth shall clip in it / A pair so famous' (5.2.358–9).

Shakespeare's achievement here in the realm of ideas is extraordinary. The magical picture he creates of a middle-aged love affair defies all expectations. Antony and Cleopatra dare to become like one another, and to cross over the hazardous boundaries of gender difference that Octavius insists upon as inviolable. Antony learns how to become tender, to weep, to be vulnerable, to yield authority to the woman he loves – sometimes, to be sure, with disastrous consequences. She, having resolved to die 'after the high Roman fashion' (4.15.92), declares at last that 'My resolution's placed, and I have nothing / Of woman in me. Now from head to foot / I am marble-constant; now the fleeting moon / No planet is of mine' (5.2.238–41). Does this erasure of the gender barrier bring with it a dissolution of social order and control, as Octavius fears, or is it liberating? Shakespeare sets these ideas in debate, as he likes to do.

He does so here, moreover, in the larger context of his study of sexual conflict in the great tragedies. Misogyny runs deep in these plays. 'Frailty, thy name is woman!' cries Hamlet, overwhelmed as he is by the speed with which his mother has forgotten how 'she followed my poor father's body, / Like Niobe, all tears' (*Hamlet*, 1.2.146–9). The play-within-the-play that is enacted for Claudius and all the Danish court, to which Hamlet evidently has contributed 'a dozen or sixteen lines' (2.2.541–2), focuses keenly on the question of whether a queen will remain true to the memory of her departed husband. 'In second husband let me be accurst! / None wed the second but who killed the first', insists the Player Queen, to which Hamlet adds his own wry comment, 'Wormwood, wormwood' (3.2.177–9). Hamlet's misogynistic outburst at Ophelia ('Get thee to a nunnery' etc., 3.1.122ff.) is perhaps an unhappy by-product of his profound disappointment about women, and about most men as well, including himself. Iago, in *Othello*, uses a misogynistic premise to undo Othello's confidence in his wife's loyalty. 'I know our country disposition well', says Iago to Othello. 'In Venice they do let God see the pranks / They dare not show their husbands; their best conscience / Is not to leave't undone, but keep't unknown' (3.3.215–18). Emilia knows all too well that Iago's fearfulness of her supposed infidelity to him is nothing but the product of his diseased imagination and his hatred of women. King Lear, in his madness, is obsessed with woman's sexual body as an image of the gates of hell:

> Down from the waist they're centaurs,
> Though women all above.
> But to the girdle do the gods inherit;
> Beneath is all the fiends'.
> There's hell, there's darkness, there is the sulfurous pit,
> burning, scalding, stench, consumption. Fie, fie, fie!
> (*King Lear*, 4.6.124–9)

The misogyny is in a sense surprising here, since Lear has not been vulnerable to sexual betrayal in his own life, so far as we know, but the idea certainly resonates in the play as a whole, especially in the yearning of both his daughters to be possessed sexually by Edmund.

Lady Macbeth terrifies us when she calls on the spirits 'That tend on mortal thoughts' to 'unsex me here / And fill me from the crown to the toe top-full / Of direst cruelty'. Her invitation to these same 'murdering ministers' to 'Come to my woman's breasts / And take my milk for gall' (*Macbeth*, 1.5.41–50) suggests that she is thinking of incubuses or evil spirits that have sexual intercourse with women while they are sleeping. Timon of Athens, in his rage at all of humanity, ironically urges Timandra and Phrynia, the mistresses of Alcibiades, to 'Be strong in whore' so as to infect with venereal disease all those men who seek sexual pleasure with them: 'Consumptions sow / In hollow bones of man . . . Down with the nose, / Down with it flat . . . Make curled-pate ruffians bald' (*Timon of Athens*, 4.3.144–62). A decayed nose and loss of hair are symptoms of syphilis. Coriolanus's mother Volumnia is a formidable Roman matron who celebrates his military achievements as a kind of love-offering intended for her. 'If my son were my husband', she lectures her daughter-in-law, 'I should freelier rejoice in that absence wherein he won honor than in the embracements of his bed where he would show most love' (*Coriolanus*, 1.3.2–5). The prospect of her son's returning from war with a bloody brow does not dismay Volumnia in the least: 'The breasts of Hecuba, / When she did suckle Hector, looked not lovelier / Than Hector's forehead when it spit forth blood / At Grecian sword, contemning' (41–4). Small wonder that when Coriolanus finally realizes that he must hold back from destroying the Rome that has exiled him as a public enemy because to do so would be to destroy his mother as well, he sees how he has been trapped and suffocated by the woman who brought him into the world. 'Oh, mother, mother!' he exclaims. 'What have you done? Behold, the heavens do ope, / The gods look down, and this unnatural scene / They laugh at' (5.3.182–5).

The threat posed by daunting, emasculating women in the great tragedies is thus symptomatic of a larger disorder. Order is restored to Scotland in *Macbeth* only when the threatening maternal presence embodied in Lady Macbeth and the Weird Sisters is expunged; Macduff, the nemesis who calls Macbeth to account, is born by Caesarian section, having been 'from his mother's womb / Untimely ripped' (5.8.15–16), and is thus, in riddling fulfillment of the second Apparition's prophecy, not 'of woman born' (4.1.80). For these reasons the daring of *Antony and Cleopatra* is all the more extraordinary. Cleopatra is a transgressive woman who does at times seem determined to invert the structure of authority in her relationship with Antony. Their story ends in military defeat and death. Yet Antony ascends into a new dimension of greatness through his relationship with Cleopatra. She is an essential feature of Shakespeare's debate, in these late plays, about the role of sexuality in adult life.

In the so-called late romances or tragicomedies – *Pericles, Cymbeline, The Winter's Tale, The Tempest*, and, somewhat more peripherally, *The Two Noble Kinsmen* and *Henry VIII* – Shakespeare moves beyond the terrifying image of the devouring woman to a more hopeful and reconstructive portrait of the family. The mother is an unstable figure, sometimes entirely absent, sometimes lost to the story and eventually recovered, sometimes transformed into a wicked stepmother. The heroine of these plays is the daughter, infinitely dear to her father but usually exiled or otherwise separated from him for many years until they are eventually reunited. The father is a central figure, usually guilt-ridden and remorseful for the unpardonable things he has done to his family but forgiven at last by those he has harmed. A son or sons may or may not be part of the picture.

Generically, the late romances do seem to represent a conscious shift on Shakespeare's part away from the burdensome existential challenges of the great tragedies toward an ameliorating cosmos in which forgiveness and reunion are possible. The human capacity for self-inflicted unhappiness is no less great in some of these plays, but it is eventually swept up into a more benign counter-movement. Genre has a lot to do with this: the structure of romance or tragicomedy necessarily moves the protagonists through separation and loss toward an eventual happiness. To that important extent, the ideas are not exclusively Shakespearean; John Fletcher and others were writing tragicomedies during these same years from 1607 or so to 1613. At the same time, we need to ask why Shakespeare chose this genre at this point in his career. One inviting possibility is that he did so because it afforded him such a useful vehicle for closure in the large architectonic sense of finishing and rounding off an artistic career in the theatre. The obvious similarities of these late romances to Shakespeare's earlier comedies (see Chapter 4 on definitions of these genres) brings the wheel full circle for Shakespeare: in his end is his beginning. At the same time, the romances' inclusion of more potentially tragic circumstance lends to the enterprise a more inclusive generic perspective, and provides Shakespeare a rich opportunity for moving comedy in a new and final direction.

One senses too an autobiographical connection in the late plays, as though Shakespeare is also attempting to sort out patterns and beliefs in his own life. To explore such possibilities is necessarily speculative, but it is inviting nonetheless. One subject of special poignancy in this regard has to do with the appearance or non-appearance of a son or sons in the late romances.

We must assume that Shakespeare cared deeply about a father's love for, and need of, a son. His only son, Hamnet, twin brother of Judith, died at the age of eleven in 1596. We do not know of what cause, or whether the father was able to be with his son when this terrible thing occurred; Shakespeare was living in London while his family resided in Stratford, a long and arduous journey in those days. Shakespeare displays in his writings a remarkable ability to dramatize the sorrow of a parent over the loss of a son, as in *1 Henry VI*, when the brave Lord Talbot, hemmed in by the French in the region of Bordeaux, is joined by his son John and must then decide how to provide for the young man's safety. John refuses to preserve his life through cowardly flight and dies in battle. His father, holding John in his arms, addresses with moving eloquence 'Thou antic Death': 'Coupled in bonds of perpetuity, / Two Talbots, wingèd through the lither sky, / In thy despite shall scape mortality' (4.7.18–22). The father then dies too. In *3 Henry VI* a father learns that he has unwittingly killed his own son in the butchery of civil war and bitterly laments what he has done:

'O boy, thy father gave thee life too soon, / And hath bereft thee of thy life too late!' (2.5.92–3). The trouble is, in terms of possible auto-biographical explanation, that these plays predate 1596. So too, perhaps, does *King John*, with its exquisite litany of a mother's sorrow at being separated from her only son under circumstances that threaten his life:

> Grief fills the room up of my absent child,
> Lies in his bed, walks up and down with me,
> Puts on his pretty looks, repeats his words,
> Remembers me of all his gracious parts,
> Stuffs out his vacant garments with his form.
> (3.4.93–7)

Shakespeare then need not have had personal experience in order to write beautifully about the deaths of sons.

But how, if at all, did Shakespeare respond to that horror of Hamnet's death when it occurred? Did he use his chief vehicle of expression, the drama, to reflect on what such a death meant to him? He certainly used the sonnet form to urge to his gentlemanly friend the vital import-ance of bearing a son, though once again these writings may well pre-cede the death of Hamnet in August of 1596. We know that in October of 1596 Shakespeare instituted proceedings to obtain a coat of arms for his father John Shakespeare, so that the father (who was to die in 1601) could style himself a gentleman. Yet despite the seemingly huge importance of the father–son relationship to Shakespeare, nothing emerges in the plays of 1596 and immediately afterwards. *The Merchant of Venice, Much Ado About Nothing, The Merry Wives of Windsor, As You Like It, 1 Henry IV, Henry V, Julius Caesar*: none of these is con-cerned with the death of a son. *2 Henry IV*, c.1598, does offer one possible instance, when the widow of Hotspur criticizes Hotspur's father, the Earl of Northumberland, for not having come to the aid of his son at the battle of Shrewsbury. Otherwise, not until *Twelfth Night*, perhaps as late as 1600–2, do we encounter a story about twins, a young man and a young woman, both shipwrecked in circumstances that lead the young woman, Viola, to think that her twin, Sebastian, has drowned. By adopting a male disguise, Viola fills her brother's place until, through the magic of romantic comedy, he is in effect brought back to life.

If this is belated dreamwork on Shakespeare's part, dealing with the painful reality of death by reuniting twin boy and girl in an imagined happy ending, the fantasizing does not end there. The late plays take up the motif of a lost son in varying ways. The story of *Pericles* does not include a son in its saga of family separation and reunion, as though Shakespeare were unwilling to face the issue at this point (and indeed his source story had no son in its roster of characters). But in *Cymbeline,* Princess Imogen's two brothers, one of them the crown prince and heir to Cymbeline's throne, have long been given up for dead; the eventual discovery that they are alive recovers not one but two lost sons. *The Winter's Tale* sadly but realistically accepts the death of a son as final and irrevocable: Mamillius, the only son of King Leontes and older brother of the heroine, Perdita, dies an unhappy death as the result of his father's cruelty. *The Tempest* concludes this spectrum of imagined possibilities with yet another pair of options: the young Ferdinand is restored to his father, King Alonso of Naples, who has supposed the son to have drowned, while simultaneously, as the husband-to-be of Miranda, Ferdinand becomes the perfect son-in-law for Prospero and hence the 'son' that Prospero has never had. It is as though Shakespeare makes a deliberate turn toward romance and tragicomedy in his late writings in order to provide some closure in regard to the loss of his only son and also in regard to the approaching end of his own artistic career.

These late plays are acutely aware of the existential challenges posed by the great tragedies – sexual jealousy, anxieties of ageing, worries about lost powers, male fears of emasculating women, and a resulting increase of scepticism, melancholy, depression, misogyny, and misanthropy. Yet the essential structure of tragicomedy, moving through near-tragic failure over a prolonged period of time to eventual restoration and forgiveness, provides Shakespeare with the means of completing a progression of ideas from thesis to antithesis and synthesis. Tragicomedy enables him to reach out to a transcendental vision of happiness, one that is presided over by the gods. These gods are pagan rather than Christian; moreover, the presentation of them verges continually on the sceptical by suggesting that they are the creations of Shakespeare's art. An intensified metatheatricality invites us to be attuned to the self-aware artifice of Shakespeare's late dramaturgy. Even so, the sense of something ultimately providential hovers over the scene. The vision is unstable, but then so is Shakespeare's theatre by its very nature. Such theatre is, as Prospero says, an 'insubstantial pageant faded' that leaves 'not a rack behind'. 'We are such stuff / As dreams are made on, and our little life / Is rounded with a sleep' (*The Tempest*, 4.1.155–8). If life itself is a dream, how can theatre be any less so?

Along with the loss of a son, the biographical circumstances of Shakespeare's life most potentially at issue in the late plays, and seemingly in need of some kind of artistic closure, have to do with his marriage and his family. He had married Anne Hathaway in late 1582 at the age of eighteen. She was eight years his senior, and already three months or so pregnant when the marriage was performed. The necessity of obtaining a dispensation from the church to wed quickly, without the customary reading of the banns (the announcement of intent to marry) on three succeeding Sundays, clearly suggests that the pregnancy had been unplanned. Their daughter Susanna was baptized on 26 May 1583, presumably right after her birth. The twins, Hamnet and Judith, were baptized on 2 February 1585. Thereafter Shakespeare and his wife had no more children, though they remained legally married until he died in 1616 at the age of 53. Anne lived till she was 67, dying in 1623. Some time between 1585 and 1592, Shakespeare moved to London and began to make his way up in the world of the professional theatre. He rented rooms and never brought his family to London, though he supported them handsomely in Stratford. There he bought a fine house for his family and another for Susanna when she married a successful physician, Dr John Hall, 1607. In 1613 he bought a house in the Blackfriars district in London, though he may not have lived in it, for he had probably retired by this time to Stratford. He made investments in real estate there, having become wealthy in his profession. His daughter Judith married Thomas Quiney in 1616. What was Shakespeare's relationship with Anne like? We have no reliable information. We have only the plays, and any attempt to connect them with the sparse biographical information is plainly speculative. At the same time, the late plays do offer plentiful grounds for investigating the author's ideas, or artistic fantasies at least, on retirement, reunion with family, and preparation for death.

Pericles is not entirely by Shakespeare, and its text is at times corrupt. For these reasons, perhaps, the play was excluded from the first complete 1623 collection of his plays edited by his fellow-actors, John Heminges and Henry Condell. Yet however defective in details of language and situation, *Pericles* usefully establishes the romance or tragicomic pattern that runs through the other late plays in the genre. The play's hero undertakes a series of adventures around the eastern

Mediterranean, first to the court of Antiochus, where he competes for the hand in marriage of the King's beautiful daughter. The terms of the competition require him to solve a riddle:

> I am no viper, yet I feed
> On mother's flesh which did me breed.
> I sought a husband, in which labor
> I found that kindness in a father.
> He's father, son, and husband mild;
> I mother, wife, and yet his child.
> How they may be, and yet in two,
> As you will love, resolve it you.
> (1.1.65–72)

As riddles go, this one is not difficult. Pericles perceives at once that the King's daughter is the incestuous sexual partner of her own father. Realizing that his life is in danger for having found out the answer to the riddle, Pericles makes a hasty retreat. This is the sole instance in all Shakespeare of overt incest, and it is plainly intended as an instructive warning.

When Pericles is shipwrecked on the shore of Pentapolis and makes his way to the court of that country, he encounters a situation that is the virtuous opposite of the danger he has just escaped. King Simonides also presides over a competition for the hand of his daughter, and briefly pretends to be wary of the attractive new candidate who has emerged out of the sea, but the anger is only a pretence (as it is later in Prospero's handling of the courtship of Ferdinand and Miranda) and lasts but a moment. Simonides is the model of what a father should be: loving of his daughter, wealthy, generous, welcoming, and eager to see his daughter married to a young man who is the right choice of both her and her father. The marriage proceeds apace and soon results in a pregnancy. When, however, Pericles and his wife Thaisa undertake a shipboard journey during the final term of her pregnancy, another fearful storm turns their story to apparent tragedy. Thaisa seemingly dies during childbirth, prompting the sailors to insist that her body be committed to the deep; otherwise, they say, the storm 'will not lie till the ship be cleared of the dead' (3.1.48–9). Superstitiously, they will not yield. Pericles, grieving, has Thaisa put over the side in a tightly-caulked chest, and commits the infant, Marina, to the care of her nurse. Yet Thaisa is not actually dead, or else is revived from death by a gentleman of Ephesus (Cerimon) who is practised in the arts of 'blest infusions / That dwells in vegetives, in metals, stones' (3.2.38–9). Thaisa is provided with a haven in Ephesus at the Temple of Diana, where she becomes a votaress of that goddess.

The father–daughter relationship is at the heart of the remainder of the play, most of which is generally thought to be the work of Shakespeare. A common feature of romance drama is that it allows for a considerable lapse of time in mid play, between the 'tragi-' and the 'comedy' of tragicomedy, sufficient in this case for Marina to grow to young womanhood. She encounters numerous mishaps and mis-adventures on the way, being assailed by the jealous wife of Cleon of Tarsus, to whom she is entrusted for a time, and by pirates that sell her into the slave trade of prostitution in Mytilene (in the Aegean), where she proceeds to save her virginity by converting would-be cus-tomers to a virtuous way of life. Pericles, meantime, has vowed to keep his hair 'unscissored' (3.3.31) until such time as his daughter is mar-ried. He arrives eventually at the port of Mytilene a deeply chastened man, in rough garments and with long hair and beard, having 'for this three months' not spoken to a soul and refusing to take any sustenance 'But to prorogue his grief' (5.1.25–7). His main grief, his attendants and followers believe, 'springs from the loss / Of a belovèd daughter and a wife' (30–1), both of whom he supposes to be dead. The 'disaster' of 'one mortal night' at sea 'Drove him to this' (38–9). Does he experience guilt at having abandoned them both, however much under the press of circumstances? The play-text does not make this clear, but the extremity of his wordless isolation suggests that his spiritual affliction is both deep and unresolved. Only when Marina is brought aboard his ship in the harbour to see if she, as miracle-worker, can do anything for Pericles does he respond to the sound of a human voice. 'My dearest wife was like this maid', he says, 'and such a one / My daughter might have been' (110–11). A tearful and joyous reunion is then followed by the appearance of Diana to Pericles in a vision, bidding that he visit her temple in Ephesus. There he finds his long-lost wife.

In this version of what is to become a recurring scenario in the late plays, Shakespeare imagines what it would be like for a husband to be reunited with a wife whom he was abandoned years ago, under constraint but with a lingering sense of guilt that only increases with time. The restoration of the lost wife and daughter is presented as a miracle in *Pericles*, so overwhelming in its undeserved happiness that Pericles asks a follower to strike him, 'Lest this great sea of joys rushing upon me / O'erbear the shores of my mortality, / And drown me with their sweetness' (5.1.196–9). Blissfully and paradoxically, his daughter has given him a second life, just as he was the first author of her being: Marina is one who 'begett'st him that did thee beget' (200). The family is successfully reconstituted; the only misogynistic element is to be found in Dionyza, the wife of Cleon, who, like a wicked stepmother, attempts to snuff out the life of Marina for outshining the merits of Dionyza's own daughter, Philoten (4 Chorus 15–45). No son takes part in this narrative, just as no son is to be found in the play's sources, John Gower's *Confessio Amantis* and Laurence Twine's *The Pattern of Painful Adventures* (c.1594–5, second edition 1607).

Cymbeline gives a frightening centrality to the murderous stepmother glimpsed at in *Pericles*'s Dionyza. King Cymbeline, recently a widower, is now married to a woman who is a caricature of the witchlike stepmother in folk tale. The Queen in *Cymbeline* is intent on marrying her oafish son Cloten ('a thing / Too bad for bad report', 1.1.16–17) to the King's daughter, Imogen. When Imogen chooses instead to marry a virtuous gentleman well below her in social station named Posthumus Leonatus, she incurs her father's wrath and the homicidal hatred of her stepmother. At the play's end, King Cymbeline learns to his astonishment and dismay that the Queen 'Affected greatness' (i.e., yearned for social advancement) by her marriage with the King. She 'Married your royalty', Doctor Cornelius tells Cymbeline, 'was wife to your place, / Abhorred your person' (5.5.38–40). Moreover, the Queen has confessed that she only pretended to love Imogen, who 'Was as a scorpion in her sight' and whose life, 'But that her flight prevented it, she had / Ta'en off by poison'. Well might Cymbeline marvel, 'Oh, most delicate fiend! / Who is't can read a woman?' (43–8). Onto this creature of malice Shakespeare has scapegoated every imaginable anxiety about the managerial, suffocating maternal figure in the nightmare world of his tragic imagination. The overthrow and defeat of this wicked Queen signals in negative terms the regenerative ending of this tragicomedy.

Imogen is coveted and envied by Cloten and the Queen for her political importance. She is the sole daughter and seemingly the heir of King Cymbeline, since her two brothers were stolen in infancy (one at the age of three, the other in swaddling clothes) from their nursery, and 'to this hour' there is 'no guess in knowledge / Which way they went' (1.1.58–61). We as audience, presumably attuned to the conventions of romantic story-telling, may well suppose that these sons will eventually show up, since the mention of them so early in the play and in such mysterious circumstances might seem otherwise inexplicable, but this insight is denied to Cymbeline and his daughter. The reason for the King's intemperate anger at Imogen's socially imprudent marriage is that she has ruinously upset his plans for the succession. Instead of tying herself to the son of Cymbeline's new queen, thus consolidating their two dynasties, Imogen has wilfully chosen one who is unacceptable to Cymbeline as a potential consort to Imogen on the British throne. 'Thou took'st a beggar', he arraigns her, 'wouldst have made my throne / A seat for baseness' (143–4). Imogen does not appear to be ambitious for royal power; she seems overjoyed when at last her brothers resurface, enabling the older of the two, Guiderius, to assume his position as crown prince while Imogen resumes her own long-interrupted marriage with Posthumus.

Imogen's arduous journeying in Wales in search of her estranged and exiled husband provides the necessary lapse of time for this tragicomic play to turn away from its tragic beginnings and toward restoration. The tragic dimensions of her saga are as marked as are the elements of adventure. Having been falsely accused by the unprincipled Italian, Iachimo, of lack of fidelity to her marriage vows, Imogen learns that her husband has ordered that she be executed. The loyal servant charged with this grim assignment, Pisanio, cannot bring himself to do the deed, and so Imogen is allowed to live, but under the necessity of adopting a male disguise and finding some means of survival in mountainous Wales, to which she has travelled at the command of Posthumus. For his part, Posthumus acts the role of the deceived and erring tragic hero. Like Othello and Leontes, he is deluded into an insane jealousy over a truly virtuous woman. Even though the tempter Iachimo is a practised villain, like Iago, Posthumus's willingness to wager rashly on Imogen's virtue and then believe the worst of her is ultimately his responsibility. In soliloquy, he sounds as tortured and miserable as the most unhappy of tragic protagonists:

> Is there no way for men to be, but women
> Must be half-workers? We are all bastards,

> And that most venerable man which I
> Did call my father was I know not where
> When I was stamped. Some coiner with his tools
> Made me a counterfeit; yet my mother seemed
> The Dian of that time.   (2.5.1–7)

The misogyny of this speech, the insistence on blaming women for his unhappiness, the mistrust and hatred, the longing for 'vengeance, vengeance' (8), all bespeak the same fear of betrayal by women that we find in Hamlet, Othello, King Lear, Macbeth, Timon of Athens, and Coriolanus. Posthumus is all the more appalled by Imogen's apparent cunning in that she seemed so hesitant to give herself even to him, her husband: 'Me of my lawful pleasure she restrained / And prayed me oft forbearance; did it with / A pudency so rosy the sweet view on't / Might well have warmed old Saturn, that I thought her / As chaste as unsunned snow' (9–13). His deepest fear is that women are deceivers, and that his wife is just like all the rest.

From these tragic dilemmas the central figures of *Cymbeline* are rescued by a series of events as improbable as they are metatheatrically self-aware. Imogen, disguised as a young man, desperately in need of help, falls in with an old man and two younger men dwelling in a cave and living off their mountainous environment as hunters. These young men turn out eventually to be Imogen's lost brothers, of course, having been taken from court years ago by a disgruntled and alienated courtier named Belarius. Brothers and sister (she still disguised as a man) remain unidentified to one another. More improbabilities follow. The loathsome Cloten, son of the Queen, dressed in some of Posthumus's garments (obtained for him by Pisanio) and searching for Imogen in order to ravish her and kill Posthumus before her very eyes (3.5.138–9), encounters Guiderius (known by the name of Polydore) and is beheaded by that brave young man for his insolence. Imogen, afflicted with some sort of illness, takes a medicine given her by Pisanio which turns out to be a sleeping potion devised by Doctor Cornelius as a means of virtuously duping the wicked Queen, who has asked him for a real poison. The seemingly dead Imogen is laid out for burial by her grieving brothers, awakens to find herself alone, falls grief-stricken on the headless body of Cloten which she takes to be her husband since the corpse is dressed in Posthumus's clothes, and is found in this desperate plight by Lucius, commander of the

Roman forces attempting to bring Britain back under the control of the Roman empire. The real Posthumus, having returned from Italy to Britain with the intent of ending his own wretched existence, doffs his Roman habit for the dress of a British peasant, but then reverts to Roman garb in order that he may be imprisoned and executed by the victorious British forces. He is brought before the King for sentencing just as Lucius and 'Fidele' (Imogen), having been captured in the battle, are led in under guard. The villain, Iachimo, is among the Italians who have come to Britain and are now assembled by their captors for a determination of their fate. Thus it is that all the characters of the play, except for the dead Cloten and his mother, are brought together for a large finale.

Why does Shakespeare make such a point of narrative improbability in weaving his tragicomic tale? In part the answer may be that the genres of romance and tragicomedy call for such devices. Then, too, some of these same devices are essentially as Shakespeare found them in his chief source, a story from the second day, story nine, of Giovanni Boccaccio's *Decameron*, along with Raphael Holinshed's *Chronicles of England, Scotland, and Ireland* (1587 edition). A deeper reason may be that Shakespeare is intent on highlighting what is wondrously unexpected and miraculous in the rescuing of Cymbeline, Posthumus, Iachimo, and others from their own worst selves. Divine deliverance of Posthumus takes an overtly mythic character. He is in prison, welcoming his bondage; he believes still that Imogen is dead, but he has forgiven her for her imagined adultery and wishes only to suffer punishment for the unforgivable thing he thinks he has done to her. In this receptive state of mind he is visited in his sleep by the apparition of his family, praying to Jupiter for his aid. Jupiter responds by descending '*in thunder and lightning, sitting upon an eagle*' and throwing a thunderbolt (5.4.92 SD). The consolation he offers is to affirm that 'Whom best I love I cross; to make my gift, / The more delayed, delighted. Be content' (101–2). He reassures them, in other words, that their sufferings have been under his supervision, and have been designed to teach them the rewards of patience. Their past tribulations will only make the happy ending of their story all the more unexpected and joyous.

This idea is the formula for tragicomedy. Jupiter is the presiding genius of that genre in *Cymbeline*. He is, moreover, the creation in this play of the dramatist, taking on the role of *deus ex machina* in order to guide the play to its happy ending. He is *deus ex machina* in almost a literal and technical sense; the term derives from the practice in ancient Greek drama of lowering the god onto the scene in the finale of a play by means of the 'machine' or crane. Here Jupiter emerges from an aperture in the 'heavens' over the Jacobean stage and is lowered by ropes and pulleys until, having played his part, he '*Ascends*' (the original stage direction at line 113). Shakespeare uses this descent from the 'heavens' only rarely, and only in his late plays; the other instance is in the masque of the gods in *The Tempest*. New technology, some of it imported from Italy into court masques, offered expanded opportunities for bravura effects of this sort in the theatre of the early 1600s. Jupiter's manifestation of himself to mortals is patently theatrical, calling attention to the artifice of the staging and the event itself. It is so theatrically self-aware, in the style of Jacobean tragicomedies by playwrights like John Fletcher, that modern productions sometimes play it as campy and oddly funny.

We might be inclined at first not to take the episode seriously, and yet the scene is vital as a comment on the nature of closure in tragicomedy. Seen from the perspective of what Jupiter tells us, the whole story retrospectively makes sense: human suffering has a purpose in the transcendental scheme of things. It teaches us to be humbly aware of our own penchant for self-destructive behaviour, and it offers an artistic vision of how our tribulations will end in harmony if we submit ourselves to a larger providential plan. 'Be content', Jupiter bids us. As the wise Pisanio has said, 'Fortune brings in some boats that are not steered' (4.3.46). Shakespeare as Jacobean dramatist is the ultimate presider over this theatrical mystery; the pagan gods are his, and they supervise the conduct of a tragicomic play as the dramatist wishes.

The Winter's Tale ends with a scene of theatrical sleight of hand no less theatrically self-aware than that of *Cymbeline*. First of all, Shakespeare leaves us for most of the play with the false impression that Queen Hermione is dead, as the consequence of her having been put on trial by her husband for an adultery that she certainly did not commit. Nowhere else in the canon does Shakespeare so deliberately mislead his audience about such an important matter. Hermione's spirit appears in a vision to the courtier Antigonus as one of 'the spirits o'th' dead', 'In pure white robes, / Like very sanctity', bidding him care for the babe to whom Hermione has given birth. Then, 'with shrieks, / She melted into air.' Antigonus can draw only one conclusion: 'I do believe / Hermione hath suffered death' (3.3.15–41). The play drops no hints of ultimate deliverance, as does *Cymbeline* when we are told, early on, about two sons of the king who have strangely disappeared from court. We have every reason to believe that Hermione is dead. The deception is essential for the great surprise of the play's final scene, when the still-grieving King Leontes is invited to view a newly finished statue of Queen Hermione, some sixteen years or more after her supposed death. The statue comes to life; the guilty husband and his innocent wife are united at last, since the statue turns out to be Hermione herself, having been hidden away all this time until that which was lost has been found (3.2.135–6, 5.1.40), i.e., their lost daughter, Perdita. ('Perdita' means 'the lost one'; the words 'lost' and 'found' have a special prominence in this play.) Once again, Shakespeare chooses to end a tragicomedy with an event that is wondrously improbable and highly metatheatrical.

The Winter's Tale is quintessential tragicomedy. It is divided into two halves at the beginning of the fourth act by the appearance of old father Time, boasting of his ability to 'slide / O'er sixteen years', to 'o'erthrow law and in one self-born hour / To plant and o'erwhelm custom'. He bids us be patient as if we 'had slept between' (4.1.5–17). This choric allegorical figure flaunts the theatrical artifice of his intervention, like the Chorus in *Pericles*. We are in his hands, necessarily submitting to his breaking the classical unities of time and place and his insistent reminder that we are watching a play in the theatre. The play up to this point has been deeply concerned with tragic events: the insane jealousy of King Leontes of Sicilia, the innocence of his Queen and his best friend (Polixenes, King of Bohemia) who stand falsely accused of adultery, the apparent death of Hermione following her trial, the actual death of the crown prince Mamillius, and the King's determination that the Queen's newly-born daughter be put to death. Mamillius's death is an especially poignant consequence of the fallen world of Sicilia; he cannot be brought back to life, even in a tragicomedy, as though by way of acknowledgement on the dramatist's part that the death of a son can indeed be final and unrecoverable. In the second half of the play, as the action moves from the wintry court of Sicilia to the make-believe kingdom of Bohemia (complete with an unhistorical seacoast), we enter into a world of springtime flowering, of sheep-shearing festivals, of song and dance, and of young people falling in love. When plot complications inevitably assail the young lovers in Bohemia, those complications are of the sort we have come to expect in romantic comedy: a father who opposes his royal son's engagement to a seeming shepherdess, the necessity of an elopement, the uncertainties of a shipboard journey, the mixup of identities when the young people reach Sicilia, and all the rest.

Leontes is, more than any husband in the late plays, terribly guilty of a jealous rage. His persuasion that Hermione and Polixenes are lovers is based on no other 'evidence' than that Hermione is nine months' pregnant and that Polixines's visit to Sicilia has lasted exactly that same period of time. No courtier supports the King in his paranoia; they all urge him to believe in Hermione's innocence. His inability to do so is clearly a product of his own diseased imagination, his fear of cuckoldry, his mistrust of women. Leontes suffers the life-destroying jealousy of Othello, or Iago. Leontes's ruminations in soliloquy are as eloquent as those of any tragic protagonist in Shakespeare:

> There have been,
> Or I am much deceived, cuckolds ere now;
> And many a man there is, even at this present,
> Now while I speak this, holds his wife by th' arm,
> That little thinks she has been sluiced in 's absence
> And his pond fished by his next neighbor, by
> Sir Smile, his neighbor. Nay, there's comfort in't
> Whiles other men have gates and those gates opened,
> As mine, against their will. Should all despair
> That have revolted wives, the tenth of mankind
> Would hang themselves. Physic for't there's none.
> It is a bawdy planet, that will strike
> Where 'tis predominant; and 'tis powerful, think it,
> From east, west, north, and south. Be it concluded,
> No barricado for a belly. Know't,
> It will let in and out the enemy
> With bag and baggage. Many thousand on 's
> Have the disease and feel't not.   (1.2.190–207)

Like other tragic protagonists, like Othello especially, Leontes learns too late that his wife has been true and chaste. She dies as a direct result of his terrible jealousy. Or so it seems, until it turns out that we are watching a tragicomedy and that a miraculous second chance is belatedly at hand.

Leontes's reunion after sixteen years of separation with his daughter Perdita, whom he had ordered to be abandoned in her infancy in 'some remote and desert place' (2.3.176) where she would be sure to die, is tearfully joyous, like the reunions of Pericles with Marina and Cymbeline with Imogen. The flawed protagonist is given a miraculous and undeserved second chance. Observers at the Sicilian court are struck with the wondrous quality of this event. It is 'so like an old tale that the verity of it is in strong suspicion', says one. It is a sight 'which was to be seen, cannot be spoken of', says another (5.2.28–44). The story of Antigonus, who carried the child to Bohemia and lost his life to a marauding bear in doing so, is 'Like an old tale still, which will have matter to rehearse though credit be asleep and not an ear open' (62–3). The play's very title, *The Winter's Tale*, bears the imprint of this idea. The coming to life of Hermione, like the coming to life of Pygmalion's statue, is an even more astonishing and nearly inexplicable mystery. The apparent explanation is that Antigonus's wife Paulina has sequestered away Hermione for some sixteen years to allow penitence to do its ultimately restorative work on Leontes and to provide time for Perdita to come of age. But this account seems implausible on its face. How would Paulina and Hermione know that in sixteen years the lost Perdita would turn up at the Sicilian court? Why would they wish to wait that long, denying Hermione and Leontes the happiness that is eventually restored to them? How conceivable is it that Leontes has 'performed / A saintlike sorrow' (5.1.1–2) all this time, begging Paulina to remind him ceaselessly of what he has done?

An alternative explanation thus suggests itself, that Hermione is miraculously brought back from death to life. Paulina speaks of herself as a kind of magician, able to 'make the statue move indeed', though she insists that in doing so she is not 'assisted / By wicked powers' (5.3.87–90). What she will do is a miracle. 'It is required / You do awake your faith', she says (94–5). The awakening fulfills the intent of the gods, who hover about this play as the presiders over its tragicomic form with Paulina as their agent. The oracle of Apollo at Delphi has spoken earlier in the play, and in terms that are remarkably unambivalent for an oracle: ' "Hermione is chaste, Polixenes blameless, Camillo a true subject, Leontes a jealous tyrant, his innocent babe truly begotten, and the King shall live without an heir if that which is lost be not found" ' (3.2.132–6). This judgemental prediction structures the narrative shift of *The Winter's Tale* from tragedy to comedy. Once again Shakespeare has chosen the pagan gods to embody the principles of his tragicomic dramaturgy. Again, the gods are his creation as dramatist; Paulina is his stand-in as theatre magician. The self-awareness of a highly contrived stagecraft brings home to us both the artifice and the deeply moving mysteriousness of the play's final scene.

Autobiographically, *The Winter's Tale* may seem applicable with a special poignancy to an authorial fantasy about husband, wife, and daughter. A guilty husband has destroyed his happiness by doing away with his guiltless wife. After a painful absence of many years, during which he has suffered endless pangs of contrition, the husband is restored to his wife as though by an undeserved miracle. She has aged, because the sculptor's genius 'lets go by some sixteen years and makes her / As she lived now', 'wrinkled, 'agèd', not as she was as a younger woman (5.3.28–32). She is older now, as is the husband, and he realizes that he loves and desires her now for what she is. 'Oh, she's warm!' Leontes exclaims, as Hermione descends from her pedestal, enabling them to touch and embrace. 'She hangs about his neck', observes Camillo (109–13). The reunion of the father with the long-lost daughter is no less precious. Whether Shakespeare thought about this in the context of his long separation from his family while he worked in London, his having had no children with Anne for some twenty-five years, and the imminence in 1610 or so of his retirement to Stratford, we cannot say for sure, but the idea is appealing. It brings together so many ideas of closure: how to end a career, how to round off a family life, how to reclaim a marriage, how to end a play. The son is inexorably gone, but other compensations remain.

The Tempest seems even more intent on bringing together the elements in drama and in life that go to make up a suitable ending. The play was given pride of first place in the First Folio of 1623, as though the editors, Heminges and Condell, Shakespeare's longtime collaborators in the King's company, saw *The Tempest* as a summing up and a demonstration of the things that Shakespeare did with such supreme skill. That helps explain why *The Tempest* has long been regarded as Shakespeare's retirement play. He continued to write afterwards, collaborating with John Fletcher, his successor as chief dramatist for the King's Men, in *The Two Noble Kinsmen* and *Henry VIII*, but *The Tempest* may have been his last solo event. It repeatedly shows an awareness that its author's career is drawing to a close.

In its relatively short span – *The Tempest* is roughly three-fifths the length of *Cymbeline* – this play is a veritable feast of Shakespearean dramaturgy. Lacking a single plot source, it turns instead to earlier Shakespearean works for models. It is a romantic comedy somewhat in the vein of Shakespeare's early writings: 'romantic' in its account of a journey by sea, of separation and loss and eventual reunion, of shipwreck (as in *The Comedy of Errors*, *Twelfth Night*, and *Pericles*); 'romantic' too in centring one of its plots on the falling in love of two young people who, as we saw in Chapter 2, cling to the idealism of holding off sexual fulfillment until marriage and are encouraged in this by the young woman's father. Like many an early comedy (*The Two Gentlemen of Verona*, *A Midsummer Night's Dream*, *Much Ado About Nothing*, *Twelfth Night*, etc.), *The Tempest* features broadly comic characters whose hilarious antics occupy a subplot or substratum of the play that is also deftly connected to the main story. At the same time, *The Tempest* shares with other late plays the sombre elements characteristic of tragicomedy. The tale of cutthroat political machination in mainland Italy, though narrated as having taken place some twelve years ago (1.2.53), is one of social injustice, of brother against brother, of forced banishment to an almost certain death. Even on the island in the present moment, two attempts are made at political assassination and takeover. The theme of penance hangs heavy over the play. Alonso, like Leontes in *The Winter's Tale*, is a guilt-ridden monarch, certain that the apparent death by drowning of his only son is the consequence of his own culpability. Forgiveness figures centrally in the play's denouement, and is associated throughout with wondrously improbable events.

Prospero is many things: a magician, an exile, the once and future Duke of Milan, a careful father, a hopeful father-in-law, a master of two slaves, a colonialist (in a limited sense), an exacting teacher and homilist, a playwright, a retiree, and perhaps in some ways a stand-in for the dramatist. He is at once overbearing and wise, vengeful and compassionate, dogmatic and willing to listen. Sometimes today he is played as autocratic and even sadistic; our modern culture is suspicious of authority figures, and Prospero is certainly in command on the island of the Tempest. This chapter will argue, on the other hand, that he can be viewed as a successful even if flawed and self-critical character, and that his achievements contribute to a kind of summing up of what an artist and father like Shakespeare might have hoped to have accomplished in his career and in his life.

As a father, Prospero succeeds in bringing about a domestic happiness that has eluded virtually all his predecessors in the late plays – in most of Shakespeare, in fact. Old Egeus, in *A Midsummer Night's Dream*, refuses to let his daughter Hermia marry according to her own choice, even when her young man, Lysander, can hardly be distinguished from her father's arbitrary choice, Demetrius. Shylock, in *The Merchant of Venice*, loses his daughter Jessica by having 'too much respect upon the world'. 'They lose it that do buy it with much care' (1.1.74–5), says Gratiano. The phrase is offered as friendly advice to Antonio, but it fits Shylock well. Brabantio, in *Othello*, distraught by what he takes to be his daughter Desdemona's desertion of him in her elopement with Othello, disappears from the play, a broken man. Desdemona learns later that her father is dead: 'The match was mortal to him, and pure grief / Shore his old thread in vain', her uncle Gratiano tells her (5.2.211–13). To King Lear, Cordelia's quiet but firm refusal to flatter her father in the hyperbolic terms he has learned to expect is tantamount to a betrayal: 'Better thou / Hadst not been born than not t' have pleased me better', he accuses her (1.1.237–8). The incestuous bond between King Antiochus in *Pericles* and his beautiful but sin-marked daughter is only an outward manifestation of a potentially unhealthy lack of willingness on the part of many fathers in Shakespeare to let go of their daughters to younger men. The sexual nature of this rivalry between father and prospective son-in-law seems evident in Cymbeline's intense disapproval of Posthumus Leonatus as a mate for the King's daughter Imogen, even if there are political reasons as well for the King's anger. King Polixenes in *The Winter's Tale*, an otherwise admirable character, cannot be reconciled to his son's romantic attachment to the seeming shepherdess Perdita, despite the fact that the King's loyal counselor, Camillo, is very much on her side.

Prospero knows well enough how to play the role of the jealous father. A romantic comedy demands plot complication of this sort, and Prospero, as author/magician/director of his own play, obliges. When young Ferdinand, the crown prince of Naples, washes ashore in Prospero's tempest and immediately encounters Miranda and Prospero, the father subjects the young man to harsh interrogation. How dare he offer such brazen advances to Miranda as to ask if she be 'maid or no' – i.e., a human young woman or some goddess, and also if she is married or not? 'What wert thou if the King of Naples heard thee?' asks Prospero (1.2.430–6), suggesting that Ferdinand's father might be taken aback to see his son and heir usurping the father's place and then committing himself to a romantic attachment with a stranger at first sight. Prospero knows that Alonso, King of Naples, is alive on another part of the island; Ferdinand sadly supposes that his father has drowned. Miranda is distraught at her father's harsh tone: 'Why speaks my father so ungently?' (449). Prospero is far from relenting, it seems: branding Ferdinand as a 'traitor', the father (as we have seen in Chapter 2) vows to manacle Ferdinand's neck and feet together. 'Seawater shalt thou drink; thy food shall be / The fresh-brook mussels, withered roots, and husks / Wherein the acorn cradled' (464–8). When Ferdinand draws his sword in defiance, Prospero charms him into motionlessness and then insults him as a coward who makes a show of bravery but dares not strike because his conscience 'Is so possessed with guilt'. Prospero is positively brutal with Miranda. 'What, I say, / My foot my tutor?' That is, how dare you, as my lowly subordinate, presume to instruct me as head? 'Hence! Hang not on my garments.' 'Silence!' (472–9). Later, we see Ferdinand '*bearing a log*' in an abject physical servitude reminiscent of the slave-work Caliban is obliged to do. Miranda is appalled that work of 'such baseness' is being forced on a prince; menial labour of this sort 'Had never like executor' (3.1.1–13).

Yet from the start Prospero makes plain to us as audience or as readers that he is only playing a role, presumably for the young people's ultimate benefit. Ferdinand has encountered Miranda because Prospero, through Ariel, has arranged matters this way. Prospero wants the marriage to take place, for dynastic reasons (uniting the kingdoms of Milan and Naples) and as a means of seeing his only daughter happily wedded. He at once conveys to us in an aside the nature of his motive for being so brusque: 'They are both in either's powers; but this swift business / I must uneasy make, lest too light winning / Make the prize light' (1.1.454–6). This motive operates simultaneously on a personal and dramaturgic level: it reinforces the play's insistent teaching that sexual fulfillment should not precede marriage, and it provides *The Tempest* with a plot complication. Every love story needs a difficulty to be overcome, or there is no plot. 'It works' (497), says Prospero in an aside, congratulating himself as dramatist that the plot is proceeding according to script. When he has occasion later on to witness Ferdinand's carrying of logs and Miranda's cries of compassion,

Prospero becomes chorus to his own work. He is either 'invisible' or otherwise unseen and unheard by the young people. 'Poor worm', he says of Miranda, 'thou art infected!' (3.1.31). He greets their exchange of vows with joyous approval: 'Fair encounter / Of two most rare affections! Heavens rain grace / On that which breeds between 'em!' (74–6). Once they have left the stage, he brings this scene to a choric conclusion by saying, to himself and to us, 'So glad of this as they I cannot be, / Who are surprised with all; but my rejoicing / At nothing can be more' (93–5).

We need not assume that this letting go is easy for Prospero. The signs of an emotional struggle are probably evident in his need to act out his own reluctance in this way. After all, he has lived for twelve years with Miranda as his sole companion other than Caliban. Prospero and Miranda have been partners, like Brabantio and Desdemona; with no mother or wife in the picture, they have been emotionally dependent on each other to an extraordinary degree. They have kept household together. Yet Prospero does let go, and embraces his prospective son-in-law as a vital new part of his own happiness. This is one important way in which *The Tempest* provides closure not just for itself as a play but for the Shakespeare canon as a whole, and for the concept embodied in the canon regarding personal right conduct.

The role that Prospero plays toward Alonso and the other shipwrecked Italians takes a similar form. As if he were the very spirit of tragicomedy, like Jupiter in *Cymbeline*, Prospero subjects his fellow countrymen to painful visions, disappointments, sorrows, and temptations that go together to make up the plot of this portion of *The Tempest*. He deliberately misleads, allowing Alonso to suppose that his son has drowned. By Ariel's means he torments the Italian party with visions of a richly laden banquet table that then vanishes before their eyes when they hungrily reach for the food. Instead of providing a feast, he subjects them to a homily on their manifold sins delivered by Ariel in the guise of a harpy – that is to say, a fabulous monster with a woman's face and breasts and a vulture's body, personifying in Greek and Roman mythology the divine retribution that some of these men deserve (3.3). They are all 'distracted' (5.1.12), overwhelmed, awed. Is Prospero prompted by a desire for revenge? Certainly his brother Antonio has given him ample cause, by having taken away the dukedom of Milan from Prospero some twelve years earlier with the aid of Alonso as King of Naples and his brother Sebastian (see 5.1.73–4).

Prospero does indeed feel the promptings of vengeance, until Ariel, the spirit who assists him in all things, offers the observation that he, Ariel, would feel some tender concern for these men 'were I human' (5.1.20). Prospero is moved by this example to do as he is advised:

> Hast thou, which art but air, a touch, a feeling
> Of their afflictions, and shall not myself,
> One of their kind, that relish all as sharply
> Passion as they, be kindlier moved than thou art?
> Though with their high wrongs I am struck to the quick,
> Yet with my nobler reason 'gainst my fury
> Do I take part. The rarer action is
> In virtue than in vengeance. They being penitent,
> The sole drift of my purpose doth extend
> Not a frown further.   (5.1.21–30)

Prospero sees his desire for vengeance as a product of corrupted human nature, to which, as a mortal, he is prone. He sees too that he has the power to do something about this sinful weakness, by subordinating it to human reason. In doing so, he aligns himself with the spirit of forgiveness that is such an essential element of structure and of idea in Shakespeare's late plays.

If Prospero has a worthy motive in deceiving Alonso into believing for most of the play that Ferdinand is drowned, the intention is presumably to lead Alonso through sorrow and penitence to the kind of joyful reunion experienced by Pericles, Cymbeline, and Leontes – as Jupiter says in *Cymbeline*, to make the gift of happiness 'The more delayed, delighted' (5.4.102). The plan seems to work with Alonso. With Sebastian and Antonio the prognosis is decidedly less optimistic. They are villains, and remain so to the very end, still cynical for all their briefly having been daunted by Ariel's strange visions. Given this hard-heartedness in Antonio and Sebastian, Prospero's plot device for the villains is quite unlike that which he devises for Alonso. Antonio and Sebastian are given an opportunity to see what they will do if temptation lies in their way. When Ariel puts Alonso and others to sleep by his magic, Antonio plots at once with Sebastian to assassinate their companions, including the King, and thus seize into their hands absolute power (2.1.188–310). Ariel is of course watching over all this, and awakens the King in time to abort the revolutionary plot. Prospero's scheme in this instance cannot be to awaken conscience, for Antonio and Sebastian have no conscience; it is instead to expose villainy for what it is, and demonstrate a benign overseeing power in the world of Shakespearean comedy, embodied in Prospero and Ariel, that will not allow such villainy to have its way. Prospero and Ariel do precisely the same thing with the clownish characters, Trinculo and Stephano: given a seeming opportunity to assassinate Prospero and thus gain control of the island, the clowns jump at the opportunity only to be exposed and ridiculed. They are incorrigible in much the way Antonio and Sebastian are incorrigible. The play suggests that such types cannot be reformed, but they can be watched, disarmed, and subjected to satirical laughter. Caliban is of a different sort: as a creature of the natural world, he is beyond the reach of most instruction (he remains impenitent about his attempt to possess Miranda sexually), but his perceptions of natural beauty are remarkably sensitive. He can be forgiven and left behind in the environment to which he belongs when the others return to Italy.

The Tempest thus rounds out Shakespeare's story in ways that seem well suited to a dramatist on the verge of retirement from the stage, and, in due course, from life itself. The happy relationship that Prospero fashions for himself with Miranda and Ferdinand may represent, at some distance of dreamwork or fantasy, the author's hopes for Susanna in her marriage with John Hall. (Judith was not to marry Thomas Quiney until 1616, well after the writing of *The Tempest* and near to the time of Shakespeare's death.) The absence of a mother for Miranda and a wife for Prospero may strike a more melancholy note; nothing resembling the ageing but beloved Hermione of *The Winter's Tale* with whom Leontes is so gratefully reunited has been introduced into *The Tempest*. On the other hand, the lost son of *The Winter's Tale* perhaps re-emerges in various guises in *The Tempest*: Ferdinand, thought dead, is restored to his father Alonso while also taking the place of the son that Prospero never had. Ferdinand is a very satisfactory son-in-law. 'Let me live here forever!' he exclaims in wonderment at the splendid masque that Prospero and Ariel have staged for the benefit of the engaged couple. 'So rare a wondered father and a wife / Makes this place Paradise' (4.1.122–4; 'wife' is sometimes read as 'wise', since the tall 's' in early modern print resembles 'f'). How nice for Prospero, and, one is tempted to imagine, for Shakespeare, at least in his dreams, to have a son-in-law who so greatly admires and loves his bride's father!

The moment is all the more fulfilling because it is a part of a denouement in which Prospero also retires from his art as creator of dramatic visions. With the aid of Ariel and his fellow spirits he has 'bedimmed / The noontide sun, called forth the mutinous winds', and opened graves to let forth their sleepers by his 'so potent art' (5.1.41–50). Now it is time for the revels he has created, the actors he has commandeered, and 'the great globe itself' to dissolve and 'Leave not a rack behind' (4.1.148–56). The 'great globe' seemingly points to Shakespeare's own theatre, the Globe, south of the River Thames right across from London, and also to the great globe of the universe. The moment of closure in this play is one of retirement from a career, of drowning one's books of magic, of saying a fond farewell to the spirit Ariel who has created Prospero's shows for him, of reconciling oneself with one's enemies, of relinquishing a daughter to a younger man, and of preparing for death. As Prospero says of his impending retirement, 'Every third thought shall be my grave' (5.1.315).

Henry VIII and *The Two Noble Kinsmen* are an aftermath, in the sense that they appear to follow Shakespeare's official swan song and are the product of collaborative work. To the large extent that they too are touched with the spirit of tragicomedy and wondrous unforeseen deliverance, they seem appropriate to an artistic career at the point of closure. *Henry VIII* tells a story, as we have seen in Chapter 5, of mighty affairs of state in which the participants unknowingly contribute to a blessed event – the birth of the future Elizabeth I – that gives meaning to the otherwise bewildering welter of historical accidents. In *The Two Noble Kinsmen*, as in Shakespeare's other late romances, pagan deities provide a theatrically sensational answer to the petitions of humans under their control. At the altar of Diana, Emilia receives her answer as to which of her two wooers she must marry. The rival claims of Mars (Arcite) and Venus (Palamon) are reconciled in the play's tragicomic ending.

A word more about *The Tempest*. For all its harmonies of reconciliation, this play remains at one level at least the work of an interestingly humanistic and even sceptical playwright. The forces that steer this play toward its conclusion are under the control of the dramatist. The pagan gods who descend in Act 4 to bless the nuptials of Ferdinand and Miranda are creations of the dramatist, as they are in *Pericles*, *Cymbeline*, and *The Winter's Tale*. Their being pagan is perhaps a way of avoiding the blasphemy of bringing the Christian God on stage; it also signals to us that the overseeing presence in *The Tempest* is Prospero himself, and, behind him, Shakespeare. This is not to deny that Providence in the more traditional religious sense needs to be accounted for. The play acknowledges the aid of Providence twice. The first is when Miranda asks how she and her father came ashore at the island; Prospero replies, 'By Providence divine' (1.2.159–60). He then goes on to explain what he means in human terms: a kindly Neapolitan, Gonzalo, 'Out of his charity', stored their leaky boat with food, fresh water, 'Rich garments, linens, stuffs, and necessaries', not forgetting Prospero's precious books of magic (61–9). The second is when Ferdinand, asked by his father whether Miranda is 'the goddess' that has severed the Italians from one another and then has brought them together, answers, 'Sir, she is mortal, / But by immortal Providence she's mine' (5.1.189–91). Providence thus does arguably have a role to play in human destiny, though at a vast distance and by indirect means. Without some cosmic workings beyond Prospero's reach, the ship full of Italians would never have come within the orbit of the artist/magician marooned on his island. Prospero acknowledges this circumstance when he tells Miranda that 'By accident most strange, bountiful Fortune, / Now my dear lady, hath mine enemies / Brought to this shore' (1.2.179–81). Even here, to be sure, Prospero identifies the controlling force as 'Fortune' rather than Providence in the accepted religious sense, so that we are left unsure as to the nature of the great unseen. In any event, on the island itself Prospero is truly godlike, even if he is also mortal. The world of Shakespeare's dramatic art is one in which the great arbiter of human behaviour and the great presider over human destiny is the dramatist himself.

In Shakespeare's late plays, then, closure is at once a theatrical device, a meditation on retirement and the approach of death, and a kind of philosophical response to the existential terrors that have haunted the problem plays and tragedies of the 1600s. The response is not an 'answer' in the sense of correcting a misleading impression; to say that a kind of providentialism takes the place of apocalyptic terror is not to argue that faith is restored in the eventual triumph of goodness. The genre of tragicomedy requires that perils eventually yield to a happy ending. The genre is self-evidently metatheatrical in its love of surprises and improbabilities. The gods of the tragicomedies are the creations of the dramatist as artist-magician; they do his work, so that all is ultimately under his control. The extent to which these plays may also embody a kind of fantasy or dreamwork on Shakespeare's part, repeatedly telling a story of a lost or abandoned family whose members are sometimes restored to the protagonist and sometimes not, again suggests the extent to which these plays are fables of dramatic illusion. They invite a sceptical reading in the sense that their profound truths do not depend on our accepting as a philosophical truth that human destiny is under the control of Jupiter, Juno, Ceres, Iris, Diana, or indeed any other deities. Shakespeare is the creator and ultimate authority of his remarkable theatrical visions.

8

Credo

Having argued all through this book that we cannot be sure, from the pronouncements of his dramatic characters, what Shakespeare himself may have thought, and that his tactic instead is to put ideas in debate, let me now throw caution to the winds, if only for the fun of it. What if Shakespeare were to have been asked, around the age of fifty, in his retirement, to address the question: What are some ideas that we human beings should strive to live by? Here, I imagine, is something he might say. Please understand that this is pure speculation, and that it probably says more about me than anything else, though I do not personally believe in some of the things that are said below; I am not a monarchist, and I no longer go to church. At least the following represents my own highly personal reading of Shakespeare:

Be generous.

Learn to forgive the unforgivable.

Honour thy father and thy mother. Especially thy father.

Do good deeds for people not because of fear of being punished in the afterlife. You can forget that idea. It makes for lively entertainment in a drama of revenge, but practically speaking it shouldn't enter into one's consideration.

Instead, do acts of kindness and generosity because the world is a better place when people do that, and you want the world to be a better place. History contains such terrifying examples of human brutality that without some compensating goodness we would have to give up in despair. You will be remembered for your kindnesses. That is incomparably better than being remembered for one's cruelty and indifference.

Therein lies a kind of immortality I believe in and try to encourage in my writings. I choose drama because it is such a vivid mirror of human life in its best and worst aspects. It can instruct and guide us. This is not to say that drama need be preachy; indeed, it can be far more effective if it is not.

At the same time, drama, like all creative arts, cannot and should not hope to change the world politically, practically. The world will go on its mostly bad ways no matter what artists write. Drama is like religion in this regard.

Both drama and religion, in other words, are poetry. Whether the personifications that they evoke are 'true' or 'real', who is to say? Should we say that we 'believe' in fairies, ghosts, dreams, visions, omens? What about the gods themselves? They are certainly 'real' enough in my plays, which is to say that they appear on stage and are immortal in my art. Please note that the gods I create in my plays are classical and pagan. (If I tried to put God on stage, I could be in trouble with the authorities.) All these supernatural beings in my plays are illusions created by the artist. They are poetry, meaning that they are only the most important thing in life. Poetry matters. It speaks truly, if one is wise enough to interpret it carefully. Most people are not wise enough, but we go on trying.

Church-going is generally a good thing. At its best it promotes a sense of social community and healing. The Christian gospel especially is filled with beautiful ideas about charity and forgiveness. The dogmatic aspects of religious worship, on the other hand, can be divisive and do not seem to me at the heart of what religion should be all about. Christianity does not hold a monopoly on wise teaching, but it is a central text, probably *the* central text, of our Western culture. The liturgy of the church has a kind of stately magnificence about it that haunts me. The Beatitudes are eloquent in their teaching that the last shall be first and that the meek shall inherit the earth. Jesus did not mean this in a literal sense; nor do I. It is an eschatological vision of a world we can only dream about, a world of perfect justice. That idea of justice seems so easy: since those who are wealthy are usually made insolent and insensitive by having too much, and since many other persons have too little to enable them to live a civilized life, why not redistribute this wealth where it might do some good? This essential idea of the Scriptures is radical in the sense of getting back to the root (radix) cause of things. It will never happen, but art can dream.

Worldly possessions can be deadening to the soul. We must all learn not to covet. This idea can benefit one's spiritual well-being by teaching contentedness and a willingness to share. It also has immense practical advantages. As the stoics teach us, if we eschew covetousness we are armed against disappointment. If we do not pin our hopes on material and worldly gain, we can have no reason to feel cheated if that sort of prosperity evades us. Conversely, we must not congratulate ourselves complacently if we are fortunate.

The teachings of the Christian church about the fallen nature of humankind seem to me compellingly insightful. The story in Genesis of the expulsion of Adam and Eve from the Garden of Eden for their disobedience, and of the first murder in history when Cain slew his brother Abel, resonate with me as with so many of my contemporaries. These are central myths. We all need to be aware that as human beings we are creatures of potentially self-destroying appetites. We need help. I find much wisdom in the teachings of the great church fathers, from St Augustine down through Martin Luther and John Calvin, that salvation is something that we cannot attain by ourselves: it is a gift from above. By 'salvation' again I do not mean an afterlife in heaven, as opposed to dwelling in the eternal darkness of some hell; I mean spiritual wholeness. At the same time, the divisive arguments among various Christian denominations about works versus faith or predestination versus free will seem to me counterproductive. Toward non-Christian faiths and ethical systems one must try also to be tolerant and understanding, even if there are limits. The larger truths of religion are simple, and are consistent with the teachings of the great pagan philosophers like Seneca.

One can be a practising Christian and still be a sceptic about so many important things. One must certainly avoid the superstitious hope that divine assistance will come to those who pray for practical help. Experience shows that it doesn't work that way at all. One must be realistic. The gods will not intervene in our daily lives. One of the few things one can be sure about is that, if one is still breathing and alive, things can get worse. Even if one is seemingly at the bottom of Fortune's wheel, having suffered every imaginable loss, one can have no logical reason to assume that things will then get better. Only when we come to terms with this existential nightmare of much human existence can we hope to achieve the self-knowledge needed for a compassionate and sane survival.

Our scepticism needs to be tempered by a faith in something we can call Providence. Whatever this may be, it operates at an immeasurably vast distance from daily life. It unquestionably appeals to faith rather than reason, since there is no way it can be proven to exist; but we should be conscious of how little we know, really. A truly sceptical attitude about such great matters acknowledges that if we have no proof of the existence of Providence, we have no evidence against it either, so long as we define it as operating at the level of faith. The idea that somehow all is ultimately for the best, and that the intentions of some higher Providence can make sense out of the welter of human history which we as humans so grossly mismanage and misunderstand, is so comforting that we cannot let go of it. Rival theories about human history as only a process without transcendental meaning cannot be dismissed, either. We simply do not know. The uncertainty does make for good drama.

In political matters we are well advised not to go against the state. Political structures take various forms. England's government, as in Western Europe generally, is a monarchy. That plan will probably do as well as any other. Experience with mob rule is generally frightening; since human appetites are by their very nature unruly, we need structures. Some rulers are wise and effective, while some others are very badly fitted for their positions. Despite our longing to idealize monarchs and other rulers as somehow uniquely dispassionate and strong, the evidence is entirely mixed. The wars they wage may be justifiable, as they proclaim, but we can often detect pragmatically self-serving motives in even the most successful of princes. Theorists of the divine right of kings make compelling arguments based on tradition, but history strongly disputes any notion that the origins of hierarchical government lie in divine will. One can regard that idea of divine right as a myth while still appreciating its beauty. In reality, history marches on, and success sometimes goes to those who break the rules. A monarch's first responsibility is to survive, and the same is true of a country like England. Somehow we muddle through.

In our personal and domestic lives we need to be compassionate and evenhanded. Men need to be aware that a patriarchal way of life bestows huge advantages on them, which it behooves them to exercise with great forbearance. Paradoxically, men are often very weak and vulnerable; their need for women's approval puts their frail sense of manhood at risk. Women are often the more even-tempered, self-knowing, and patient, and thus able to prop up men's wavering egos when help is most needed. Women can also seem threatening and even terrifying, but at least some of the time one can interpret this misogynistic vision as a result of a diseased male imagination. Most of all, men and women need each other. Courtship and marriage are filled with difficult challenges, but on the whole one can see that we have no other choice. Men and women must learn to get along with one another and to practise forbearance, because otherwise human life will have no way to continue. Friendships between men and men, women and women, are no less precious.

Any questions?

Further Reading

The following list is meant to accomplish two purposes: first, to offer suggestions for reading in case you would like to follow up on questions that have been raised by the chapters of this book, and second, to acknowledge my indebtednesses. Although this book lacks detailed citations, I do need to give credit for many of the ideas in what I have written. I have read and taught Shakespeare for so long (going back to 1957, in fact) that I am sure I no longer remember all my indebtednesses, but the list here is at least a significant effort in that direction.

Throughout this book, act-scene-and-line references to the plays of Shakespeare are to David Bevington, ed., *The Complete Works of Shakespeare*, 6th edn., New York: Pearson Longman, 2008. The line numberings may differ from those of other editions, owing chiefly to different column widths in the printing of prose and to differing editorial views as to where line breaks occur in verse, but generally the user of any reputable edition of Shakespeare ought to be able to find a particular passage close to where it is cited in this book.

Chapter 1: A Natural Philosopher

Beauregard, David N. *Virtue's Own Feature: Shakespeare and the Virtue Ethics Tradition*. Newark: University of Delaware Press; London: Associated University Presses, 1995.

Bullough, Geoffrey, ed. *Narrative and Dramatic Sources of Shakespeare*. 8 vols. London: Routledge and Kegan Paul; New York: Columbia University Press, 1957–75.

Curry, Walter Clyde. *Shakespeare's Philosophical Patterns*. Baton Rouge: Louisiana State University Press, 1937, 1959.

Garber, Marjorie B. *Shakespeare After All*. New York: Pantheon, 2004.

Greenblatt, Stephen. *Will in the World: How Shakespeare Became Shakespeare*. New York: Norton, 2004.

Gurr, Andrew. *Playgoing in Shakespeare's London.* 2nd edn. Cambridge: Cambridge University Press, 1996.

Gurr, Andrew. *The Shakespearian Playing Companies.* Oxford: Oxford University Press, 1996.

Gurr, Andrew. *The Shakespeare Stage, 1574–1642.* 2nd edn. Cambridge: Cambridge University Press, 1980.

Harbage, Alfred. *As They Liked It.* New York: Macmillan, 1947.

Horowitz, David. *Shakespeare: An Existential View.* London: Tavistock, 1965.

Joughin, John J., ed. *Philosophical Shakespeares.* London and New York: Routledge, 2000.

Kimpel, Ben. *Moral Philosophies in Shakespeare's Plays.* Lewiston, ME: Edwin Mellen, 1987.

Kinney, Arthur F. *Shakespeare and Cognition: Aristotle's Legacy and Shakespearean Drama.* New York and London: Routledge, 2006.

Lowenthal, David. *Shakespeare and the Good Life: Ethics and Politics in Dramatic Form.* Lanham, MD: Rowman & Littlefield, 1997.

Lütgenau, Franz. *Shakespeare als Philosoph.* Lepizig: Zenien-Verlag, 1909.

Marquis, Don. 'pete the parrott and Shakespeare.' *archy and mehitabel.* London: Faber, 1931, pp. 95–9.

McGinn, Colin. *Shakespeare's Philosophy: Discovering the Meaning Behind the Plays.* New York: HarperCollins, 2006.

Schoenbaum, S. *William Shakespeare: A Documentary Life.* Oxford: Oxford University Press, 1975.

Schoenbaum, S. *William Shakespeare: Records and Images.* Oxford: Oxford University Press, 1981.

Spalding, K. J. *The Philosophy of Shakespeare.* Oxford: George Ronald, 1953.

Zamir, Tzachi. *Double Vision: Moral Philosophy and Shakespearean Drama.* Princeton: Princeton University Press, 2007.

Zeeveld, W. Gordon. *The Temper of Shakespeare's Thought.* New Haven: Yale University Press, 1974.

Chapter 2: Lust in Action: Shakespeare's Ideas on Sex and Gender

Bamber, Linda. *Comic Women, Tragic Men: A Study of Gender and Genre in Shakespeare.* Stanford: Stanford University Press, 1982.

Barber, C. L. *Shakespeare's Festive Comedy.* Princeton: Princeton University Press, 1959.

Belsey, Catherine. *Shakespeare and the Loss of Eden: The Construction of Family Values in Early Modern Culture.* New Brunswick, NJ: Rutgers University Press, 1999.

Bevington, David. ' "Jack Hath Not Jill": Failed Courtship in Lyly and Shakespeare.' *Shakespeare Survey* 42 (1990), 1–13.

Boose, Lynda E. 'The Father and the Bride in Shakespeare.' *PMLA* 97 (1982), 325–47.

Cook, Ann Jennalie. *Making a Match: Courtship in Shakespeare and His Society.* Princeton: Princeton University Press, 1991.

Dubrow, Heather. *Captive Victors: Shakespeare's Narrative Poems and Sonnets.* Ithaca: Cornell University Press, 1987.

Garber, Marjorie B. *Coming of Age in Shakespeare.* New York: Methuen, 1981.

Harbage, Alfred. *Shakespeare and the Rival Traditions.* New York: Macmillan, 1952.

Kahn, Coppélia. *Man's Estate: Masculine Identity in Shakespeare.* Berkeley: University of California Press, 1981.

Leggatt, Alexander. *Shakespeare's Comedy of Love.* London: Methuen, 1974.

Neely, Carol Thomas. *Broken Nuptials in Shakespeare's Plays.* New Haven: Yale University Press, 1985.

Novy, Marianne. *Love's Argument: Gender Relations in Shakespeare.* Chapel Hill, NC: University of North Carolina Press, 1984.

Rose, Mary Beth. *The Expense of Spirit: Love and Sexuality in English Renaissance Drama.* Ithaca: Cornell University Press, 1988.

Smith, Bruce R. *Homosexual Desire in Shakespeare's England.* Chicago: University of Chicago Press, 1991.

Smith, Bruce R. *Shakespeare and Masculinity.* Oxford: Oxford University Press, 2000.

Stone, Lawrence. *The Family, Sex and Marriage in England, 1500–1800.* London: Weidenfeld & Nicolson, 1986.

Wells, Robin Headlam. *Shakespeare on Masculinity.* New York and London: Harvester Wheatsheaf, 2000.

Wheeler, Richard P. *Shakespeare's Development and the Problem Comedies: Turn and Counter-Turn.* Berkeley: University of California Press, 1981.

Chapter 3: What is Honour? Shakespeare's Ideas on Politics and Political Theory

Alexander, Catherine, ed. *Shakespeare and Politics.* Cambridge: Cambridge University Press, 2004.

Calderwood, James L. *Metadrama in Shakespeare's Henriad: 'Richard II' to 'Henry V'.* Berkeley: University of California Press, 1979.

Dollimore, Jonathan, and Alan Sinfield, eds. *Political Shakespeare: Essays in Cultural Materialism.* Manchester: Manchester University Press, 1985. 2nd edn., Ithaca: Cornell University Press, 1994.

Drakakis, John, ed. *Alternative Shakespeares.* Two separate collections. London: Methuen, 1985; London and New York: Routledge, 2002.

Hazlitt, William. *Characters of Shakespear's Plays.* London: Printed for C. H. Reynell, 1817.

Hodgdon, Barbara. *The End Crowns All: Closure and Contradiction in Shakespeare's History.* Princeton: Princeton University Press, 1991.

Howard, Jean E., and Phyllis Rackin. *Engendering a Nation: A Feminist Account of Shakespeare's English Histories.* London and New York: Routledge, 1997.

Jorgensen, Paul A. *Shakespeare's Military World.* Berkeley: University of California Press, 1956.

Kamps, Ivo, ed. *Shakespeare Left and Right.* New York and London: Routledge, 1991.

Kantorowicz, Ernst H. *The King's Two Bodies: A Study in Medieval Political Theology.* Princeton: Princeton University Press, 1957.

Kastan, David. *Shakespeare and the Shapes of Time.* Hanover, NH: New England Associated Presses, 1982.

Kelly, Henry A. *Divine Providence in the England of Shakespeare's Histories.* Cambridge, MA: Harvard University Press, 1970.

Kettle, Arnold, ed. *Shakespeare in a Changing World.* London: Lawrence & Wishart, 1964.

Marx, Karl. *The Eighteenth Brumaire of Louis Napoleon.* New York: International Publishers, 1963.

Patterson, Annabel. *Shakespeare and the Popular Voice.* Oxford: Oxford University Press, 1989.

Rackin, Phyllis. *Stages of History: Shakespeare's English Chronicles.* Ithaca: Cornell University Press, 1990.

Saccio, Peter. *Shakespeare's English Kings: History, Chronicle, and Drama.* New York: Oxford University Press, 1977, 2000.

Shaw, George Bernard. *Shaw on Shakespeare,* ed. Edwin Wilson. New York: Dutton, 1961, Applause, 2000.

Tillyard, E. M. W. *The Elizabethan World Picture.* London: Chatto & Windus, 1943; New York: Vintage Books, 1967.

Tillyard, E. M. W. *Shakespeare's History Plays.* London: Chatto & Windus, 1944; New York: Barnes & Noble, 1969.

Underdown, David. *Revel, Riot, and Rebellion: Popular Politics and Culture in England, 1603–1660.* Oxford: Oxford University Press, 1985.

Watson, Robert N. *Shakespeare and the Hazards of Ambition.* Cambridge, MA: Harvard University Press, 1994.

Wells, Robin Headlam. 'Julius Caesar, Machiavelli, and the Uses of History.' *Shakespeare Survey* 55 (2002), 209–18.

Chapter 4: Hold the Mirror Up to Nature: Shakespeare's Ideas on Writing and Acting

Bednarz, James P. *Shakespeare and the Poets' War*. New York: Columbia University Press, 2001.

Bevington, David. 'Shakespeare vs Jonson on Satire.' *Shakespeare 1971: Proceedings of the World Shakespeare Congress*, Vancouver, August 1971, eds. Clifford Leech and J. M. R. Margeson. Toronto: University of Toronto Press, 1972, pp. 108–22.

Charney, Maurice. *Style in 'Hamlet'*. Princeton: Princeton University Press, 1969.

Dawson, Anthony B. *Hamlet*. Shakespeare in Performance. Manchester: Manchester University Press, 1995.

Donaldson, Ian. 'Shakespeare, Jonson, and the Invention of the Author.' *Proceedings of the British Academy* 151 (2007), 319–38.

Frye, Northrop. *Anatomy of Criticism*. Princeton: Princeton University Press, 1957.

Frye, Northrop. 'The Argument of Comedy.' *English Institute Essays 1948*. New York: Columbia University Press, 1949, pp. 58–73. Reprinted in *Shakespeare: Modern Essays in Criticism*, ed. Leonard F. Dean. New York: Oxford University Press, 1961; *Shakespeare's Comedies: An Anthology of Modern Criticism*. Harmondsworth and Baltimore: Penguin, 1967; and *Essays in Shakespearean Criticism*, ed. James L. Calderwood and Harold E. Toliver. Englewood Cliffs, NJ: Prentice-Hall, 1970.

Ingram, W. G., and Theodore Redpath, eds. *Shakespeare's Sonnets*. New York: Barnes & Noble, 1964.

Knight, G. Wilson. *The Mutual Flame: On Shakespeare's Sonnets and 'The Phoenix and the Turtle'*. London: Methuen, 1955.

Mack, Maynard. 'The World of Hamlet.' *Yale Review* 41 (1952), 502–23.

Rose, Mark. '*Hamlet* and the Shape of Revenge.' *English Literary Renaissance* 1 (1971), 132–43.

Skura, Meredith. *Shakespeare the Actor and the Purposes of Playing*. Chicago: University of Chicago Press, 1993.

Chapter 5: What Form of Prayer Can Serve My Turn? Shakespeare's Ideas on Religious Controversy and Issues of Faith

Adelman, Janet. *Blood Relations: Christian and Jew in 'The Merchant of Venice'*. Chicago: University of Chicago Press, 2008.

Ball, Bryan W. *A Great Expectation: Eschatalogical Thought in English Protestantism to 1660*. Leiden: E. J. Brill, 1975.

Barber, C. L. *Shakespeare's Festive Comedy*. Princeton: Princeton University Press, 1959.

Calvin, John. *The Institutes*, trans. Henry Beveridge. 2 vols. Grand Rapids, MI: Calvin Society, 1962.

Cox, John D. *Seeming Knowledge: Shakespeare and Skeptical Faith*. Waco, TX: Baylor University Press, 2007.

Frye, Roland M. *Shakespeare and Christian Doctrine*. Princeton: Princeton University Press, 1963.

Greenblatt, Stephen. *Hamlet in Purgatory*. Princeton: Princeton University Press, 2001.

Hunter, Robert Grams. *Shakespeare and the Comedy of Forgiveness*. New York: Columbia University Press, 1965.

Knappen, M. M. *Tudor Puritanism: A Chapter in the History of Idealism*. Chicago: University of Chicago Press, 1939.

Kocher, Paul. *Science and Religion in Elizabethan England*. San Marino, CA: Huntington Library, 1953.

Lovejoy, A. O. *The Great Chain of Being*. Cambridge, MA: Harvard University Press, 1936.

Marotti, Arthur F., ed. *Catholicism and Anti-Catholicism in Early Modern English Texts*. Basingstoke: Macmillan; New York: St Martin's, 1999.

Matchett, William H. *Shakespeare and Forgiveness*. McKinleyville, CA: Daniel & Daniel, Fithian Press, 2002.

Matheson, Mark. 'Hamlet and "A Matter Tender and Dangerous".' *Shakespeare Quarterly* 46 (1995), 383–97.

Mattingley, Garrett. *The Armada*. Boston: Houghton Mifflin, 1959.

Mattingley, Garrett. *Catherine of Aragon*. Boston: Little, Brown, 1941; New York: Vintage Books, 1960.

McEachern, Claire, and Debora Shuger, eds. *Religion and Culture in Renaissance England*. Cambridge: Cambridge University Press, 1997.

Shapiro, James S. *A Year in the Life of William Shakespeare*. New York: HarperCollins, 2005.

Shapiro, James S. *Shakespeare and the Jews*. New York: Columbia University Press, 1996.

Targoff, Ramie. *Common Prayer: The Language of Public Devotion in Early Modern England*. Chicago: University of Chicago Press, 2001.

Chapter 6: Is Man No More Than This? Shakespeare's Ideas on Scepticism, Doubt, Stoicism, Pessimism, Misanthropy

Adelman, Janet. *Suffocating Mothers: Fantasies of Maternal Origin in Shakespeare's Plays, 'Hamlet' to 'The Tempest'*. New York: Routledge, 1992.

Adelman, Janet. ' "This Is and Is Not Cressid": The Characterization of Cressida.' *The (M)other Tongue: Essays in Feminist Psychoanalytic Interpretation*, eds. Shirley Nelson Garner, Claire Kehane, and Madelon Sprengnether. Ithaca: Cornell University Press, 1985.

Auden, W. H. *Lectures on Shakespeare*, ed. Arthur Kirsch. Princeton: Princeton University Press, 2000.

Bertram, Benjamin. *The Time Is Out of Joint: Skepticism in Shakespeare's England*. Newark: University of Delaware Press, 2004.

Boose, Lynda E. 'Othello's Handkerchief: "The Recognizance and Pledge of Love".' *English Literary Renaissance* 5 (1975), 360–74.

Bowen, Barbara E. *Gender in the Theater of War: Shakespeare's 'Troilus and Cressida'*. New York: Garland, 1993.

Bowers, Fredson T. 'Hamlet as Minister and Scourge.' *PMLA* 70 (1955), 740–9.

Bradley, A. C. *Shakespearean Tragedy*. London: Macmillan, 1904.

Bradshaw, Graham. *Shakespeare's Scepticism*. New York: St Martin's, 1987.

Cavell, Stanley. *Disowning Knowledge in Seven Plays of Shakespeare*. Cambridge: Cambridge University Press, 2003. An updated edition, incorporating an essay on *Macbeth*, of *Disowning Knowledge in Six Plays of Shakespeare*, 1987.

Chaudhuri, Sukanta. *Infirm Glory: Shakespeare and the Renaissance Image of Man*. Oxford: Clarendon Press, 1981.

Erlich, Avi. *Hamlet's Absent Father*. Princeton: Princeton University Press, 1977.

Greenblatt, Stephen. *Renaissance Self-Fashioning: From More to Shakespeare*. Chicago: University of Chicago Press, 1980.

Jacobus, Lee A. *Shakespeare and the Dialectic of Certainty*. New York: St Martin's, 1992.

Kaula, David. 'Will and Reason in *Troilus and Cressida*.' *Shakespeare Quarterly* 12 (1961), 271–83.

Kirsch, Arthur. *The Passions of Shakespeare's Tragic Heroes*. Charlottesville: University Press of Virginia, 1990.

Kott, Jan. *Shakespeare Our Contemporary*, trans. Boleslaw Taborski. Garden City, NY: Doubleday, 1964; New York: Norton, 1974.

Landau, Aaron. ' "Let Me Not Burst in Ignorance": Skepticism and Anxiety in Hamlet.' *English Studies* 82 (2001), 218–30.

Mack, Maynard. *King Lear in Our Time*. Berkeley: University of California Press, 1965.

Mallin, Eric. 'Emulous Factions and the Collapse of Chivalry: *Troilus and Cressida*.' *Representations* 29 (1990), 145–79.

Matchett, William H. 'Some Dramatic Techniques in *King Lear*.' *Shakespeare: The Theatrical Dimension*, eds. Philip C. McGuire and David A. Samuelson. New York: AMS, 1979, pp. 185–208.

Miola, Robert. *Shakespeare and Classical Tragedy: The Influence of Seneca.* Oxford: Oxford University Press, 1992.

Ornstein, Robert. 'Donne, Montaigne and Natural Law.' *Essential Articles for the Study of John Donne's Poetry*, ed. John R. Roberts. Hamden, CT: Shoe String, 1975, pp. 129–41.

Pierce, Robert B. 'Shakespeare and the Ten Modes of Scepticism.' *Shakespeare Survey* 46 (1993), 145–58.

Popkin, Richard H. *The History of Scepticism from Erasmus to Spinoza.* Berkeley: University of California Press, 1979.

Rabkin, Norman. *Shakespeare and the Common Understanding.* New York: Free Press, 1967.

Spivack, Bernard. *Shakespeare and the Allegory of Evil.* New York: Columbia University Press, 1958.

Srigley, Michael. *The Problem of Doubt: Scepticism and Illusion in Shakespeare's Plays.* Uppsala: Studia Anglistica Upsaliensia, 2000.

Strier, Richard. 'Shakespeare and the Skeptics.' *Religion and Literature* 32 (2000), 171–96.

Toulmin, Stephen. *Cosmopolis: The Hidden Agenda of Modernism.* New York: Macmillan Free Press, 1990.

Velz, John. 'Undular Structure in *Julius Caesar.*' *Modern Language Review* 66 (1971), 21–30.

Wells, Robin Headlam. *Shakespeare's Humanism.* Cambridge: Cambridge University Press, 2005.

Wiley, Margaret L. *Creative Sceptics.* London: Unwin, 1966.

Wiley, Margaret L. *The Subtle Knot.* London: Unwin, 1952.

Willey, Basil. *The Seventeenth Century Background.* London: Chatto, 1934.

Williamson, George. 'The Libertine Donne.' *Philological Quarterly* 13 (1934), 276–91.

Chapter 7: Here Our Play Has Ending: Ideas of Closure in the Late Plays

Adelman, Janet. *The Common Liar: An Essay on 'Antony and Cleopatra'.* New Haven: Yale University Press, 1973.

Barber, C. L. ' "Thou That Beget'st Him That Did Thee Beget": Transformation in *Pericles* and *The Winter's Tale.*' *Shakespeare Survey* 22 (1969), 59–67.

Bevington, David. ' "Is This the Promised End?" Death and Dying in *King Lear.*' *Proceedings of the American Philosophical Society* 133.3 (1989), 404–15.

Dreher, D. E. *Domination and Defiance: Fathers and Daughters in Shakespeare.* Lexington: University Press of Kentucky, 1986.

Ewbank, Inga-Stina. 'The Triumph of Time in *The Winter's Tale*.' *Review of English Literature* 5.2 (1964), 83–100.

Frey, Charles. '*The Tempest* and the New World.' *Shakespeare Quarterly* 30 (1979), 29–41.

Hunter, Robert Grams. *Shakespeare and the Comedy of Forgiveness*. New York: Columbia University Press, 1965.

James, D. G. *The Dream of Prospero*. Oxford: Oxford University Press, 1967.

Kermode, Frank, ed. *The Tempest*. The Arden Shakespeare. London: Methuen, 1958.

Kernan, Alvin B. *The Playwright as Magician: Shakespeare's Image of the Poet in the English Public Theater*. New Haven: Yale University Press, 1979.

Kirsch, Arthur C. '*Cymbeline* and Coterie Dramaturgy.' *ELH* 34 (1967), 285–306.

Mowat, Barbara A. *The Dramaturgy of Shakespeare's Romances*. Athens: University of Georgia Press, 1976.

Neill, Michael. *Issues of Death: Mortality and Identity in Renaissance English Tragedy*. Oxford: Oxford University Press, 1997.

Orgel, Stephen. 'Prospero's Wife.' *Representations* 8 (1984), 1–33.

Siemon, James Edward. ' "But It Appears She Lives": Iteration in *The Winter's Tale*.' *PMLA* 89 (1999), 10–16.

Watson, Robert N. *The Rest is Silence: Death as Annihilation in the English Renaissance*. Berkeley: University of California Press, 1994.

Wheeler, Richard P. 'Deaths in the Family: The Loss of a Son and the Rise of Shakespearean Comedy.' *Shakespeare Quarterly* 51 (2000), 127–53.

Index